Reflections of Change

Recent Titles in
Contributions to the Study of World Literature

Postcolonial Discourse and Changing Cultural Contexts
Gita Rajan and Radhika Mohanram, editors

Prometheus and Faust: The Promethean Revolt in Drama from Classical Antiquity
to Goethe
Timothy Richard Wutrich

English Postcoloniality: Literatures from Around the World
Radhika Mohanram and Gita Rajan, editors

The Vonnegut Chronicles
Peter Reed and Marc Leeds, editors

Satirical Apocalypse: An Anatomy of Melville's *The Confidence-Man*
Jonathan A. Cook

Twenty-Four Ways of Looking at Mary McCarthy: The Writer and Her Work
Eve Stwertka and Margo Viscusi, editors

Orienting Masculinity, Orienting Nation: W. Somerset Maugham's Exotic Fiction
Philip Holden

A Matter of Faith: The Fiction of Brian Moore
Robert Sullivan

Samuel Johnson and the Essay
Robert D. Spector

Fighting Evil: Unsung Heroes in the Novels of Graham Greene
Haim Gordon

Pearl S. Buck: A Cultural Bridge Across the Pacific
Kang Liao

A Systems Approach to Literature: Mythopoetics of Chekhov's Four Major Plays
Vera Zubarev

Reflections of Change

Children's Literature Since 1945

Edited by
Sandra L. Beckett

Published under the Auspices of the International Research Society for Children's Literature

Contributions to the Study of World Literature,
Number 74

GREENWOOD PRESS
Westport, Connecticut • London

Library of Congress Cataloging-in-Publication Data

Reflections of change : children's literature since 1945 / edited by
    Sandra L. Beckett.
        p.   cm.—(Contributions to the study of world literature,
    ISSN 0738-9345 ; no. 74)
        Selected papers of the Twelfth Biennial Congress of the
    International Research Society for Children's Literature (IRSCL),
    held 1995 in Stockholm.
        "Published under the auspices of the International Research
    Society for Children's Literature."
        Includes bibliographical references and index.
        ISBN 0-313-30145-X (alk. paper)
        1. Children's literature—20th century—History and criticism.
    I. Beckett, Sandra L., 1953-   . II. International Research Society
    for Children's Literature. Congress (12th : 1995 : Stockholm,
    Sweden) III. International Research Society for Children's
    Literature. IV. Series.
    PN1009.A1R425   1997
    809'.89282'09045—dc20   96-22004

British Library Cataloguing in Publication Data is available.

Library of Congress Catalog Card Number: 96-22004
ISBN: 0-313-30145-X
ISSN: 0738-9345

First published in 1997

Greenwood Press, 88 Post Road West, Westport, CT 06881
An imprint of Greenwood Publishing Group, Inc.

Printed in the United States of America

The paper used in this book complies with the
Permanent Paper Standard issued by the National
Information Standards Organization (Z39.48-1984).

10 9 8 7 6 5 4 3 2 1

Copyright Acknowledgments

The editor and publisher gratefully acknowledge permission for use of the following material:

Poem by Wiel Kusters, "Now It's You and Me Again" (Original Dutch title: "Goed, dan nu weer jij en
ik") in *Salamanders vangen*. Amsterdam: Em. Querido, 1985. Reprinted with permission.

Every reasonable effort has been made to trace the owners of copyright materials in this book, but in
some instances this has proven impossible. The author and publisher will be glad to receive information leading to more complete acknowledgments in subsequent printings of the book and in the
meantime extend their apologies for any omissions.

Contents

Introduction: Reflections of Change
Sandra L. Beckett   ix

Part I. Theory and Children's Literature

1. Fear of Children's Literature: What's Left (or Right) After Theory?
   Perry Nodelman   3

2. "Is This the Promised End . . .?": *Fin de Siècle* Mentality and
   Children's Literature
   John Stephens   15

3. Ramona the Underestimated: The Everyday-Life Story in Children's
   Literature
   Deborah Stevenson   23

Part II. Shifting Boundaries Between Children's and Adult Literature

4. The Disappearance of Children's Literature (or Children's Literature
   as Nostalgia) in the United States in the Late Twentieth Century
   Jerry Griswold   35

5. Literature for All Ages? Literary Emancipation and the Borders of
    Children's Literature
    Anne de Vries   43

6. The Changing Status of Children and Children's Literature
    Eva-Maria Metcalf   49

Part III. Experimental Writing and Postmodern Trends

7. From Grand Narrative to Small Stories: New Narrative Structures
    in Recent Scandinavian Children's Literature
    Åsfrid Svensen   59

8. The Status of Sequels in Children's Literature: *The Long Secret*
    and *Beyond the Chocolate War*
    Bettina Kümmerling-Meibauer   65

9. Gillian Cross's *Wolf*: An Exploration of Patterns and Polarities
    Susan Clancy   75

Part IV. Paradigm Shifts

10. Reflections of Change in Children's Book Titles
     Maria Nikolajeva   85

11. High and Wild Magic, the Moral Universe, and the Electronic
     Superhighway: Reflections of Change in Susan Cooper's Fantasy
     Literature
     Carole Scott   91

12. "Terror is Her Constant Companion": The Cult of Fear in Recent
     Books for Teenagers
     Roderick McGillis   99

13. Suburban Scenarios in Simon French's *All We Know*: The
     Emergence of the Suburbs as the Spatial Framework for Australian
     Children's Fiction
     Beverley Pennell   107

14. Reading Children's Literature Multiculturally
     Daniel D. Hade   115

Part V. National Literatures

15. The Journey Inward: Adolescent Literature in America,
    1945–1995
    Anne Scott MacLeod   125

16. The Novel for Adolescents in Quebec: Stereotypes and New
    Conventions
    Danielle Thaler   131

17. Realistic Stories for Children in the Federal Republic of
    Germany, 1970–1994: Features and Tendencies
    Dagmar Grenz   141

18. Text and Context: Factors in the Development of Children's
    Literature in Taiwan, 1945–1995, and the Emergence of
    Young Adult Literature
    Shu-Jy Duan   153

Part VI. Reconceptualizing the Past

19. An Awfully Big Adventure? Representations of the Second
    World War in British Children's Books of the 1960s and 1970s
    Dieter Petzold   163

20. Topsy-Turvy World: New Trends in Modern Russian Children's
    Literature
    Olga Mäeots   171

21. Children's Literature in Totalitarian and Post-totalitarian Society
    Vincas Auryla   177

Selected Bibliography   183

Index   189

About the Editor and Contributors   199

Introduction: Reflections of Change

Sandra L. Beckett

The Twelfth Biennial Congress of the International Research Society for Children's Literature (IRSCL), held in Stockholm in 1995, brought together children's literature scholars from some twenty-five countries to reflect on the changes that have taken place in children's literature and children's literature theory and criticism since 1945, a period that has seen rapidly accelerating innovation in so many fields. This volume, a selection of the papers given at the Congress, is representative of the variety of ways in which children's literature around the world has been evolving over the last half-century. In many countries, particularly those of the West, the process of change has been steadily ongoing since the end of the Second World War. In others, however, for social, political, or economic reasons, periods of growth have been followed by periods of stagnation. And when countries have existed in isolation from the international community, it is often only in very recent years that any significant innovation in children's literature and its criticism has been possible. The keynote address given at the Congress by Vincas Auryla of Lithuania shows very clearly how differently children's literature in Eastern Europe evolved over this period.

Clearly, one of the most dramatic changes has been the new, privileged status that children's literature has begun to enjoy in recent decades. In the early part of the twentieth century, children's literature was undervalued, marginalized, excluded from mainstream literature. Children's literature, like texts by women and other minority groups, owes a great debt to postmodernism and its tendency to eliminate barriers, level hierarchies, and give equal voice to all. There is no doubt, as Eva-Maria Metcalf points out in her essay, that postmodernism has had a significant liberating and empowering effect on children's literature. In the 1990s, children's book publishing is booming in most Western countries, and many publishing houses attribute their survival in a slumping economy to their children's departments.

The changing status of children's literature has been accompanied by an unprecedented growth in children's literature research internationally. Since 1970, children's literature, as a significant field of scholarship, has been growing steadily, gradually securing its place in the academy. The Stockholm Congress marked the twenty-fifth anniversary of the IRSCL, founded at Frankfurt in 1970. Already one of the most exciting and vibrant fields of literary research in much of the Western world, children's literature theory and criticism are now emerging rapidly in many other parts of the world as, in the global village of the end of the twentieth century, scholars from around the world have increasing opportunity to exchange ideas, a dialogue that is facilitated by organizations such as the IRSCL.

In its early years, children's literature theory and criticism were marked, and no doubt marred, by a perceived need to demonstrate the seriousness and value of the literature and to justify their own existence. This sometimes resulted in a tendency to adopt somewhat conservative critical approaches that did not always take into considersation the unique merits of children's literature. More recently, however, some of the most innovative and exciting literary research is being done in the field of children's literature theory. The essays in Part I of this volume reflect on where children's literature theory has come from and where it seems to be heading at the end of the millennium. Taking as a point of departure Paul Hazard's groundbreaking work *Books, Children, and Men* (*Les livres, les enfants et les hommes*), published in 1944, and showing how developments in literary theory in the ensuing fifty years have led to the understanding that children's literature embeds its readers in ideology, and consequently to a fear of the genre, Perry Nodelman, one of the keynote speakers at the Congress, asks a provocative question: "Is there anything worth salvaging after theory gets through with literature?" Nodelman goes on to assure us that we can go beyond the fear that knowledge of theory engenders, and to suggest that we can use it to create a new world. Children's literature theory has indeed come a long way in the last fifty years.

The demarginalization and emancipation of children's literature has led to a broadening of horizons, in content as well as in form. During the last half-century, children's literature has gradually freed itself of many of the traditional restrictions, and the rigid moral codes and taboos, that had long governed it. It now offers authors and readers the wide range of topics addressed in adult fiction, including philosophical, political, sociocultural, and economic issues.

The boundaries of children's literature are shifting, and several essays in this volume explore these changing borders. Children's literature has always been difficult to define, but there seems to be less and less consensus about what constitutes a text for children. Is it possible that the integration of children's literature into the mainstream is actually the beginning of its demise? Are children's literature writers and critics, in their zeal to prove the seriousness of the genre, sometimes guilty of attaching too great a value to children's literature that imitates adult literature? Postmodernism has contributed to the emergence of a more complex literature for more sophisticated child readers. This evolution has led some critics to speculate upon the disappearance of childhood and children's literature as we approach the end of the twentieth century. Boundaries between children's and adult literature seem to be collapsing in favor of literature for all ages. More and more authors are addressing books to a dual audience of adults and children. Does this widespread phenomenon of literature for all ages signal the death of children's literature? The essays in this volume suggest that children's literature will continue to place special demands on authors writing for young readers, but that this literature will continue to evolve rapidly as we move into the twenty-first century.

Not only do contemporary children's authors have a vast range of topics from which to choose, they also have much greater freedom to experiment with form. Since the 1970s, postmodernism has left its mark on the formal aspects of children's literature, which thus has reflected dominant trends in adult fiction. In some countries, children's literature did not just leave the literary fringe to assume its place in mainstream literature; it actually became part of the literary avant-garde, leading the way in postmodern stylistic experimentation, once totally foreign to children's literature. A multitude of complex narrative strategies—including focalization, polyphony, composite genres, fragmentation, absence of closure, metafiction, intertextuality, irony, increasing metaphorical sophistication, the carnivalesque—transgress the traditional demarcations separating children's literature from adult literature. Paradigms are shifting. Traditional narrative patterns are undergoing innovative reconstruction. Literary genres are breaking with conventions, evolving and transforming, assuming new roles and functions. Retellings of grand narratives reflect shifts in sociocultural values and patterns. Fluctuating, inconstant characters challenge traditional concepts of identity. As accepted modes of perception are redefined, readers are confronted with new temporal, spatial, and human dimensions. Texts have become more obscure, more symbolic, with multiple levels of meaning. Much greater demands are placed on child readers as they are confronted with increasing skepticism, ambivalence, and contradictions, and are asked to participate critically, often to play an active role in the unfolding of the plot.

As a result of these changes, children's literature has become more complex, more ambiguous, more noncommittal, but also more interesting, more colorful, more diversified. The papers in this volume show that children's literature at the end of the twentieth century offers its readers a multitude of representations and possible responses to the rapidly altering modern world in which they live. At the dawn of a new millennium, we can only hope that children's literature and children's literature theory will continue to reflect our changing world, and perhaps will even provide the means of creating a new world for future generations of child readers.

Part I

Theory and Children's Literature

1

Fear of Children's Literature: What's Left (or Right) After Theory?

Perry Nodelman

The year is 1944. As war rages in Europe and elsewhere, Americans can open a newly published book and read these words:

Children and grownups belong to different worlds. . . . How far removed is the world of childhood! Its inhabitants seem of another species. . . . Reason does not curb them, for they have not yet learned its restraints. Happy beings, they live in the clouds, playing light-heartedly without a care.[1]

Not surprisingly, such beings require their own special kind of stories: "those that offer children an intuitive and direct way of knowledge, a simple beauty capable of being perceived immediately, arousing in their souls a vibration which will endure all their lives".[2]

The book expressing these convictions was *Books, Children, and Men*, a translation into English of *Les livres, les enfants, et les hommes*, first published in France in the early 1930s by Paul Hazard. From the viewpoint of 1995, it's hard to imagine that children could ever have been so innocent, or that children's books could ever have been so innocent—or, above all, that an adult could ever have been so innocent as to believe so wholeheartedly in that childhood innocence. It's especially hard not to remember that, as Americans read these words, children were starving and dying and otherwise being abused, not only in European concentration camps but also in many of the poorer parts of the United States—and that they continue to be so treated now, all these decades later.

But Hazard wasn't alone in his views. They represent ideas about children and literature that most people took for granted for many decades. I bought my own copy of *Books, Children, and Men* in the late 1970s, as a newcomer to children's literature wishing to find out what the respected authorities had to say about my newly chosen subject. I knew the book was respected because it was still in print, more than thirty years after its first American publication, and it remained in print for some years after that. Furthermore, it wouldn't take more than a quick browse through journals that publish reviews of or articles about children's books to find comments similar to the ones by Hazard with which I began. A lot of people still share these views.

Yet much has happened since 1944. There has been half a century more of news about the astonishing persistence and prevalence of child abuse in all its despicable forms. There has also been half a century of developments in our theoretical understanding both of child psychology and of literature. Nowadays, it's pretty difficult for people to maintain the conviction that childhood is ever as innocent as Hazard wanted to imagine it always was. More significantly for those of us professionally interested in this subject, it's almost impossible to maintain that literature for children could ever be as simple, as direct, or even as wise as Hazard claims.

If anything, what we have come to know—and how we have come to think five decades later as a result of that knowledge—can encourage only one clear response in us to children's literature, perhaps to all literature. That response is, quite simply, fear. After having learned what theory has to tell us about the nature of childhood and the nature of literature, we can logically conclude only that literature in each and all of its forms and manifestations is very, very bad for children and other human beings.

And indeed, many people do reach that conclusion—or get uncomfortably close to it.

Most obviously, there are the censors: those people of every political stripe who are convinced that literature representing values other than the ones they themselves know to be right and true is incredibly dangerous and exceedingly powerful, and inevitably will pervert young readers' minds. If this logic is ever correct, then surely it is always correct. All children's literature is at least suspicious, if not downright horrifying.

But even those of us who are committed to freedom of speech and who know that children almost always grow up with a deep belief in their parents' or peers' values, no matter what books they read—even *we* aren't free from our fears about literature. Some of us believe that children who read too much of what we consider to be inferior or tasteless literature will themselves remain inferior and without taste, and so we deeply fear popular series like the Babysitters Club or Goosebumps. And some of us, deeply learned in our knowledge of theory and ineffably wise, have even deeper and more all-encompassing fears. We see literature, all literature, as a means of enmeshing children in repressive ideology. In an article I wrote a few years ago, in which I explored the similarities between the intellectual basis of the European colonial project, as described by Edward Said in *Orientalism*, and our common assumptions about childhood, I concluded that children's literature is best understood as a means by which adults claim power over children and force them to accept our repressive versions of who they really are. Scary stuff, that children's literature—very dangerous indeed. Maybe the only way to protect children from being ruined for life is to keep them illiterate—that, and drown all the TV sets.

In 1994, I gave a paper at a children's literature conference in the United States about a series of picture books by the American writer and illustrator David Wiesner. While Wiesner's books claim to be celebrations of the freed imagination, I argued that even they were profoundly manipulative and repressive. After the talk was over, a member of the audience, my friend Lois Kuznets—a critic who has done fine work of revealing repressive ideologies in apparently harmless texts—asked this question: "Is nothing safe anymore? Is it *all* dangerous?"

My immediate, automatic answer was, "Yes, Lois, of course, it *is* all dangerous." But I surprised myself by saying it, and I've been wondering about Lois's question ever since she asked it. It's a good question, and a very important one. Is there anything left worth salvaging after theory gets through with literature? Is the whole enterprise of adults providing texts for children ever anything but oppressive and repressive? *Can* it be?

I'd like to explore those questions here—and then try to find some answers to them.

Let me begin once more with Paul Hazard. When I was asked to talk about what's happened to our theoretical understanding of children's literature since 1945, my first thought was to reread his book—it seemed like an easy way to recall where we'd all come from. As I browsed through *Books, Children and Men* for the first time in almost twenty years, I found myself noticing things in it I didn't remember having noticed in 1977, and that I suspect no adult interested in children's literature in 1944 would be likely to have noticed at all. My knowledge of theories of various sorts was making the book seem different than I remembered it.

My strongest response was to Hazard's faith that some texts might "offer to children an intuitive and direct way of knowledge, a simple beauty capable of being perceived immediately, arousing in their souls a vibration which will endure all their lives."[3] This now bothers me on two accounts: what it says about children's literature, and what it says about children.

About literature: literary theories of many kinds, from reception theory to gender studies, has encouraged me to understand that texts, all texts, exist within a complex network of ideas and images and cultural values—and that includes apparently simple texts written for children. I can no longer believe that any text is ever direct or simple, and I've come to mistrust critics like Hazard who claim that some are. Hazard takes all of his own knowledge of French life and culture for granted when he assumes that young children will automatically read Charles Perrault's fairy tales as he does.

I also find myself noticing how strangely contradictory it is that Hazard offers detailed analyses of a number of the books he claims speak so perfectly and so directly to children, from Perrault's fairy tales to *Robinson Crusoe*. If they are so simple and so direct, why do they need to be explained?

Which takes me to what Hazard says about children. What children understand so intuitively needs to be explained to adults like me because, Hazard asserts, we adults have lost the ability to think like children. That's a doubly dangerous generalization. First, it *is* a generalization: surely not all children are alike in any way whatsoever, except in being young. Second, it assumes the shared likeness is a deficiency in relation to adults: if nothing else, it's surely a little insulting for us to assume that children, any children, are closer to nature than we are, less sophisticated, and therefore, presumably, less evolved.

As I read Hazard's descriptions of children and their reading, I found myself doing an act of translation. He might well be right, but not, I told myself, about actual children who might actually be reading books—for the real children I know are nothing like that, and they are not freaks. Rather, these might be accurate descriptions of what reader-response theorists call *implied* readers: the imaginary constructs of ideal audiences that writers had in their minds when they wrote, and therefore implied in the contents of their texts, and that actual readers might need to transform themselves into, in order to make best sense of the texts. In other words, Hazard may have confused the cart and the horse. In order to celebrate a certain kind of text, he had to pretend there already existed an audience, now defined as essentially childlike, exactly suited to respond to it. But in point of fact, the text precedes, and might even help to create, the audience.

Obviously, my act of translation changes what was apparently harmless in Hazard's text into something deeply suspicious. If a text invites and requires a real child to become the ideal reader—the ideal child—it implies, then the text is manipulative. And if that ideal child represents an ideal I don't myself share, then I have no choice but to see the manipulation as dangerous—something to fear.

I certainly fear Hazard's view of childhood—and recognize it as a very popular one even now. In insisting that children are exactly opposite to adults, an alien species who belong in a different and presumably better world, proponents of this idea force me either to share their views and despise adults for not being childlike, or to disagree with them and despise children for not being fully evolved humans. Both positions insist that children are more significantly different from adults of their own species than similar to them. As Hazard suggests in the first sentence of his that I quoted, "Children and grownups belong to different worlds."

As I consider that sentence, I can't help but notice the parallel between Hazard's view of children as an alien species and the kind of thinking that led too many human beings to believe for too many centuries that, for instance, woman and men belong to different species, that white Europeans and black Africans belong to different species, that Englishmen and Frenchmen belong to different species. In this kind of thinking, the species are not only different but opposite in every way. If men are reasonable, women are intuitive, and if Europeans are pragmatic, then Africans live only for the day. The Other is always and inevitably the opposite—and Hazard's children are clearly opposite to adults in every important way: imaginative where adults have lost the ability to imagine, playful where adults insist on serious purposes even in their play. Childhood, says Hazard, "remains healthy because it has not yet reached the age for analysing the soul's emotions."[4]

Or to put it another way, adults are all sick—including the adult who wrote these words. For Hazard makes this comment in the midst of a carefully organized and presumably rational analysis. Thus we have to conclude that he, himself an analytical adult, is sick also—a sick being envying the health of those in a category so opposite to himself that he could not possibly enter it. For an adult cannot become a child, just as a white cannot become black or, except through extreme and still relatively rare measures, a man cannot become a woman. Thus, another thing Hazard's view of childhood shares with certain forms of racism or sexism is praise of those qualities that mark the other and opposite to oneself as a stick with which to beat oneself and one's kind.

Always, in this kind of thinking, there is more than a hint that what is being celebrated is, exactly, inadequacy, inhumanity, incapacity—the state of being less than completely human. Women are wonderful because they aren't restricted by the narrow confines of truth or rational logic, blacks are full of the joy of life because they don't have the corruptly sophisticated white sense of how the world really works, children are blissfully innocent because they're just too dumb (or, in this logic, too smart) to know any better— lucky things. As James Kincaid says in his remarkable book *Child Loving: The Erotic Child and Victorian Culture,* we see being childlike as "a kind of purity, an absence and an incapacity, an inability to do. . . . Unencumbered by any necessary traits, the emptiness called a child can be constructed any way we like."[5]

And so Hazard, I see, constructed it to his taste—which was, mostly, to privilege and celebrate its emptiness. "It is sweet, sometimes," he says, "to see the world again with a child's eyes." He goes on to say, "It is true that they lure us away from the feast of ideas, taking no pleasure there themselves. They place small value on the abstractions that are so useful to our grown-up pastimes." But it's clear that what he presents here supposedly as a qualification is exactly the reason why he wants to think like a child: "Let us admit that they have no skill in handling ideas. What they have is enough for them."[6] It would be enough for him, too, it seems, if only he weren't cursed with his awful adult superiority—the terrible knowledge of how very bad knowledge is. Thus he has it both ways: he is superior, and he knows how bad it is to be superior enough to hate it—which presumably makes him even more superior than the rest of us adults. This kind of thinking is still surprisingly common in children's literature criticism, in which sophisticated adults often celebrate the wonderful innocence of childhood.

If I fear this sort of thinking, and I find it so blatantly present in Hazard, then what am I to make of the children's books he prefers—that the many adult experts who still share his basic principles prefer? They are ones that celebrate the childlike as something directly antithetical to what we might normally see as mature or thoughtful or responsible. Their wisdom is to deny that most of what we usually consider to be true is wise. If children did indeed learn what it means to be childlike from these books as Hazard understands them, they would be learning to be proud of their immaturity, thoughtlessness, and irresponsibility. They would learn that it is good to be self-indulgent and egocentric and careless of the feelings or needs of others. I find myself asking why this should be seen as a good thing.

Hazard's own answer to that question is a little strange, I think, and once more suggests a profound degree of self-hatred. He says he admires books that provide children "with pictures, the kind that they like. . . . enchanting pictures that bring release and joy, happiness gained before reality closes in upon them, insurance against the time, all too soon, when there will be nothing but realities."[7] Children must be childlike, unreal, or else there is nothing but the brute horror of the bare truth, despicable and unbearable reality itself. I can't imagine anything more pessimistic or more life-denying. Hazard's paean of praise for the jolly, happy childhood he has imagined and tries so desperately to impose on children disguises an exceedingly negative and very ugly view of the world he knows as an adult. In teaching me how to see this aspect of Hazard, theory has taught me to fear all forms of praise for the delights of childhood—and that means just about all children's literature.

At this point, I'm reminded again of theorists like James Kincaid and Jacqueline Rose, who talk about how and why we adults attempt to persuade children that our imaginary visions of childhood are true. Rose believes that the actual nature of childhood—she focuses particularly on children's confused experience of sexual desire—frightens adults. We protect ourselves from knowledge of the chaotic confusion children really experience by constructing images of childhood that eliminate everything threatening, leaving only what Kincaid described as "a kind of purity, an absence and an incapacity, an inability to do."[8] We then present the images we have constructed to children in their literature, in order to persuade them that their lives actually are as we imagine them to be. "If children's fiction builds an image of the child inside the book," says Rose, "it does so in order to secure the child who is outside the book, the one who does not come so easily within its grasp."[9]

Children's literature, then, represents a massive effort by adults to make children believe that they ought to be the way adults would like them to be, and to make them feel guilty about or downplay the significance of all the aspects of their selves that inevitably don't fit the adult model.

It's all too frighteningly easy to read Hazard from this point of view. He insists both that children are inherently and always imaginative, and also that they need help from adults in being imaginative—need the right kinds of books to feed their imaginations and the right kind of adults, supposedly childlike ones, to write those books. So it is adults who must write children's books. But as we've already seen, all adults are afflicted by reality, and cannot see as children see. Only one conclusion is possible: adults no longer childlike must imagine—invent, contrive, create, make up—how children *should* see, and then impose what they imagine upon children, lest children see the actual ugly truth and therefore force adults to acknowledge that it is in fact the only truth. Let us create a lie of childhood and then force children to believe in it.

Hazard gets very angry at most writers for children: "Entirely pleased with themselves, they offered the child books that represented themselves, with all their attributes thrown in."[10] Yet the books that he himself recommends, he admires exactly because they represent himself and his ideas of wisdom. He is himself one of the people he attacks.

From this point of view, obviously, the books Hazard admires are exceedingly dangerous ones—greatly to be feared. And yet, of course, the danger is unavoidable. For there is one other thing theory has taught me: the aspects of children's books I've been describing—that Hazard takes for granted as good and true, and that I fear as bad and dangerous—are always and inevitably present. There would be no children's books if we didn't believe children were different enough from adults to need their own special kinds of books; and of course it is adults—the ones with the ideas about just how it is that children differ—who write those books. All children's books always represent adult ideas of childhood—and inevitably, therefore, work to impose adult ideas about childhood on children.

Furthermore, the process works. Children do become what we believe they are; assumptions about childhood, like those of Hazard, have the potential to become self-fulfilling prophecies. If we believe, as many adults do, that children are limited in various ways, then we deprive them of experiences that might make them less limited. If we believe that children have short attention spans, we won't expose them to long books. If we believe they cannot understand complicated language, we will give them only books with limited vocabularies. If we believe they are susceptible, we will keep them away from interesting books that may contain potentially dangerous ideas or attitudes. And if we believe they like only certain kinds of books, we won't give them access to other kinds. Deprived of the experience of anything more than the little we believe them capable of, children often learn to be inflexible, intolerant of the complex and the unconventional.

And clearly, children's literature plays an important part in this process. As a wide range of ideological theorists like Antonio Gramsci and Louis Althusser and Raymond Williams have suggested, and as John Stephens in particular has so persuasively pointed out in *Language and Ideology in Children's Fiction,* whatever else literary texts are, and whatever pleasure they may afford us, they are also expressions of the values and assumptions of a culture and a significant way of embedding readers in those values and assumptions—persuading them that they are in fact the readers that the texts imply.

The reader whom Hazard suggests good children's books imply is one who luxuriates in a supposedly childlike freedom. Paradoxically, therefore, he implies the unsettling truth that good children's literature is that which constrains and represses children in the process of pretending to liberate them. To believe oneself childlike in this supposedly freeing way is to accept limited and limiting adult ideas—to be childlike rather than mature, simple rather than sophisticated, intuitive rather than reasonable, empty rather than full.

Writing before theory, then, Hazard neatly reveals all the ways in which theory has taught us to be suspicious of our assumptions about children and children's literature—why we might fear them. Too neatly, perhaps—you might well wonder why I have spent so much time attacking such an obvious target. I have done it simply because so much of what I read in Hazard could still appear in adult discussion of children's literature today—still does appear, albeit, perhaps, in less poetic and more scientific language, influenced by brands of developmental psychology and pedagogical theory whose unspoken and uncontested myths of origin are very much like the ideas and assumptions that Hazard expresses so boldly.

And they appear for a good reason. I find it hard to imagine a third position in addition to the one Hazard presents and the one that shows me the dangers of the one Hazard presents. Theory tells me to fear Hazard; logic tells me that as long as children's literature exists as an endeavor of adults, it will always emerge from adult representations of childhood, and therefore, will always be in some way what Hazard describes it as being. To attack Hazard and to learn to fear him is, in some fundamental way, to learn to fear the entire project of children's literature, its very existence.

Is there then any third way possible? That's what I'd like to consider next.

My first step beyond fear comes, I realize, as I think about whom or what I fear for.

If I talk about embedding children or constructing their subjectivity as misrepresentation or oppression or limitation of their full potential, I'm assuming the existence of a child larger than, outside of, and complete beyond the construction—a whole, unified, coherent being whose unity and completeness I am fearing for. To be repressed is to be forced to be less than this whole.

But another kind of theory has taught me that such a child could exist only outside of human consciousness—beyond human life as we know it and could ever possibly be aware of it.

Before what the psychoanalytical theorist Jacques Lacan calls the mirror stage, that moment in infancy in which a child identifies itself with its image in a mirror, Lacan imagines that the child lives in a posited but in actual fact unknowable and utterly seamless universe, and makes no distinction between itself and other things—it is whole, complete, unified in the most absolute of senses. This pre-oedipal stage sounds very much like Hazard's vision of childhood: a prelapsarian paradise before knowledge of distinctions and divisions intervenes. What's interesting is that for Lacan it occurs early in infancy, at the very moment when self-consciousness first develops; what Hazard views as characteristically childlike actually disappears for Lacan at the moment when a child becomes conscious of itself as a child—or, more exactly, as just a human being. What Hazard calls childlike, Lacan might well define as not yet quite human.

In the mirror stage, the child develops an ego, a sense of self, and does so by realizing that there are things outside it, such as the space around its image in the mirror. It perceives that it exists as a separate being only inside a context that is larger than itself, and that makes the child feel small in relation to it. Once we identify ourselves with the smaller versions of ourselves we see in the mirror, therefore, we are always conscious of ourselves as diminished, lacking a wholeness we once had, eternally striving for and never achieving it, as Hazard strives for but never achieves what he perceives as the blissful delights of childhood. The mirror image, then, constrains and constricts us—as I believe the images of children that appear in children's literature work to constrict the children they attempt to embed in their images of the suitably childlike—and as, perhaps paradoxically, Hazard's idea of childhood as prelapsarian bliss constricts less blissful real children. For prelapsarian wholeness is hard to imagine as anything but empty—a state less confusing and less complex than maturity. And it isn't much of a leap to conclude that children who are successfully embedded in the limited or empty images of the childlike offered in so many children's books might well feel diminished by them—defined as being *less,* as lacking.

Inevitably, furthermore, to be conscious of oneself in terms of the imagery of mirrors is to be divided. Lacan speaks of the "bipolar nature of all subjectivity."[11] A self is both that which thinks or views, the separate, detached consciousness, and that which is being viewed or thought about. I am *that* which sees myself as *this:* in demanding and therefore confirming this relationship—a reader sees himself or herself as a character or an implied reader—literary texts for children play their part in establishing what Lacan calls "an alienating identity" built on what is only an "illusion of autonomy."[12] We are both what the books have encouraged us to believe we are *and* the reader thus encouraged, a separate being who thinks about and acknowledges the truth of that representation. To identify is to see oneself as something else in two senses—as being the thing seen *and* as being the one who does the seeing.

If Lacan is at all right, then this divided subjectivity is inevitable—is in fact, and exactly, human consciousness as humans of any age past early infancy always know it. To rail against it, to fear the ways in which books help to create it, is to rail against life itself—to hate the human condition.

I can put that in another, and much simpler, way. To fear texts because they embed children in ideology is to fear all of the social and communal aspects of human existence—and all the pleasures they offer.

To be embedded is to learn to understand oneself as a social being—in terms of the obligations and responsibilities one has toward others, and also in terms of the kinds of behavior acceptable to others that will allow individuals to survive and prosper as members of groups. To embed children is to encourage them to think of themselves as the kinds of people who can live and interact with and take pleasure from other people in the human community as currently constructed around them.

There can be no question about the fact that the demands of community can—indeed, inevitably do—repress individual freedoms and limit individual potential. But they are also and inevitably necessary as the medium of our mind-expanding and deeply pleasurable exchanges with each other. *All* societal interactions occur in a language of gestures and behaviors that allow us to express our private selves in the very act of replacing, and therefore repressing, those private selves. These social conventions are like any other language, and as repressive of choice as any language. In order to communicate within them, we must agree to use the signs and structures shared by others. If we choose to invent our own signs and structures, we will be both totally free and totally unable to communicate with anybody else. I conclude, then, that children who did somehow manage to escape the apparently fearful process of being embedded in ideology might indeed retain their freedom to be whole—but they would do so only at the cost of being involved in any way at all with other people. That's more fearful than losing a little freedom. What seems like the fearful repressive tendency of children's literature from one point of view is, from another point of view, its rich ability to provide children with a means of making enriching connections with other human beings.

There is still, of course, the danger of the mask becoming the face. It is possible, as I suggested earlier, that children encouraged by an adult world to see themselves as being childlike in a particular way might well *become* childlike in exactly that way.

Furthermore, it's unquestionably true that some of the most popular ways of being childlike, as conveyed by literature and the mass media, are decidedly repressive and exceedingly limiting. And it's also unquestionably true that powerful forces in mainstream culture work hard to impose these repressive and limiting ideas of themselves upon children. Witness, as just one example, the ways in which Disney films continue to confirm decidedly dangerous ideas about what desirable girls' and women's bodies should look like. Girls who accept these images, most often unthinkingly, as the one and only way to be attractive and powerful work very hard to conform themselves to these supposed ideals, at great expense and often at great danger to their health. In fact, then, the real danger is *not* that literature might work to fragment childhood sensibility and provide children with a divided and incoherent view of themselves. It's just the opposite of that. It might persuade children that one particular and partial representation is the complete and only truth.

Theory, which has helped me to perceive and understand this problem, also suggests a possible solution to it: knowledge of theory.

Representations possess the fearful potential to repress and envelop us without our being aware of it only to the degree to which we are unconscious of the fact that they *are* representations—and therefore accept them as the way things naturally and obviously are. Althusser says:

It is indeed a peculiarity of ideology that it imposes (without appearing to do so, since these are "obviousnesses") obviousnesses as obviousnesses, which we cannot *fail to recognize* and before which we have the inevitable and natural reaction of crying out (loud or in the "still small voice of conscience"): "That's obvious! That's right! That's true!"[13]

N.B.

The potential for freedom, then, comes in realizing that the obvious may *not* be true—may just be a representation, just one possible way of being out of a vast spectrum of other possible ways of being that one might consider, try on, adopt. In the matter of ways of being human, one has a choice only at the point at which one realizes one has a choice.

Theory taught me that. If it worked for me, then why can't it work for children?

I believe that it can. I believe, indeed, that we adults must do everything we possibly can to make children aware of the "obviousnesses" that texts work to impose on them and to give them the means to weigh and consider the implications of the subject positions that texts offer. If we are not to fear for what texts might do to them, in other words, we must teach them to be divided subjects in their reading and in their lives—to be involved as both implied readers of texts and critical observers of what texts demand of them in that process. The texts I refer to here include literature—and also all the physical and social representations and gestures and conventions that make up our life in society.

To read the world in this way is to *be* this way—divided, fragmented, always aware of how the faces one puts on are merely masks, how there is always more to us than whatever particular way we've decided to represent our selves to others (and therefore, presumably, to ourselves) at any particular moment. This is not I that you see standing here talking to you—it is the I that I have chosen to represent myself as today.

In discussing how we perceive ourselves in terms of gender, Judith Butler argues that it always a question of performance—that we become male or female by enacting in our minds and bodies our culture's ideas about maleness or femaleness. What's true of gender, an aspect of our self-perception, seems to me to be generally true of all aspects of our self-understanding. As representations, personalities are roles we put on and perform—and, perhaps, nothing more. We are, in fact, fragmentary, collections of roles or representations, each of which is merely partial, not unified at all. Rather than fear that fact and work toward some illusory utopia of unity and wholeness, we might instead celebrate the fragmentary. We might simply revel in and rejoice in the playful possibilities of the various masks and roles we can choose to put on, and the various beings we can inconsistently, at various points, choose to become.

In the end, then, theory teaches me that a foolish consistency is indeed the hobgoblin of little minds—minds that foolishly choose to perceive themselves as littler than they actually are. There is really no such thing as a complete or whole or coherent individual—and that's something to celebrate, not something to fear.

If we can learn to celebrate it, and teach children to celebrate it, then children's literature can be a source of much more than fear. It can, in its various manifestations, offer children a vast repertoire of ways of being human to choose from, to play with, to celebrate.

All we adults have to do, then, is not to fear—to fear neither children nor books. Not to fear children means to trust their ability to make wise decisions and enjoy playful possibilities once equipped with the strategies for doing so—the knowledge of theory I've just talked about. Not to fear literature is to not eliminate from children's experience books whose representations personally distress us, but instead to allow children access to as wide a range of representations as possible, in books of all sorts from places of all sorts by people of all sorts.

If we can be that fearless, then children will indeed learn to belong to a different world than our current repressed and limiting world of grown-ups. But then we grown-ups will belong to that different world, too.

NOTES

1. Paul Hazard, *Books, Children, and Men*, trans. Marguerite Mitchell (Boston: Horn Book, 1944), pp. 1–2.

2. Ibid., p. 42.

3. Ibid.

4. Ibid., p. 167.

5. James Kincaid, *Child-Loving: The Erotic Child and Victorian Culture* (New York and London: Routledge, 1992), pp. 70–71.

6. Hazard, *Books, Children, and Men*, p. 166.

7. Ibid., p. 42.

8. Kincaid, *Child-Loving*, p. 70.

9. Jacqueline Rose, *The Case of Peter Pan; or, The Impossibility of Children's Fiction* (London: Macmillan, 1984), p. 2.

10. Hazard, *Books, Children, and Men*, p. 3.

11. Jacques Lacan, *Écrits: A Selection*, trans. Alan Sheridan (New York and London: Norton, 1977), p. 10.

12. Ibid., pp. 4, 6.

13. Louis Althusser, "Ideology and Ideological State Apparatuses," trans. Ben Brewster, in *Critical Theory Since 1965*, ed. Hazard Adams, and Leroy Searle (Tallahassee: University Press of Florida and Florida State University Press, 1986), p. 245.

REFERENCES

Althusser, Louis. "Ideology and Ideological State Apparatuses." Trans. Ben Brewster. In *Critical Theory Since 1965*. Ed. Hazard Adams and Leroy Searle. Tallahassee: University Press of Florida and Florida State University Press, 1986.

Butler, Judith. *Gender Trouble: Feminism and the Subversion of Identity*. New York and London: Routledge, 1990.

Hazard, Paul. *Books, Children, and Men*. Trans. Marguerite Mitchell. Boston: Horn Book, 1944.

Kincaid, James. *Child-Loving: The Erotic Child and Victorian Culture*. New York and London: Routledge, 1992.

Lacan, Jacques. *Écrits: A Selection*. Trans. Alan Sheridan. New York and London: Norton, 1977.

Nodelman, Perry. "The Other: Orientalism, Colonialism, and Children's Literature." *Children's Literature Association Quarterly* 17, no. 1 (Spring 1992): 29–35.

Rose, Jacqueline. *The Case of Peter Pan; or, The Impossibility of Children's Fiction*. London: Macmillan, 1984.

Stephens, John. *Language and Ideology in Children's Fiction*. London and New York: Longman, 1992.

2

"Is This the Promised End . . . ?": *Fin de Siècle* Mentality and Children's Literature

John Stephens

Although what is associated with the *fin de siècle* mentality has not obviously permeated contemporary children's literature, its influence is nevertheless evident in some recent narrative fictions. By *fin de siècle* mentality I refer, of course, to ways of thinking shaped by the sense of an approaching end: the end of a century and of a millennium, and the apparent disappearance of ideas and values that had been used to give order and meaning to existence for the last couple of hundred years. It's hard to speak convincingly about this, needless to say, because the ideas seem to have been developing over the past half-century, and in accelerated modern time, the idea of the *fin de siècle* began rather early.

We can, though, at least in Western societies, point to attitudes that parallel those perhaps more obviously present during the last *fin de siècle*, especially pessimism, cynicism, and a mixed sense of anxiety, unease, and exhilaration. Interlocked with such attitudes is the realization that as the century moves to its close, we find ourselves more and more acting and thinking collectively, and less and less individually. These effects have been muted to some extent by another ending, that of the Cold War, with its accompanying reduction in anxiety about apocalypse through nuclear warfare. They have also been muted, as Stjepan Meštrović argues, because "these things are disguised under the rubric of 'postmodernism.'"[1] Many attributes of postmodernism are also attributes of *fin de siècle* mentality: a cultivation of radical indeterminacy; a preference in representation for transparency, for surfaces-without-depth; the return of surrealism (of which Gothic horror fiction for the children's market is perhaps a pertinent example); hostility toward "high" culture; and so on. These are tendencies that *may* create anxiety about the directions in which society is heading at the *fin de siècle*.

The question I want to consider is, if *fin de siècle* mentality is being represented in children's literature, what forms is it taking? It becomes most apparent, I suggest, in fictions that concentrate thematically on the interface between destructivity and creativity, and in particular in two main kinds of such fiction. The first kind encompasses a broad range of fictions that deal with humanity's crises—displacement and homelessness, urban decline, ecological crisis, epidemic drug use—often projected into apocalyptic themes, and that forecast a bleak future for humanity, or that reaffirm "traditional" values over against the pervasive values of postmodernity. This type of fiction has appeared in children's literature only since about 1970.[2]

A second kind of fiction that deals with *fin de siècle* themes is to be found in books that focus on art and creativity, and that reaffirm the meaningfulness of individual creative acts of the imagination, as against *fin de siècle* absence of meaning, and thence reaffirm such key humanistic ideas as freedom, self-expression, self-awareness and self-realization, and individual agency. Thus many books published in the early 1990s at least implicitly situate themselves against a social tendency to empty events of value or meaning, and at least implicitly address what Meštrović describes as "the burning question left over from the 1880s: how to secure a humane, decent, and just society and government?"[3] I will be referring to seven books published between 1992 and 1994, examining their representations of social structure and projected futures, and commenting on "the sense of an ending" in each as it moves toward some point of closure that interrogates the values of postmodernity.[4]

The issues of human subjectivity and individual agency have been widely debated since about 1970, albeit with relatively minor impact on children's literature, which in general still conforms to modernist notions of subjectivity and agency. However, whenever these issues become problematized in children's literature, as in most of the books I'm concerned with here, they are nuanced with a sense of anxiety that at least conforms with *fin de siècle* anxiety. This is expressed most obviously as loss of meaning in the world and of purpose for the individual. It is articulated most clearly by Guy, a young artist in Sonya Hartnett's *Wilful Blue*, a few days before he kills himself. In part, he says:

it's a miserable thing, being empty of belief. Not just in religion—in everything. I have no faith in anything any more. What I have is a huge disappointment. In the world, in myself. That the world is not as interesting as it should be, as I imagined it would be when I was young. That I am not the person I wanted to be. I wanted to be someone remarkable, someone memorable. I had such big plans for myself when I was a child. But I won't ever be like that. I'll never be who I wanted to be, where I wanted to be. Disappointment and doubt—not what I imagined. Not what I was taught.[5]

Through Guy's disappointment in the world and himself, Hartnett raises a crucial issue facing children becoming adults during this *fin de siècle*: social ideology teaches them that individual agency exists in a world of large possibilities, but they are likely to grow up to discover that this is not true. On the other hand—and I think this is characteristic of how *fin de siècle* mentality is controlled in children's fiction—this bleak worldview does not become authoritative. Rather, Hartnett uses a complex narrative structure to depict Guy as largely unknowable because finally deeply solipsistic. The story unfolds as a retrospective narrative, told to Guy's sister, Grere, by two other young artists, Jesse and Walt, the only people who know that his death by drowning was suicide rather than accidental. Because they have decided not to reveal this, they must falsify the story they tell. Further, readers are unable to determine what has been told and what only remembered, because the narration is situated in at least three different times—the time of the events related, the time of the narrating, and the time of Guy's funeral—and events are almost entirely focalized by Jesse (apart from a few paragraphs focalized by Grere in the opening and closing chapters). These strategies have the effect of demanding that readers think very hard about cause-and-effect relationships that usually structure narrative.

Hartnett also makes a space for interrogating Guy's worldview through the novel's central concern with creativity. Guy, Jesse, and Walt are part of a group of young artists employed by a would-be patron of the arts to try to found an artists' colony, and she has commissioned Guy and Jesse to collaborate on a large painting of four Australian artists of the late nineteenth century "Heidelberg School."[6] They set the painting in 1889, and depict the four as "pioneers—'young radicals in revolt'":[7] that is, they are creative artists working during the last *fin de siècle* who are inspired by confidence and optimism. This positive worldview is strongly brought out in an extended two-page ekphrasis describing the finished painting, and especially in the forward-looking "[their work] would be derided, savaged by critics, perhaps some people on the beach had already sneered at it; but history would look kindly upon it and call it masterly, and the four artists looked as if they knew this: they looked badly worn, but they also looked . . . sure."[8] Guy's loss of faith in his own talent, in his capacity for intersubjective relationships, and in any teleological meaning, is thus placed as one possible response to the world, but not a necessary response.

Of the other novels, those by Francesca Lia Block, Catherine Jinks, Susan Price, Gillian Rubinstein, and Cynthia Voigt explore social conditions under which the loss of independent agency can occur. Block and Voigt, in different ways, use the classical Orpheus myth to examine relationships between creativity and cultural formations (audience expectations, pop music culture). Jinks, Price, and Rubinstein use science fiction to project future crises as the outcomes of contemporary tendencies. In Jink's *The Future Trap*, for example, Paula, a fourteen-year-old girl, is snatched 5000 years into the future, to a scientific research station on a desolate, uninhabitable planet, which turns out to be Earth. Here she finds a regimented society in which populations have been specialized by genetic engineering—"Ironclads," for example, are a human form engineered for strength and endurance in harsh environments. Such projected futures reflect an apprehension that modern societies are moving toward structures in which human functions are specialized and restricted, with little space for individuality or agency. The novel is about resisting the contemporary factors that might produce such a future, and moves toward a quite exhortatory closure. When Paula is about to be returned to her own time, she is advised: "Try not to let what you have seen affect what you do. Try to forget that it ever happened."[9] Instead, however, looking around her own garden, she expresses a resolution that must be considered the antithesis of *fin de siècle* mentality: "And she thought: I've got to save it. Somehow I've got to save it. Even if I have to spend the rest of my life doing it, I've *got to save this planet.*"[10]

Jinks's genetically engineered humans overlap with another area through which science fiction enables themes of subjectivity and agency to be foregrounded, that of the introduction of robots, androids, or cyborgs as major characters: the possibility that technology can be used to create a living being with human self-awareness has been imagined for a long time. O. B. Hardison, Jr., points to two nightmares that "hover just below the surface of machine life": that machine life may turn out to be malevolent, and that robots may become indistinguishable from people.[11] The former has been treated in, for example, the *Doctor Who* "Robots of Death" series; the grounding text for the latter is Philip Dick's *Do Androids Dream of Electric Sheep* (more widely known in its derivative form as the film *Blade Runner* [1982]). Price's *Coming Down to Earth* incorporates a large bundle of these concerns.

In this novel, Price projects late-twentieth-century social tendencies into the future and explores their implications through the experiences of Azalin, an eleven-year-old girl from Newarth, a utopian space colony built by people who had chosen to escape the social and economic ills of Earth. As in many other utopias, social consensus in Newarth functions to suppress difference, dissent, or discontent. People lead highly regulated lives in a state where there is full employment but no choice of occupation, where life is communal and private space very restricted, and where there is little place for inquiry, imagination, or enterprise. Dissatisfied with the life predetermined for her on Newarth, Azalin runs away while on a school trip to Earth, and inadvertently makes her way to Birmingham, where she eventually takes refuge in an urban wasteland that Price represents as the inevitable outcome of the late-twentieth-century Conservative government's social and industrial policies.

The problem of human agency in a regulated society is accentuated by the companion Azalin finds—a humanoid robot named Houdin who has developed self-awareness and a desire for agency, and is running away to avoid reprogramming designed to strip away these attributes. Neither of them succeeds, except that when Azalin is traced and returned to Newarth and her future as a storekeeper, she takes with her Houdin's hard disk. This is his subjectivity in process of becoming, and Azalin is able to install it in a small, unobtrusive maintenance robot. Both must therefore operate in a more restricted domain than they had desired but, importantly, they still have something all of these novels assume to be a basic human quality—an intersubjective relationship, reciprocated empathy, concern for the other. If human beings forget that they fully exist only as individual selves in states of intersubjectivity, they will bring about the wasteland Price images as the product of *fin de siècle* England.

The idea that *fin de siècle* society is transforming itself into something inhuman and inhumane informs the social allegory that is the basis of Donna Jo Napoli's *The Prince of the Pond* (1994), which deals overtly with the recuperation of some traditional social values. A re-versioning of the "Frog Prince" story, this narrative encodes *fin de siècle* apocalypse in the figure of the hag who enchants the prince—that is, deprives him of humanity and, initially, of agency—and then hunts him. For his part, the Prince, now the frog Pin, begins civilizing the pond by introducing concepts

such as love, family, community, and concern for others into an environment that
otherwise functions as a mere foodchain. As the aggressive bullfrog remarks, "What's
going on? Since when do frogs care about what happens to other frogs?"[12] In other
words, by affirming conservative, even nostalgic, values, the book rejects the
relativism and nihilism of the postmodern world. When, near the end of the novel, Pin
decides to take his fifty small children back to the palace well, where they will be safe
from the hag, even though this seems against all frog logic ("Where will we find food?
How will we all swim about?"), his wife finally decides: "Yes, I would follow that
crazy frog and all those crazy froglets. I would follow them, and we would find a way
to survive. I didn't know how, but I knew we would."[13] The suggestion that survival
depends on resistance to and transformation of contemporary social conditions is an
overt message in this fairy tale, enforced by the end when, Pin having been
inadvertently transformed back into a human being, the values he has introduced
continue on.

The premise that social and family values are collapsing also grounds the
apocalyptic vision of Rubinstein's *Galax-Arena*. It's also comparable with Price's
Coming Down to Earth, in projecting a future from the widening socioeconomic gap
between the haves and the havenots at the end of the twentieth century. These elements
of social crisis are emphasized by a narrative strategy that turns on a process of
horrific disclosure: for about two-thirds of the novel, the story is apparently set in a
fantastic, alien world—a group of children have been kidnapped and deceived into
thinking they have been transported to another world, Vexak, where they are made to
perform sometimes fatal gymnastic routines in the Galax Arena for the amusement of
the inhabitants, who regard the children merely as circus animals. When one of the
children (Joella, the narrator) discovers that they are still on Earth, and their captors
are human, the effect is that the familiar, known world becomes threatening and
disturbing.

The enclosed fantasy world enables the representation of society as a system, with
the world of the gym functioning as a microcosm of the power relations of the social
world. The morally reprehensible actions of the children's captors act as a scathing
comment on social power relations in postmodern society. *Galax-Arena* is one of the
most pessimistic children's novels published in Australia, moving to a closure
characterized by loss and despair: the book ends, in effect, with the narrator awaiting
the arrival of her executioners. It is possible—indeed proper—to argue that *Galax-
Arena* negatively asserts positive values because it evokes anger at social injustice and
lack of moral or human values, but there is no certain guarantee that adolescent
readers will not, rather, see its bleakness as merely expressing the *fin de siècle*
mentality.

The gymnastic exhibitions in *Galax-Arena* represent a breakdown in the proper
reciprocal relationship between artistic production and audience, which is perhaps
another important trait of *fin de siècle* postmodernism. As in three of the other
books—*Coming Down to Earth*, *Orfe*, and *Ecstasia*—this novel assumes an
interrelationship between entertainment and responsibility that parallel's Meštrović's
account of how apocalyptic themes are emptied of meaning in contemporary media:
"Postmodernist audiences are exposed routinely to apocalyptic themes that are

camouflaged in 'fun' images, so that they are not permitted to feel indignation, outrage, real concern, nor even a desire to act. The threat of the apocalypse is converted into entertainment."[14] *Galax-Arena* and *Orfe* both deal with versions of an entertainment industry, with *Orfe* in particular examining the operation of apocalyptic themes in popular culture and the shallowness of audiences that crave Orfe's "It Makes Me Sick" song (which ends with projectile vomiting) as a substitute for actual empathy with human suffering. At this novel's close, Orfe bitterly attributes her failure to retrieve her lover from the hell of drug addiction to an element of escapism from existential engagement with life processes in the *fin de siècle* mentality: "What kind of fools are they if they think life is never going to hurt? If they think they can be safe and never hurt and still be alive?"[15]

Orfe and *Ecstasia* use the Orpheus and Eurydice myth to comment on and interrogate modern culture, and finally to reaffirm forms of liberal humanism in the face of a culture whose formations seem to promote meaninglessness. The myth's pivotal motifs of music and lost love enable the implications about creativity and relations between individuals and societies to be worked out in the contexts of pop culture and the dream of romantic love.

Ecstasia, a novel for older and rather sophisticated readers, is written in the postmodernist style that Block characteristically uses to deconstruct postmodernism. It consists of a mixture of genres and modes, including such things as narrated stretches, focalized by various characters; visions; drug-induced stream-of-consciousness utterances; and song lyrics. The novel depicts a schematized, futuristic world that is a projection of contemporary postmodern society—the world of surfaces, of ecstatic experiences, of a youth culture devoted exclusively to an irrational pursuit of pleasure and striving to deny temporality, especially in its aspects of aging and death. The main settings in the novel are Elysia, the pleasure world of the young, and Under, the Hades beneath the city where "Old Ones" go to await death at the first signs of aging or the young go to obtain drugs that offer them the illusion of memory or transcendence. Beyond Elysia is the Desert, a hard world inhabited by people of all generations that signifies community, intersubjective relationships and commitments, love, and Being as a state of reflective self-awareness. The Orpheus figure, Rafe, cannot recover his dead beloved from the underworld, but he does finally take his music out into the world and use it to effect change. In his final recuperation of his grief, at the novel's close, he uses his music to call a garden into existence in the desert. By the close of the novel, the representation of Orphic desire has transcended the ultimately solipsistic focus on the recovery of a lost Eurydice—the faith in love between two people as a panacea for social ills—to find expression within and for sociality.

The blending of mythological frame and postmodernist narrative modes in *Ecstasia* is used to affirm a sense of good in the world, of purpose, and of the permanence of human values. Against the tendency to meaninglessness in modern existence, Block pits a sense of a deep and recuperated past, human relationships based on love, and human creativity in the form of music (especially that of musicians working in a group), asserting the power of art to effect change. In doing this, it seems to me to epitomize the response of contemporary children's fiction to the *fin de siècle* mentality which I've attempted to trace through this bundle of books.

NOTES

1. Stjepan Meštrović, *The Coming Fin de Siècle: An Application of Durkheim's Sociology to Modernity and Postmodernity* (London and New York: Routledge, 1991), p. 2.

2. For further discussion, see John Stephens, "Post-Disaster Fiction: The Problematics of a Genre," *Papers: Explorations into Children's Literature* 3, no. 3 (1992): 126–130.

3. Meštrović, *The Coming Fin de Siècle*, p. 2.

4. The "apocalyptic" group is Catherine Jinks, *The Future Trap* (Norwood, N. J.: Omnibus Books, 1993); Susan Price, *Coming Down to Earth* (London: Lions, 1994); Gillian Rubinstein, *Galax-Arena* (Melbourne: Hyland House, 1992). The "art" group is Francesca Lia Block, *Ecstasia* (New York: Penguin, 1993); Sonya Hartnett, *Wilful Blue* (Ringwood, Australia.: Viking, 1994); Donna Jo Napoli, *The Prince of the Pond* (New York: Puffin, 1994); Cynthia Voigt, *Orfe* (London: Lions, 1992). *Ecstasia, Coming Down to Earth*, and *Galax-Arena* contain elements of both kinds.

5. Hartnett, *Wilful Blue*, p. 123.

6. Charles Conder, Frederick McCubbin, Tom Roberts, and Arthur Streeton.

7. Hartnett, *Wilful Blue*, p. 41.

8. Ibid., pp. 143–144.

9. Jinks, *The Future Trap*, p. 183.

10. Ibid., p. 184.

11. O. B Hardison, Jr., *Disappearing Through the Skylight* (New York: Viking, 1989), p. 320. See also Lois Kuznets, *When Toys Come Alive* (New Haven and London: Yale University Press, 1994), chap. 10.

12. Napoli, *The Prince of the Pond*, p. 131.

13. Ibid., p. 137.

14. Meštrović, *The Coming Fin de Siècle*, p. 3.

15. Voigt, *Orfe*, p. 120.

REFERENCES

Block, Francesca Lia. *Ecstasia*. New York: Penguin, 1993.

Hardison, O. B., Jr. *Disappearing Through the Skylight: Culture and Technology in the Twentieth Century*. New York: Viking, 1989.

Hartnett, Sonya. *Wilful Blue*. Ringwood, Australia: Viking, 1994.

Jinks, Catherine. *The Future Trap*. Norwood, N. J.: Omnibus Books, 1993.

Kuznets, Lois. *When Toys Come Alive*. New Haven and London: Yale University Press, 1994.

Meštrović, Stjepan. *The Coming Fin de Siècle: An Application of Durkheim's Sociology to Modernity and Postmodernity*. London and New York: Routledge, 1991.

Napoli, Donna Jo. *The Prince of the Pond*. New York: Puffin, 1994.

Price, Susan. *Coming Down to Earth*. London: Lions, 1994.

Rubinstein, Gillian. *Galax-Arena*. Melbourne: Hyland House, 1992.

Stephens, John. "Post-Disaster Fiction: The Problematics of a Genre." *Papers: Explorations into Children's Literature* 3, no. 3 (1992): 126–130.
Voigt, Cynthia. *Orfe*. London: Lions, 1992.

3

Ramona the Underestimated:
The Everyday-Life Story
in Children's Literature

Deborah Stevenson

Stories of everyday life, of family, and of school exist for children of all ages, and such stories provide the bulk of contemporary American children's literature for readers aged eight to twelve. They are popular with children and often cherished by adult practitioners and critics, yet they are frequently lost in the shadow of books more stimulating to adult readers and scholars. Taking as synecdoche and as example Beverly Cleary's extremely successful books about Ramona, I examine the light this undervaluation casts upon children's literature's history, practices, and criticism, and the ways in which this undervaluation ironically mirrors the treatment children's literature itself has frequently received.

Children's literature is not, of course, monolithic, nor are children's literature authorities, a term I employ to include practitioners—librarians, teachers, and parents—who work with children as well as critics who write upon or teach the subject. There is no choric voice speaking one overriding viewpoint, and there have been adults who have championed this kind of children's fiction or considered it worthy of analysis. These adults, however, are exceptions to the field's general disinclination to consider the everyday-life story not just a worthwhile but also a creditable literature.

The treatment of everyday life is not, of course, a concern unique to children's literature. Discourse about the importance and authenticity of daily life has figured prominently in sociology and cultural theory, treated by scholars such as Agnes Heller, Michel de Certeau, and Henri Lefebvre. The issues surrounding theories of everyday life, unsurprisingly, parallel those of the everyday-life story: Michel Maffesoli notes, for instance, the tendency for sociologies of everyday life to be overlooked in favor of apparently grander subjects, and Mike Featherstone points out both the difficulty of defining everyday life and the linkage of that concept with women.[1] Most useful for my discussion, however, is Featherstone's examination of the polarization of everyday life and heroic life, and the different valuations of these two modes of interpreting existence. This polarization, and the valorization of the heroic mode at the expense of that of everyday life, pervade the critical treatment of children's literature.

At the heart of this question of undervaluation is the question of value itself. What makes a book singularly meritorious? Originality or familiarity? Entertainment or education? Understandability or challenge? What kinds of books make a genre meritorious? What kinds of books will make the world take this literature seriously? The topics of the Newbery medalists in the past few years include death, morality, and race relations, all subjects that adults respect as worthy matter, all subjects that demonstrate how serious and substantial children's literature can be. Even if Louis Sachar's *Marvin Redpost: Why Pick on Me?* had been considered the best children's book of 1994, children's literature authorities would not have awarded their ultimate prize to a book about nose-picking—what would the neighbors say?

One manifestation of children's literature's attempts at self-justification is the valorization of books that most strongly resemble adult books. Although everyday-life stories feature prominently on children's-choice award lists and circulate to a feverish degree, the adult-judged awards and the adult critical attention tend to go to books of a more traditionally "weighty" nature: those that treat, in Featherstone's terms, heroic life rather than everyday life. Critics find their material in dramatic fantasies, controversial problem novels, and pivotal coming-of-age sagas, shying away from the challenge of books where the family does not break down and where no great tragedy occurs—from, in short, books whose merits may uniquely depend upon their audience.

Francelia Butler suggests that English departments sneer at children's books as "the literature with the washable covers";[2] the response of children's literature authorities has generally been outraged denial and a claim that young-adult fiction is nearly as good as adult fiction, rather than an invitation to such sneerers to discover the merits of washable covers. Even critics writing on Beverly Cleary seem more at ease discussing her novel for older readers, *Dear Mr. Henshaw* (1983), than they do the Ramona books: Geraldine DeLuca applauds *Dear Mr. Henshaw* for handling "many matters that the bulk of her work avoids," and Pat Pflieger, in her monograph on Cleary, states that *Dear Mr. Henshaw* "deserves deep analysis on its own," which presumably the remainder of Cleary's works do not.[3] Children's literature authorities often seem to feel that their literature needs to grow up to become adult literature, just as its readers need to grow up to become adults; praise is often meted out according to how close a book comes to that adult ideal.

Attempts to demonstrate that children's literature can tackle serious subjects often produce books that seem to be watered-down versions of adult literature: there are quite a few dystopias, I would argue, superior to Lois Lowry's *The Giver* (1993), many of them understandable to children of the same reading level.[4] The fact that such a book is in many ways like an adult book seems often to blind adult readers to the fact that those adult books are, by most traditional literary standards, better books. *The Giver* is, however, a more exciting book for children's literature critics than are most everyday-life stories. American children's literature offers a few dystopias, but they are almost exclusively post-apocalyptic tales written for a young-adult audience, so Lowry's book deals with issues of morality in a way that seems innovative within the genre. The appearance of innovation fades, unfortunately, when one views the book in terms of both adult and children's literatures; it resembles an adult book only so long as no one actually compares it with adult literature. Even this illusory and ephemeral resemblance, however, gives the book and, correspondingly, the genre of children's literature a glamour that the workaday everyday-life story never can.

The classic everyday-life heroine, Ramona first appeared as a supporting, albeit never minor, character in Beverly Cleary's books about Henry Huggins; she pushed her way to a title role in *Beezus and Ramona* (1955) and then took her rightful place in the spotlight in six books: *Ramona the Pest* (1968), *Ramona the Brave* (1975), *Ramona and Her Father* (1977), *Ramona and Her Mother* (1978), *Ramona Quimby, Age 8* (1981), and *Ramona Forever* (1984). Initially a wayward toddler, she has triumphantly become a big sister and a third-grader by the final book, but she is essentially the same impulsive person dealing with the same difficult demands of getting through daily child life throughout the series. She has been a favorite of young readers from the very beginning and continues to be even today, over a decade after her last appearance. Many of the characteristics that have made these books successful, however—their humor, their quotidian subject matter, their proclivity toward serial appearances—and even that very popularity inhibit their serious critical consideration.

Like many everyday-life stories, the Ramona books rely extensively on humor. Humor is in some ways a double-edged sword: books that are particularly humorous may win more attention for this feat but will rarely garner the serious attention given to books of a more sober tone. Light comedy is a traditionally undervalued field in virtually every art: when it is done well, it looks too easy, and humor in children's fiction offers delicate directorial challenges to which many authors fail to rise. American awards committees rarely select a comedy for the ultimate prizes; to state that a funny story is the ultimate in children's literature is, it seems to be feared, to suggest that children's literature is as light and insignificant as it has often been painted.

Nor does the subject matter of these books help stave off skeptical charges of insignificance—there is no human death or life-threatening illness, no global crisis, no painful realizations of racism or sexism in the chronicles of Ramona; these are not stories of great heroism. While there is conflict in Cleary's books, that conflict is not the point of the books in the way it is in other children's fictions. Everyday-life stories describe interaction with peers at school, struggles with sibling rivalry at home, or anticipation of a holiday; they end usually for temporal reasons (e.g., summer is over) rather than reasons of climax or resolution. It often seems that each volume simply chronicles the struggle to make it to the next book.

Everyday-life stories not only demonstrate but also depend upon predictability: friends fall out; teachers teach, or upset, or both. In such fictions for older audiences, protagonists as young as fifth and sixth grade start wondering about members of the opposite sex. Perry Nodelman notes that "most children's books are 'simple,' undetailed, and consequently, so similar to each other that their generic similarities and their evocations of archetypes are breathtakingly obvious."[5] Such "simple" books can begin to seem homogeneous to the adult reader, and series of everyday-life stories featuring the same protagonist begin to blend together.

Such a lack of episodic differentiation is, to a certain extent, the point. Were a new Ramona book to appear, one would not ask (nor would one with books about most other classic everyday-life stories) what the book is "about," because it is about Ramona. They are all about Ramona. What overtly differs in each book is the season, or perhaps how her father's efforts at finding a job he likes have been rewarded, or if she likes her new teacher, but these differences do not necessarily distinguish the events in one book from those in another. What is important is Ramona's overall growth and reflection, not the events that cause them. Each of Cleary's books shows Ramona at a different stage of Ramonaness than she was in the previous book, as she, like the reader, matures, but she is still Ramona, and therein lies the point of continuing to read her exploits. With their focus on recurrent visits with the same character, everyday-life stories as exemplified by the Ramona books are devoted to the sheer literary pleasure found, as Wayne Booth says, in his book so titled, in "the company we keep."[6]

As Jane Tompkins points out, these characteristics of predictability, circumscription of pleasure, and apparent literary safety are not those that critics are accustomed to venerating.[7] As child readers relish the return of their favorites and appreciate the books all the more for the familiarity of the hero or heroine, adults grow less interested in what appears to be more of the same, no matter how well crafted the same is. To practitioners and critics, who read a great many everyday-life stories, the subject matter can begin to seem clichéd regardless of the merit of the writing or the memorableness of the main character. Where child readers value familiarity, adult authorities distrust it; to hold up as meritorious a book that is conspicuously lacking in originality, obviously resembling the author's other works about the same character, is to suggest that this book is good in spite of—or, more challengingly, because of—its flouting of the traditional merit of originality.

Some of the most significant feminist criticism since the mid-1970s has challenged the devaluation of literature popular with and written for a devalued class; much of this criticism is meaningful for the discussion of children's literature as well. Jane Tompkins points out that "the *popularity* of novels by women has been held against them almost as much as their preoccupation with 'trivial' feminine concerns." If one replaces "by women" and "feminine" with "for children" and "childish," that statement applies to contemporary children's everyday-life stories much as it did to nineteenth-century domestic fiction. I would go on to contend that, despite the strong presence of women in nearly every aspect of the production of children's literature, Tompkins' charge that criticism equates "popularity with debasement, . . . domesticity with triviality, and all of these, implicitly, with womanly inferiority" still and often applies to academic criticism of children's literature.[8]

Like feminist criticism, "children's literature criticism has had to come out of a corner fighting";[9] like much feminist criticism, children's literature criticism often displays a strongly defensive tone, repeatedly explaining, in the face of anticipated opposition, the worth of studying these books and frequently commenting, sometimes bitterly, about the critical underestimation of such texts. Such defensiveness is not necessarily misplaced in either kind of criticism; both kinds of scholarship have been denigrated as trivial, dismissed as an unimportant women's concern, and ignored.

Since both women and children operate from positions of diminished power, it would be inappropriate to overlook this effect on their literatures. It is nonetheless notable that, in criticism of both kinds of literature, the criticism's perception that it is itself struggling against opposition infuses the scholarship to such a degree and for such a duration.

Children's literature, especially in America, is a female-dominated genre, and the everyday-life story is historically a strongly female literature, "written always by women for the reading of girls."[10] Yet everyday-life stories are rarely valorized by the feminine discipline that judges them; behind this devaluation of the daily is a struggle against the perceived femininity of children's literature. While the female shaping of children's literature sometimes works to the genre's advantage, the counterreaction to that female predominance, that determination to fight the categorization of children's literature criticism as "nursery" criticism, contributes to keeping these "feminine" books from receiving the ultimate accolades. Practitioners and critics of both sexes underplay the role of these domestic fictions in children's literature in order to prove the genre's seriousness. These books evoke too much affection both from adult practitioners and from child readers to disappear from libraries and bookshelves because of this undervaluation, but these fictions are, as a result of this struggle for recognition, casualties of critical regard.

This constant struggle for justification, this "generic self-image," as Zohar Shavit terms it,[11] permeates much critical writing on children's literature and influences children's literature authorities' recognition of individual titles and of types of literature. The field's newness to the academy and its uncertainty encourage it to adopt conservative views of literary merit and critical purpose, views that adult literary criticism has seriously challenged for some time. As children's literature attempts to establish and justify itself according to those views, it treats the everyday-life story with the same affectionate condescension with which adult literary criticism has often viewed children's literature.

Nicholas Tucker describes children's literature as "backward-looking";[12] there is a widespread, albeit not unanimous, opinion that children's literature's very merit lies in its resistance to new forms, that it is, as Isaac Bashevis Singer called it, "a last refuge from a literature gone berserk and ready for suicide."[13] The literature tends to replicate the tastes of the past, the childhood of the adult rather than the experience of the contemporary child; the criticism, in its attempt to justify the literature and itself, tends similarly to cling to venerable methods of scholarship, which offer an illusion of solidity. While other literary genres are contemplating dismantling their canons, children's literature, in volumes such as the Touchstones series, or Charles Frey and John Griffith's *The Literary Heritage of Childhood: An Appraisal of Children's Classics in the Western Tradition* (1987), is attempting to build one. Karín Lesnik-Oberstein points out that even Peter Hunt's important criticism incorporates a subtle and apparently unquestioning reliance on adult literary theories, such as canonization, literary influence, and reader theory, whose validity has been seriously challenged.[14] Aidan Chambers' classic essay "Three Fallacies About Children's Books" opines that many children's literature critics like finding in children's literature the kind of solid, old-fashioned story they appreciate, and that they intend to ensure the continued existence of such literature;[15] I would suggest that many such critics employ a "solid, old-fashioned criticism" that overlooks some of the greatest merits of the genre.

Using awards to judge a genre can be misleading, but the choice of recipients for major distinction, such as the Newbery Medal, is still revealing. Awards are by their very nature designed to reward important books. They are also tacit statements about the genres from which the awardees come, demonstrating not only which books are important within a particular genre but also that the genre, by extension, is itself important. The series of judgments of importance that make up the Newbery list offer an interesting insight into what has appeared significant to representatives of the children's literature community over the years. The last everyday-life story to win even an honor citation was *Ramona Quimby, Age 8*, in 1982, and these fictions did not feature prominently before that (the last time a classic everyday-life story won the Newbery Medal itself was in 1952).

Most recent medal winners combine a social challenge of some kind with a straightforward, almost old-fashioned telling of a tale; in short, the books have been very literarily conservative, in terms of literature as a whole, and have thematically acknowledged a contemporary concern either overtly or metaphorically. And while committee members are limited to judging the books published in one particular year, it is nonetheless significant that Beverly Cleary won her Newbery Medal not for her everyday-life stories about Ramona but for her serious novel about dealing with divorce; Lois Lowry not for her everyday-life stories about Anastasia but for her serious novels about the Danish resistance and about the soul-destroying immorality of a repressive system; Phyllis Reynolds Naylor not for her everyday-life stories about Alice but for her serious novel about a boy who earns his maturation by championing an abused dog.

Random House has an easy-reader imprint, Stepping Stone Books, that includes several everyday-life stories. That series title is revealing. Adults tend to consider everyday-life stories as stepping stones, paths to something else that is the real destination. These are the books we give children to read until they are capable of reading "real" books. Yet all children's literature is, essentially, a stepping stone on the way to somewhere else; the more children's literature authorities suggest or imply that the stepping stoneness of everyday-life stories makes them insignificant, the more such critics implicitly devalue the entire genre of children's literature.

The very existence of children's literature depends on an acceptance of the mutability of evaluative criteria; if literature that is superlative for one is superlative for all, then children's literature, with its acknowledgment of the effect of experiential, biological, and conceptual differences on reading, should not exist. Yet critics often seem to hold all books within the genre to a single standard of literary merit, occasionally conceding the usefulness of successful books for younger readers but clearly considering them inferior as literature. This tendency results in a fundamentally flawed approach to notions of merit, since to take this standard to its end would suggest that the book of excellence can exist only for the reader of excellence, that excellence is a knowable and fixed trait in readership and literature, and that excellence in literature is more important than significance in reading experience. One cannot consider the relative merits of *Ramona the Pest* and, say, *Great Expectations* or even *The Chocolate War* without considering their respective readerships.

Jane Tompkins regrets "a long tradition of academic parochialism" that depends on "a series of cultural contrasts: light 'feminine' novels vs. tough-minded intellectual treatises; domestic 'chattiness' vs. serious thinking";[16] these theories of dichotomy exist in children's literature, too, and have resulted in criticism that fails to consider that very parochialism and its cost. Children's literature will never become the adult literature it wishes to emulate; if it does, it will cease to be. Its strengths lie, as Jane Tompkins suggests, in continuing to push beyond this parochialism and in appreciating its own productions as they walk their peculiar and intriguing tightrope between adult desires and children's responses. Let us learn from the error of adult literary criticism and recognize the power of literature that we might otherwise dismiss as cute, or insignificant, or trivial, or safe. Everyday-life stories are children's literature in microcosm; without valuing them, children's literature cannot value itself.

NOTES

1. Michel Maffesoli, "The Sociology of Everyday Life (Epistemological Elements)," *Current Sociology* 37, no. 1 (Spring 1989): 1; Mike Featherstone, "The Heroic Life and the Everyday Life," in *Cultural Theory and Cultural Change,* ed. Mike Featherstone (London: Sage, 1992), p. 159.

2. Francelia Butler, "Children's Literature: The Bad Seed," in *Signposts to Criticism of Children's Literature,* ed. Robert Bator (Chicago: American Library Association, 1983), p. 38.

3. Geraldine DeLuca, "'Composing a Life': The Diary of Leigh Botts," *The Lion and the Unicorn* 14, no. 2 (1990): 58; Pat Pflieger, *Beverly Cleary* (New York: Twayne, 1991), p. x

4. It is interesting to note that science-fiction fans among young readers and adult critics alike seem to hold the book in less repute than those less familiar with that genre; I would suggest that science-fiction readers are more likely to be familiar with other dystopias and therefore have a clearer sense of the ways in which *The Giver* falls short.

5. Perry Nodelman, "Interpretation and the Apparent Sameness of Children's Novels," *Studies in the Literary Imagination* 18, no. 2 (Fall 1985): 5.

6. Wayne C. Booth, *The Company We Keep: An Ethics of Fiction* (Berkeley: University of California Press, 1988).

7. Jane Tompkins, *Sensational Designs: The Cultural Work of American Fiction 1790–1860* (New York: Oxford University Press, 1985), p. xvi.

8. Ibid., pp. xiv, 123.

9. Karín Lesnik-Oberstein, *Children's Literature: Criticism and the Fictional Child* (Oxford: Clarendon Press, 1994), p. 7; two not-so-random and relatively recent examples of such defensiveness in feminist criticism appear in Elaine Showalter's introduction to Louisa May Alcott's *Little Women* (New York: Penguin, 1989), p. vii, and in Carey Kaplan and Ellen Cronan Rose, *The Canon and the Common Reader* (Knoxville: University of Tennessee Press, 1990), p. 173n.

10. Cornelia Meigs, *Louisa May Alcott and the American Family Story* (London: Bodley Head, 1970), p. 14.

11. Zohar Shavit, *Poetics of Children's Literature* (Athens and London: University of Georgia Press, 1986), pp. 33–59.

12. Nicholas Tucker, *Suitable for Children?* (Berkeley: University of California Press, 1976), pp. 33–34.

13. Isaac Bashevis Singer, "I See the Child as a Last Refuge," in *Signposts to Criticism of Children's Literature*, ed. Robert Bator (Chicago: American Library Association, 1983), p. 50.

14. Lesnik-Oberstein, *Children's Literature*, p. xx.

15. Aidan Chambers, "Three Fallacies About Children's Books," in *Signposts to Criticism of Children's Literature*, ed. Robert Bator (Chicago: American Library Association, 1983), pp. 54–59.

16. Tompkins, *Sensational Designs,* p. 125.

REFERENCES

Booth, Wayne C. *The Company We Keep: An Ethics of Fiction.* Berkeley: University of California Press, 1988.

Butler, Francelia. "Children's Literature: The Bad Seed." In *Signposts to Criticism of Children's Literature.* Ed. Robert Bator. Chicago: American Library Association, 1983.

Chambers, Aidan. "Three Fallacies about Children's Books." In *Signposts to Criticism of Children's Literature.* Ed. Robert Bator. Chicago: American Library Association, 1983.

Cleary, Beverly. *Beezus and Ramona.* New York: William Morrow, 1955.

———. *Ramona the Pest.* New York: William Morrow, 1968.

———. *Ramona the Brave.* New York: William Morrow, 1975.

———. *Ramona and Her Father.* New York: William Morrow, 1977.

———. *Ramona and Her Mother.* New York: William Morrow, 1978.

———. *Ramona Quimby, Age 8.* New York: William Morrow, 1981.

———. *Ramona Forever.* New York: William Morrow, 1984.

DeLuca, Geraldine. "'Composing a Life': The Diary of Leigh Botts," *The Lion and the Unicorn* 14, no. 2 (1990): 58–65.

Featherstone, Mike. "The Heroic Life and the Everyday Life." In *Cultural Theory and Cultural Change.* Ed. Mike Featherstone. London: Sage, 1992.

Kaplan, Carey, and Ellen Cronan Rose. *The Canon and the Common Reader.* Knoxville: University of Tennessee Press, 1990.

Lesnik-Oberstein, Karín. *Children's Literature: Criticism and the Fictional Child.* Oxford: Clarendon Press, 1994.

Maffesoli, Michel. "The Sociology of Everyday Life (Epistemological Elements)." *Current Sociology* 37, no. 1 (Spring 1989): 1–16.

Meigs, Cornelia. *Louisa May Alcott and the American Family Story.* London: Bodley Head, 1970.

Nodelman, Perry. "Interpretation and the Apparent Sameness of Children's Novels." *Studies in the Literary Imagination* 18, no. 2 (Fall 1985): 5–20.

Pflieger, Pat. *Beverly Cleary.* New York: Twayne, 1991.

Shavit, Zohar. *Poetics of Children's Literature.* Athens and London: University of Georgia Press, 1986.

Showalter, Elaine. Introduction to *Little Women* by Louisa May Alcott. New York: Penguin, 1989.

Singer, Isaac Bashevis. "I See the Child as a Last Refuge." *Signposts to Criticism of Children's Literature.* Ed. Robert Bator. Chicago: American Library Association, 1983.

Tompkins, Jane. *Sensational Designs: The Cultural Work of American Fiction 1790–1860.*
    New York: Oxford University Press, 1985.
Tucker, Nicholas. *Suitable for Children?* Berkeley: University of California Press, 1976.

Part II

Shifting Boundaries Between
Children's and Adult Literature

4

The Disappearance of Children's Literature (or Children's Literature as Nostalgia) in the United States in the Late Twentieth Century

Jerry Griswold

THE CREATION OF CHILDHOOD AND CHILDREN'S LITERATURE

To entertain even the possibility of the disappearance of children's literature, we first have to take notice of the fact that there was a time when childhood, as we know it, did not exist. In his now familiar observation, Philippe Ariès has argued that the concept of "childhood" was unknown before the Renaissance. Until then, children (after they attained the "age of reason") were regarded as small adults who mingled, competed, and worked with mature adults.[1]

Many people find it difficult to imagine a time when "children" did not exist because our own acceptance of the cultural construct of "childhood" has been so pervasive that it is now confused with biological fact. Our imaginations are taxed when we try to imagine a culture where children are not distinguished from adults. For us, it seems to mean imagining incongruities—say, legions of ten-year-olds in business suits, swinging their briefcases and talking on car phones; or children mingling with grown-ups, say, in Las Vegas, drinks in hand, on their way to risqué shows.

As Marie Winn has noted, it is easier to imagine a time when childhood didn't exist if we remember that in preindustrial times, the world of labor meant agriculture and arts and crafts, conducted at home and with the help of child labor.[2] A visit to the museum is also an aid to conception because, as J. H. Plumb has observed, in the world revealed by old paintings, there is no separate realm of childhood: in a painting by Brueghel, for example, a "coarse village festival [is] depicted . . . , showing men and women besotted with drink, groping each other with unbridled lust, [and] children eating and drinking with adults."[3]

The concept of "childhood," Ariès argues, first appeared in the 1600s and gradually developed as children began to be distinguished from adults in everything from clothing to norms of acceptable behavior. Speculation about the special nature of the "child" began then, along with the development of schools and curricula. By the same token, "adulthood" became something to achieve—a guild with its own knowledge (e.g., reading) and secrets (e.g., sex) that "children" had to be prepared for or initiated into.

Childhood did not, however, arise full-blown overnight. Its development was gradual and fitful. While at first a luxury of the privileged classes, "childhood" and its perquisites came to be seen (under the inspiration of John Locke and Jean-Jacques Rousseau) as the birthright of any child (qua "child"). But this democratic impulse suffered setbacks along the way—for example, during the Industrial Revolution, when youths once again found themselves laboring alongside adults; indeed, the popularity of Dickens' novels, for example, might be said to reflect the cultural collision that occurred when "children," trailing Wordsworthian "clouds of glory," were seen working in mines and sweatshops. At the same time, "childhood" did not occur in all places at once; even today, in some places in the world, it seems for many never to have occurred at all.

In the United States, a pervasive notion of childhood might be reckoned to have begun in the mid-nineteenth century. While there were certainly some well-to-do parents before that time who were aware of European fashions and who had the means to coddle their offspring in that special and leisurely period of time known as childhood, for the most part (in a largely agrarian culture and in the busy beginnings of the country) children were required to put childhood behind them and enter adulthood with dispatch, to help on the farm and become mature providers as soon as possible. A real interest in children and in the special nature of childhood did not occur in America until after 1865, when, for example, child-labor laws were introduced, the public school movement was begun, pediatrics was accepted as a legitimate specialty in medical schools, social and governmental agencies concerned with child welfare were created, and so forth. As Neil Postman has observed, "If we use the word *children* in the fullest sense in which the average American understands it, childhood [in America] is not much more than a hundred and fifty years old."[4]

If "childhood" is a relatively new concept, "children's literature" might be reckoned an even more recent phenomenon. Historians generally point to its origin with John Newbery, the English bookseller who in the 1740s established the trade of publishing books intended solely for children. During that era, however, "children's literature" was not as discrete as we have come to think of it; in addition to imaginative works, it included folklore, which had always had an audience of all ages (fairy tales, ballads about Robin Hood, legends of King Arthur, and the like), and works that seem more an adjunct to child-raising than imaginative literature (ABC and toy books, volumes on courtesy and manners, exemplary spiritual biographies, and lessons about good and bad apprentices). Generally speaking, prior to the 1850s, children's literature was in its infancy and a feeble branch of letters; few people besides literary historians are likely to recognize, for example, the names of Hannah More and Peter Parley. After the 1850s, however, children's literature became a genuinely robust genre, with the appearance of such authors as Lewis Carroll, Louisa May Alcott, Mark Twain, Jules Verne, and Robert Louis Stevenson.

Henry Steele Commager explains the situation in this way: In the past, children and adults shared equally in "the great tradition of literature"—which extended from Aesop, Plutarch, King Arthur, and Charles Perrault, through *Pilgrim's Progress,*

Robinson Crusoe, and *Gulliver's Travels,* to Scott, Austen, the Brontës and Dickens in England, and, in America, to Cooper, Poe, and Longfellow.[5] But somewhere along the way, in the nineteenth century, arose a distinct category of children's literature. This occurred, some scholars have suggested, when something called "adult literature" was invented and veered away from the mainstream of "the great tradition." The remnant, "children's literature," arose by default.[6]

THE DISAPPEARANCE OF CHILDHOOD AND THE BOOM IN CHILDREN'S BOOKS

Now let us jump to the present. During the 1980s, social critics began to lament (as the title of Neil Postman's book had it) "the disappearance of childhood." These critics—besides Postman, Marie Winn in *Children Without Childhood*, David Elkind in *The Hurried Child*—predicted a return to an earlier condition when children were not separated from adults. As proof of their contentions, they point to an abundance of evidence—for example:

- In talking about the development of the concept of childhood, Ariès had spoken of the rise of taboo knowledge (particularly sex). Now, television programs at any time of day routinely address subjects (from hermaphroditism to spouse swapping) that were once deemed too sensitive for tender years.

- In an earlier era, films featured Jackie Coogan and Shirley Temple, actors and actresses who were conspicuously children—in fact, exaggerated children. Nowadays, we are given transistorized adults and Lolitas; and it is difficult to imagine their contemporary counterparts (Gary Coleman and Brooke Shields, for example) dipping and swaying to a song like "The Good Ship Lollipop."

- While the distinction between juvenile and adult court systems seemed important in an earlier era, it now seems arbitrary when the label "gang member" is no longer applied to Al Capone-like adults but usually is used to describe metropolitan youths not yet old enough to vote.

I am citing only some of the abundant evidence these social critics offer as proof of the disappearance of childhood. That change is something they lament. They argue that the humane and liberal concept of childhood (invented in the sixteenth century, according to Ariès) is being dismantled before our eyes.

If these critics are correct, then we might reasonably expect a waning of interest in and the disappearance of children's literature. Here, however, we are faced with apparently contradictory evidence. Children's book publishing is booming, and interest in children's literature has been growing by leaps and bounds.

The most remarkable trend in American publishing circles since the 1980s is what magazines have termed the "boom in kiddie lit." While sales in all other areas have been down, between 1982 and 1990 sales of children's books quadrupled in the United States; in fact, some publishers have said that their children's departments have kept their firms afloat during economic hard times. In addition, in 1990, circulation figures from the children's sections of public libraries indicated that book borrowing was up 54 percent from the already high figures of the year before.

This same interest in children's books has been occurring at American universities. Children's literature used to be a minor enterprise, a class offered only to would-be schoolteachers by a university's education department. All that has changed. Now, by my count, more than 200 universities (including major universities like Princeton, Dartmouth, and Cornell) regularly offer courses in children's literature in their English departments. Given the chance, students have poured into these courses. A course taught at the University of Connecticut regularly enrolls more than 300 students a term. My own experience has been no different: in 1982 I offered a course in children's literature at UCLA, and 325 students signed up; since then, my courses elsewhere have been equally swollen. Across the country, the story is no different: enrollments are likewise measured in hundreds.

This same growing interest in children's literature can be seen in literary scholarship in the United States. Since the 1970s, the field has begun to enjoy some of the prestige it has long had in Europe, and has even become something of a boom industry. University presses have begun to publish monographs in what they see as a "coming" field. Scholarly journals have appeared. Professional organizations have sprung up. The prestigious Modern Language Association has raised children's literature from a discussion group to the status of a division. And the National Endowment for the Humanities has regularly begun to fund institutes devoted to its study.

NOSTALGIA AND THE MERGING OF CHILDREN'S AND ADULT LITERATURES

Thus, we encounter a paradox. On the one hand, social critics point to an abundance of evidence and argue convincingly that in America the notion of childhood is disappearing. On the other hand, evidence points to an extraordinary growth of interest in children's books—in the sales figures posted by publishers, in university classrooms, and among literary scholars. How can this paradox be explained?

Many may not be pleased with the likely answer. If childhood is truly disappearing, then tremendous growth of interest in children's books may reflect adult nostalgia for a notion in its evanescence, in a twilight period just before its disappearance.

This may explain many things. Take the extraordinary growth in the sales of children's books. This has been occurring at a time when the number of children in the population is decreasing. While sales of children's books nearly quadrupled between 1982 and 1990, in 1985 the number of children (aged five to thirteen) reached a twenty-five-year low, and in 1987 births were just a little more than half (58 percent) of what they were in 1957. Moreover, the numbers of childless couples and single-person households have risen considerably.[7] What the dramatic increase in the sales of children's books may suggest, then, is a considerable *adult* interest in children's books. In fact, several years ago, writer James Marshall told me that marketing studies done by publishers indicated that one-third of all illustrated children's books are purchased by adults who don't plan to pass them along to children.

As for the incredible surge in enrollments in children's literature classes offered by universities, I have no statistical or hard information to draw upon. I can only proceed anecdotally. When I ask the hundreds of students who enroll in my classes what brings them there, what I hear most often is that they have come to read the works they didn't have a chance to read in childhood.

And as for the dramatic growth of interest in children's literature in scholarly circles, Postman may have an answer: "The best histories of anything are produced when an event is completed, when a period is waning. . . . Historians usually come not to praise but to bury. In any event, they find autopsies easier to do than progress reports."[8] The genuine subject of literary scholars, in other words, may be "what was children's literature."

Henry Steele Commager's point was that children's literature arose when the great tradition of literature shared equally by children and adults (Aesop, King Arthur, fairy tales, and the like) parted into two streams: children's and adult literature. If the notion of childhood is disappearing, then what we are likely to see is what we are now, in fact, seeing: those two streams are merging once again and children's literature per se is disappearing.

In the last few decades, we have seen the rise of the kind of book that Randall Jarrell (thinking of his own work) described as "half for children, half for grown-ups."[9] Isaac Bashevis Singer's work provides an example. Russell Hoban's provides another; in this era, Hoban has said, "Books in a nameless category are needed—books for children and adults together."[10] And, of course, the rise of adolescent "problem novels"—which take up previously taboo subjects (prostitution, incest, drug-taking, etc.)—also suggests the evaporation of boundaries between children's and adult literature. From Hoban's existential fable *Mouse and His Child* (with its joking reference to Sartre) to Judy Blume's sexually explicit *Forever*, what we are encountering are works not written for "children of all ages" but for "adults of all ages."

Another kind of evidence of the collapse of boundaries between children's and adult literature may found in the last few decades in the renewed interest in classic fairy tales—in works as diverse as Anne Sexton's collection of poems titled *Transformations*, Stephen Sondheim's play *Into the Woods*, the Disney film *Beauty and the Beast*, and Bruno Bettelheim's scholarly study *The Uses of Enchantment*. As Commager suggested, fairy tales were read by both children and adults before the great tradition of literature parted into two age-determined streams. The contemporary interest in this shared literature may now suggest that these streams are once again merging.

One final suggestion of this erasure of boundaries between adult and children's literature might be found in a least likely place—in the world of picture books. Beginning with the publication of *Outside over There* in 1981, Maurice Sendak's publisher (Harper & Row) has simultaneously announced his subsequent books (including *Dear Mili* and *We Are All in the Dumps with Jack & Guy*) on both their adult's and their children's lists. During the 1980s, two of Dr. Seuss's books—his parable about the arms race (*The Butter Battle Book*) and his geriatric fable (*You Only Grow Old Once!*)—appeared on adult best-seller lists.

Of course, in this short period of time I have been able to provide only a few examples that offer intimations that children's literature per se is disappearing. Let me end by telling you of a conversation I had with a former student who now works in Hollywood. For the last few years, her job has been to search out and identify children's books that may be made into films. She has now concluded that it is no longer possible to make traditional films like *Old Yeller* or Disney's *Cinderella* and *Pollyanna*. Despite the fact that movie studios still try to market such concoctions (e.g., *Pocahontas*), children who have grown up with Bart Simpson or Beavis and Butthead no longer care for them. Children have become more cynical, more parodistic, more adultlike. Sensibilities have changed.

As an example, we might point to Stephen Spielberg's *Hook*. This film is a gloss on James Barrie's *Peter Pan* and its sequel. But what is important to note is that it no longer seemed possible simply to put Barrie's children's story on film. What was additionally needed in Spielberg's film was a parodistic overlay, the insertion of the fast mouth and witticisms of the actor Robin Williams, the addition of an adult and an adult perspective—as if Bart Simpson were retelling the story of *Peter Pan*.[11] In this way, let me suggest, we have another example of the disappearance of children's literature per se, and of the gradual erosion of barriers between children's and adult literature and the emergence of a "shared" story.

But Spielberg's *Hook*, like other contemporary movies,[12] shows something else. The story line that is laid down on top of a retelling of *Peter Pan* is the story of a workaholic adult whose life has become sterile and valueless. He is redeemed when he is stripped of everything adultlike (from his cellular phone to his very maturity) and is transformed when he finally becomes a kid again (even engaging in a food fight). In other words, what frames this presentation of Barrie's classic children's story is an account of an adult "getting in touch" with his "missing child." Let me suggest that there is a parable here: what we see is not only the disappearance of childhood and children's literature per se in our own time, but also the nostalgia felt for their loss.

NOTES

1. Philippe Ariès, *Centuries of Childhood: A Social History of Family Life*, trans. Robert Baldick (New York: Random House, 1962).

2. Marie Winn, *Children Without Childhood* (New York: Pantheon Books, 1983), p. 88.

3. J. H. Plumb, "The Great Change in Children," *Horizon* 13, no. 1 (Winter 1971): 7; quoted in Neil Postman, *The Disappearance of Childhood* (New York: Delacorte Press, 1982), pp. 15–16.

4. Postman, *The Disappearance of Childhood*, p. xi.

5. Henry Steele Commager, "Introduction to the First Edition," in *A Critical History of Children's Literature*, ed. Cornelia Meigs, rev. ed. (New York: Macmillan, 1969), pp. xii–xiv.

6. Felicity A. Hughes, "Children's Literature: Theory and Practice," *ELH* 45, no. 3 (Fall 1978): 542–561

7. Information from the U.S. Bureau of Census. See "Fertility of American Women: June 1987," series P-20, no. 427; March 2, 1990, press release (CB90-38), "Population Aged 35 to 44 Growing the Fastest."

8. Postman, *The Disappearance of Childhood*, p. 5.

9. Mary Jarrell, "Note" to recording of Randall Jarrell reading *The Bat-Poet*, Caedmon record TV 1364. See Jerry Griswold, *The Children's Books of Randall Jarrell* (Athens: University of Georgia Press, 1988), pp. 52–53, 61.

10. Russell Hoban, "Thoughts on a Shirtless Cyclist, Robin Hood, Johann Sebastian Bach, and One or Two Other Things," *Children's Literature in Education* 4 (March 1971): 23.

11. In the film *Aladdin*, Williams had a similar role.

12. Compare Tom Hanks in *Big*, George Burns in *Eighteen Again*, and Dudley Moore in *Like Father, like Son*.

5

Literature for All Ages?
Literary Emancipation and the
Borders of Children's Literature

Anne de Vries

In the Netherlands, it is a common notion that the development of children's literature since the 1940s can be characterized as a "literary emancipation." Concerning the increasing esteem of children's literature, this is obvious. But with respect to the development of children's literature itself, it is more complicated: here the "literary emancipation" relates to different phenomena that may be valued in different ways.

Roughly, one can distinguish three stages in the development since 1945. In the 1950s and 1960s, strict moral codes disappeared and the horizon in children's books broadened. In the 1970s, there was an abolition of all kinds of taboos and an increasing attention to the emotions of children. Since the 1980s, there has been a "literary emancipation" in a narrower sense, affecting the literary form: the traditional restrictions of children's literature are being rejected by many authors and critics, and children's literature shows an increasing complexity.

I will illustrate this with some observations concerning three different genres. First, children's books about the German occupation of the Netherlands during the Second World War, a popular genre in Dutch children's literature. In books from the 1950s, the image of this period was similar to the perception of wars in traditional history education: the main theme was the resistance against the occupiers; everyday life was scarcely depicted, and certainly children's experiences were not. That didn't happen until the 1970s, when the first autobiographical children's novels about the occupation appeared, written by people who had been children at that time.

For the first time, children got an authentic and differentiated image of the war. Apart from different circumstances, these books show great differences in the emotional perceptions of the events by the protagonists. Because of this, the image of the occupation disintegrated, like pieces of a jigsaw puzzle, allowing or forcing readers to construct their own images of this period.

In these books, the narrator identifies completely with the child he or she has been; as a result, the distance between the narrator and the intended reader has disappeared. Because of the resulting child's perspective, these books have a high literary quality, and at the same time they are very recognizable for children.

In some respects, the developments after 1980 are similar, but sometimes the effect is rather different. In general, the number of autobiographical elements in children's literature has increased. In poetry for children, the traditional child's perspective is often mixed with childhood memories, either concealed or from an explicitly adult point of view. Of course, memories may be very recognizable or intriguing for children: "Please, Dad, Granddad, tell me about the old days again!" But sometimes it gets more complicated—for instance, in a series of poems by Wiel Kusters, *Catching Salamanders*, in which a protagonist returns to his childhood in his thoughts. In one of these poems, he plays with time:

> Now it's you and me again.
> To the brook the two of us.
> Backwards has the water streamed,
> while a moment no one looked.
>
> It has to be like this, of course,
> even the brook should lose some time.
> How much, then? Five or thirty years?
> At *thirty*, there the mine still smokes.
>
> At *five*, all salamanders are dead.
> Perhaps even the brook has gone.
> The water came out of the mine,
> pressing itself all through the stone.
>
> At *three*, my father's gone as well.
> Fern of stone, that withered there.
> So his years should be increased.
> Let's grow older now, again.[1]

For me, this is a fascinating poem. The magical wish to turn time back and forth, and to be able to prolong your father's life, is something I have experienced quite often myself. Certainly, most children will recognize the element of magical fantasy. But how much life experience does it take to recognize the nostalgia in this poem?

Controversial themes are not avoided in recent poetry for children: for instance, in the work of Ted van Lieshout, one of the most talented young Dutch poets, we find a series of four poems dealing with a pedophile experience. The secret is not referred to by name, but implied; again, the child's perspective is disguised in the perspective of an adult looking back: "*in a child's eyes* no one can / be greater than the one you love" and "unseemingly to say his name out of *nostalgia* / and so it's been erased again."[2]

Again, this perspective doesn't make these poems easier for children. In a certain sense, it indicates emancipation that poems like these are included in a collection for children: it proves that the distinction between the adults' world and the world of children is disappearing. With respect to the literary form, this distinction has become faint as well: poetry for children has become more complex; even to adults, some poems are not very accessible, and obscure verses are no longer exceptions.

So, in more than one respect, there is hardly any distance between the poet (narrator) and the intended reader. However, sometimes it is not clear who the intended reader is. More and more authors state that they don't write for children deliberately. In 1987, Ted van Lieshout said in an interview: "I write for myself: for the adult I am, for the child I used to be and have remained ever since."[3] Other authors have made similar statements; it is the topos of our time, whereas in the 1960s or 1970s, every author could explain which specific qualities writing for children required.

This causes a striking decrease of formal adaptation. In recent children's literature, one finds fewer idiomatic restrictions and more complex structures, more symbolism and other hidden levels of meaning than ever before. Because of this, the books I mentioned may be characterized as literature for all ages. Among children they reach a smaller public than traditional children's books, and certainly young readers will not comprehend all elements, but this also applies quite often to adult readers of adult's literature.

Still, one may wonder, Doesn't children's literature require any restrictions at all? And doesn't writing for children require at least some specific qualities? Among the authors stating that they write for themselves first of all, there is only one who can explain why the result happens to be a children's book: Joke van Leeuwen, the author of *Deesje* (1985). She said:

My books are written from a child's perspective. One element of being a child is experiencing things for the first time, seeing things for the first time, not taking them for granted. Besides, a child has no power in our society . . . Fear and uncertainty are a part of its existence. This is symbolized by Deesje's journey to a large city, alone among all those tall people hindering her view. Literally, she is too small to get a view of things: her eyes are too low.[4]

But Joke van Leeuwen is an exception, at least among authors gaining literary recognition. As a result of the "literary emancipation," there is no consensus about the concept of children's books anymore. With respect to the books and poems I have mentioned so far, this affects the content first of all: they contain elements many children will not comprehend, especially at an emotional level. With respect to the last genre I want to discuss, it's the literary form that causes the problem. It has quite often been asked whether these are children's books at all.

This concerns complex, obscure fantasy books like Imme Dros's *Annetje Lie in het holst van de nacht* (1987; *Annelie in the Depths of the Night*, 1991). From a psychological point of view, it certainly has a child's perspective: it deals with a child's emotions. However, many children don't see this: the emotions are not depicted directly, but symbolized in a very subtle way by the action, which consists almost solely of the dreams of the protagonist. Annelie's father left her with her grandmother without any explanation. Her confusion, later increased by a feverish illness, reveals itself in fearful dreams about mysterious, threatening characters from her grandmother's stories and songs.

In this respect the book is very similar to Maurice Sendak's *Where the Wild Things Are*, in which the story also symbolizes the emotions of the protagonist. There is one difference, however: if a five-year-old doesn't comprehend the symbolism in Sendak's book, it still remains an exciting story. In *Annetje Lie* this is not the case: if you can't break the code, there is hardly any plot; and because of the whimsical, associative jumps of thought that are characteristic of dreams, you lose track all the time. The book is written in an evocative language, and for adult readers the quality is increased by quite a few examples of intertextuality, which children don't recognize either. Thus, it is a remarkable work of art, but it has very little appeal for children—or, rather, for most children.

Of course, the question of whether this is a children's book leads to circular reasoning. But it seems clear that critics, and certainly critics with a literary approach, will overvalue books like this rather than undervalue them—as has been confirmed by important awards for *Annetje Lie* and other obscure books. After all, these books meet with their adult literary values.

Traditionally, children's literature has two different canons, one from the adults' and one from the children's point of view. We can't confine ourselves to this observation: both researchers and critics should draw the obvious conclusions. In his article "Criticism and Children's Literature" (1994), Peter Hunt defends the proposition that criticism must reject "inappropriate" adult literary values, and recognize the difference between "adults' children's books" and "children's children's books."[5]

I could not agree more. This means that we have to pay more attention to the surface structure of a children's book, to the story itself, and ask ourselves what it has to offer children, according to their literary values, and which skills it requires from the reader. With respect to children's literature, an interesting literary development is hardly an emancipation if children don't benefit from it.

On the other hand, we should avoid generalizations. I don't feel any nostalgia for the traditional restrictions of children's literature. It is important that the borders of children's literature are being explored. Even if some of the books I mentioned are too difficult for most children, they remain very interesting for adults, both from a literary point of view and because they may help us to better understand the nature of children's literature.

NOTES

1. Wiel Kusters, *Salamanders vangen* (Amsterdam: Em. Querido, 1985), p. 56. Translation mine.

2. Ted van Lieshout, *Als ik geen naam had kwam ik in de Noordzee uit* (Amsterdam: Leopold, 1987), pp. 32, 34. Italics added.

3. Victor Frederik, interview with Ted van Lieshout, *Elke dag schrijf ik het boek*, no. 2 (1987–1988).

4. Interview with Joke van Leeuwen, *De literatuurmachine*, RVU Television, October 16, 1991.

5. Peter Hunt, "Criticism and Children's Literature: What Can We Say, and Who Wants to Listen?" *International Review of Children's Literature and Librarianship* 9, no. 1 (1994): 1.

REFERENCES

Dros, Imme. *Annetje Lie in het holst van de nacht*. Houten, Netherlands: Van Holkema & Warendorf, 1987.

————. *Annelie in the Depths of the Night*. Trans. Arno Pomerans and Erica Pomerans. London: Faber and Faber, 1991.

Frederik, Victor. Interview with Ted van Lieshout. *Elke dag schrijf ik het boek*, no. 2 (1987–1988).

Hunt, Peter. "Criticism and Children's Literature: What Can We Say, and Who Wants to Listen?" *International Review of Children's Literature and Librarianship* 9, no. 1 (1994): 1–7.

Kusters, Wiel. *Salamanders vangen*. Amsterdam: Em. Querido, 1985.

Lieshout, Ted van. *Als ik geen naam had kwam ik in de Noordzee uit*. Amsterdam: Leopold, 1987.

Interview with Joke van Leeuwen, *De literatuurmachine*. RVU Television, October 16, 1991.

6

The Changing Status of Children and Children's Literature

Eva-Maria Metcalf

Certainly, in no century before the twentieth have children been studied so intensely, gained so much recognition, and been valued so highly, and the same can be said for children's literature. The German scholar Gundel Mattenklott argues in her book *Zauberkreide* that the opportunity for children's literature to leave the literary periphery and become part of the literary avant-garde had never before been as great as it was during the late 1960s.[1] I fully agree with her argument and would like to take it a step further. In what follows, I will examine some of the preconditions and point to a few manifestations of this new status in German children's literature from the 1960s through the 1990s. Children's literature, as I approach it, is situated in the field of tension delineated by social and institutional structures, technological advances, market forces, pedagogical and political claims, literary norms, and discursive practices, and is defined by the currently dominant concept of childhood. Subtle or more substantial changes in any or all of these factors will affect the role and the makeup of children's literature. Here, I will highlight a few threads in this complex web of interrelationships, focusing on those that are linked to questions of power and prestige.

Before I embark on an analysis of the status of children's literature since the late 1960s, however, let me set the scene with some anecdotal and statistical evidence about its status and shape before the 1950s. In 1944, the Swedish publisher Hans Rabén launched a competition for the best Swedish manuscript for a girl's book, in an effort to boost the sales of children's books. When it came to opening the envelope containing the name of the winner, his worst fear came true: the winner of the prize was an unknown housewife. Fortunately both for the publisher and for children all over the world, it was an unusually gifted housewife who won the prize that year. The winner was Astrid Lindgren, who set a new tone in children's literature with the publication of *Pippi Longstocking* the following year.

The publisher's fear that the prize might go to a housewife was not unfounded. In fact, the likelihood was great, as evidenced by statistical data cited by the German author Erich Kästner, in an article in the Stockholm newspaper *Dagens Nyheter* in 1957.[2] According to this source, 30 percent of all Swedish children's books that year were written by housewives. Another 30 percent were written by teachers and 30 percent by other professionals, such as doctors and engineers. The remaining 10 percent were written by self-proclaimed authors, fully 70 percent of whom were no longer alive. In other words, only 3 percent of Swedish children's books on the market were written by currently active, professional authors.[3] If we believe the children's author James Krüss, who cited Kästner, the situation was very similar in Germany at that time, and we can assume it was the same all over Europe as well. Even if we grant that these statistics are somewhat inaccurate, they clearly reflect the low status of children's literature in the 1950s, when it was a field in which teachers and housewives with time on their hands could, and did, dabble. Children's literature, designed as the sugar coating around the bitter pill of education two centuries earlier, continued to be primarily a vehicle for educators with some talent for storytelling. Despite calls for better-quality children's literature like Heinrich Wolgast's at the turn of the century, literary quality was at best a secondary issue, and at worst, inconsequential. At the beginning of the twentieth century, children's literature was a totally separate and marginalized entity in the polysystem of literature, confined within its own system and guided by its own laws. It was effectively barred from the literary world of modernity by its association with the premodern world of folklore and fairy tale, discovered during the age of Romanticism and further cemented during the latter part of the nineteenth century. The belief that the child's naive, unadulterated, and uncritical view of the world should remain intact informed the idea of a separate world of childhood and children's literature, which, combined with a heritage of didacticism and an aura of dilettantism, barred children's literature from mainstream literature and even more so from the privileged status of high literature, which had raised its barriers by celebrating art for art's sake. Almost by definition, then, modernist stylistic experimentation and creative potential were anathema to children's literature, which, as a result, became stigmatized as imitative, backward, and unworthy of attention by any serious, self-respecting author.

Were we to conduct a survey about who writes children's books in Sweden, Germany, or the United States today, the results would be quite different. Lately, children's literature has experienced an unparalleled professionalization and literarization, as well as a concomitant and unprecedented growth in status. In *Criticism, Theory, and Children's Literature*, Peter Hunt argues that in order to accede to the privileged status of literature, from which children's literature has historically been excluded, either it must become part of the power structure, or the power structure must change.[4] I contend that the power structure has indeed changed, and that this has affected status, form, and content of children's literature. Two parallel developments have helped children's literature gain a more prominent voice: the demythification and democratization of childhood—on both conceptual and experiential levels—and the demythification and democratization of the literary establishment through attacks on the canon and the razing of hierarchical structures.

Postmodernism's attacks on logocentrism and its proclivity to erase barriers and flatten hierarchies have had a liberating and empowering effect on children's literature. It has become less provincial and, as a consequence, has gained greater access to and presence in the marketplace of ideas. As Alison Lurie remarks: "Once upon a time children's books were the black sheep of fiction . . . quarantined from the rest of literature. . . . Recently, though, children's literature is beginning to be discovered by mainstream theorists and scholars. Learned volumes on its significance crowd the library shelves, and the professional journals are full of articles that consider every classic from *Alice* to *Charlotte's Web* as a 'text.'"[5] Lurie might be overstating the case slightly, but it is certainly a fact that articles about and reviews of children's books have gained greater substance and prominence during the past decades.

THE FORERUNNERS

The children's literature of the 1990s owes an enormous debt to the cultural revolution of the late 1960s and early 1970s, and to the philosophers and social scientists who prepared the ground for that revolution. In 1962, Philippe Ariès published his groundbreaking history of childhood. Its revelation of the bourgeois concept of childhood as myth and cultural construct still reverberates in theoretical discussions about childhood today. At the time, it renewed the debate about the status of children and adults, gave rise to a fundamental rethinking of intergenerational relationships, and cleared the way for a new social and cultural construct of the child that has affected much of the literature created for children since then. Children's literature also was affected by the cultural-revolutionary euphoria. In the wake of the civil rights movement, voices were raised for children's rights as well. The debunking of canons, of authority figures, and of authoritarian structures that took place in the streets and at universities in the late 1960s entered children's books surprisingly quickly, resulting in a creative push. Carnivalesque techniques of subversion, which were among the favored discourse strategies used in this social and cultural revolt, had had a long tradition in folklore and children's literature, and could easily be filled with new content to become part of the social and cultural protest movement. Publishers cooperatives—many of them with leftist and Marxist leanings—published children's books for the new child, and scholars and critics formed alternative working teams (*Arbeitsgruppen*). The most notable of these grassroots anti-establishment movements was Red Elephant (*Roter Elefant*), founded in 1975 by Jörg Becker, Malte Dahrendorf, and Wolfgang Frommlet. It later included other leading German children's literature scholars, among them Klaus Doderer.[6] Its mission and goal was to promote books that adopted the new model of childhood. To this end, the group presented alternative prizes for a number of years, in open opposition to Deutscher Jugendbuchpreis, the prize awarded each year by the German government.

Let me give you an example of the experimental character of a book published by Basis Verlag—a leftist publishing cooperative of children's books in Berlin, that is specifically interesting in light of my argument. *Die Geschichte von der Verjagung und Ausstopfung des Königs* (The Story About How the King Was Chased out and Stuffed) violates cultural taboos not only in subject matter and message but in narrative structure as well. It is a thinly disguised story about storytelling. Two not very imaginative and innovative poets, who are part of the plot, invent a traditional tale about a king in order to amuse the child protagonists. But the fictional children—and by extension the implied readers—reject these old-fashioned tales and throw them out along with the king, thus making room for new and more socially responsible, participatory ways of living and thinking. The new, politically correct, and quite utopian happy ending depicts everyone living together in peace and harmony in a country that now belongs to everyone. This story remains in the strong grip of socialist ideology and didacticism and seems outdated in the post–Cold War period, but its respect for—and overestimation of—the child's ability to read critically and its innovative use of narrative strategies have survived or, better, have been revived in postmodern writing. This tale about storytelling that uses the Brechtian alienation effect to get its point across has no single author. It is the product of a joint creative effort of children and adults, and in its introduction the authors reveal the production process much as John Scieszka does in *The Stinky Cheese Man and Other Fairly Stupid Tales*.

The rather slim production of leftist book cooperatives was admittedly the radical fringe. But skepticism of the established order, critical reading, and demythologizing soon became the order of the day in mainstream children's literature of the 1970s. Stories abounded in which children were taught to distrust adults and to question a dehumanized consumer culture. *The Cucumber King* (*Wir pfeifen auf den Gurkenkönig*, 1972), by Austrian author and Andersen Medal winner Christine Nöstlinger, is another throw-out-the-king story, exposing the father-knows-best, happy middle-class nuclear family as a myth. It, too, addresses class and gender conflicts head-on, drawing parallels between political dictatorship and power relationships in the patriarchal family. The novel ends predictably enough for its kind: the father and his alter ego, the Cucumber King, are deposed, preparing the way for a democratic family structure within a democratic society. The social and political awareness that entered children's fiction broke open the traditional "small world" of childhood, and liberated and challenged authors to use a variety of approaches and narrative techniques to coax readers into active and critical participation.

A NEW SELF-DEFINITION

How does children's literature in the 1990s differ from that of the 1970s? What has survived, and what has changed? In the 1970s, children's literature constituted an arena for assertiveness training of both author and reader. Authors assumed the role of children's advocates and spoke largely *for* children as they let children speak up in their fiction. Children's literature simply modeled behavior to be emulated. Contrary to that approach, cutting-edge children's books today do not want to patronize or colonize readers by speaking up for them or even by guiding them. Along with the teleological certainty of the socialist cause, agency and activism have mostly disappeared. Authors, like teachers, have resigned their authority as preachers and educators, choosing to function instead as "facilitators." Behind the open problematization of the authorial position lies the deeply democratic idea of empowerment and power sharing. Modeling several modes of action, authors let readers find their own temporary and unstable solutions in multivalent texts. The double-voiced discourse of anti-authoritarian literature that pitched the voice of the oppressor against that of the oppressed, refuting and ridiculing the dominant voice by means of carnivalesque subversive strategies, has grown into multi-voicedness or, rather, voicelessness.

We should not forget that the empowerment of children and a revaluation of children's literature would be unthinkable if the emancipatory drives of the countercultures had not conformed with information society's demands for a more sophisticated and flexible workforce and "capitalist society's hunger for incessant innovation".[7] Mainstream culture—including children's literature—has responded to the deprivileging of dominant groups and their discursive practices by annexing and appropriating parts of fringe discourses and counter-discourses, as well as aspects of avant-garde experimentation, while blunting and undermining their revolutionary potential in the process. As a result of these impulses, mainstream culture has become more diversified, more colorful, and more noncommittal in recent decades. Much of children's fiction today presents readers with choices, but without the hope and the vision of the 1970s or the stable and uniform ethical guidelines of a bygone era. Child readers are asked to embrace the kind of critical, even cynical, stance—previously reserved for adults only—that is replayed in the eclecticism and cynical indifference of mainstream culture and youth culture today.

The empowerment of the child has its price, and one may ask whether children are not overtaxed, confronted as they are with skepticism, contradictions, and ambiguities, and left awash in choices between sometimes equally valid ethical and behavioral codes. Nevertheless, the ability to make more or less informed choices even in the absence of grand narratives is a vital lesson for a child growing up in a democratic, consumer-oriented, information society. In a world in which competing authoritative discourses vie with each other for ever shorter durations of time, children are forced to grow up sooner, learn the language games, and participate in them. With the shift in the perception of childhood and in childhood experiences, authors are addressing more precocious children who share more experiences with adults than children did a generation or two ago. In content as well as in form, authors have severed themselves from traditional restraints. Issues raised in today's books no longer center on everyday concerns of school, friendship, and family only. Often, the family and school settings remain, but political, social, and economic issues, from AIDS to xenophobia, from ecology to homophobia are addressed. Increasingly, philosophical and epistemological questions enter children's fiction as well, and all this occurs very much in synchrony with issues that capture the public debate.

Highlighting the function of narrative and questioning author and reader positions within the work of fiction are becoming common in postmodern children's books. These books give readers an active part in the unfolding of the plot by admitting them into the writer's workshop. The demythification and decentering of the author and of the creative process of fiction writing erase borderlines between readers and writers, and make them accomplices by lowering the author and elevating readers, regardless of age or gender. Child readers are given a voice of their own, not by model or decree, as was the case in the early phase of empowerment, but by being expected to perform and consciously participate in the creative process. A growing number of books are on a par with books written for adults in terms of their poetics. Increasingly, "readerly texts," to use Roland Barthes's term, have been replaced by more interactive "writerly" texts whose messages to readers are more diffuse and subtle. These frequently elliptical texts require profound attention and cooperation on the part of the reader.

Still, it would be silly to argue that children's books are *intellectually* at the same level as books for adults. Maria Lypp's concept of asymmetric communication as it concerns children's literature still applies. The gap in life experience and cognitive development between children and adults has shrunk but not disappeared. It will continue to place special demands on authors writing for children and on critics reviewing children's books. The range of topics, as well as the complexity and ambiguity of the narrative, may seduce critics into treating these books as adult books or looking at them as "texts" only—as Alison Lurie suggested—and applying methods of literary analysis without taking into consideration the audience and the context in which they were written. *Functionally*, however, children's literature mirrors that of adults. There are high-brow and low-brow books for children, and both are part of the public debate.

Let me add one final consideration to my observations about the changing status of children's literature. The "mainstreaming" of children's literature has much to do with the specific qualities of postmodern discursive practice. It is imitative by nature, thus doing away with the stigma of children's literature not being original and on the cutting edge. In the postmodern replay of Dada and surrealism in children's literature, I find reflected the same questioning of social and symbolic hierarchies and power structures, the same fragmentation and absence of closure, the same self-reflection, and the same metaphorical language that characterized modernist adult literature, but it is presented with a levity, playfulness, and superficiality that characterizes postmodern sensibilities. "Post-Modernism," Charles Newman argues, "carries out the aesthetics of anti-realism in an external fashion, while rejecting the varieties of Modernism in both its extreme Transcendent and Nihilistic modes."[8] Postmodernism's levity and playfulness, its superficiality and ahistoricity, and its secondary orality (a term taken from Walter Ong's work *Orality and Literacy*) are all elements of postmodern culture that correspond closely to the developmental stage and language of childhood.

The ludic, fantastic, and kaleidoscopic elements characteristic of postmodern writing and culture have a long tradition in children's literature's wordplay, nonsense, and fantasy tales going back to nursery rhymes, *Alice in Wonderland*, and Lear's nonsense verse. German author Jörn Peter Dirx consciously picks up on that tradition in *Alles Rainer Zufall* (All Pure Coincidence, 1987). (The title is a play on words that remains pervasive in the book. Rainer is a German first name, but its homonym means "pure.") It is a pastiche of *Alice in Wonderland* in which serendipity and ambiguity reign and no causal logic ties the various episodes together. The "wonderland" into which Rainer Zufall falls is nothing but the fictional rendition of an already absurd yet commonplace world. In a fashion similar to the book about the king who was chased out and stuffed (from the early 1970s), Dirx makes the author an integral part of the plot, with the added twist that here Roman Dichter (literally "novel poet," again an untranslatable play on words), the author, is both inside and outside of the plot at the same time. As he types words and sentences on his keyboard, they instantly become real, and thus the protagonists are at his mercy. On the other hand, the plot moves forward through the actions of the child protagonists and seemingly independently of the author.

The creative process thus merges the imaginative powers of author and reader, and appears as a blend of serendipity and intentionality. In Dirx's work, nonsense no longer affirms sense, as it does in Carroll's *Alice*, yet through the intrusion of the absurd and the fantastic into fictional reality, the world assumes a Kafkaesque quality of illogic and absurdity. It is probably no "coincidence" that in one of the illustrations that exquisitely catches the play of illusion and allusions that makes up this book, Kafka appears next to Alice, Mary Poppins, Struwwelpeter, Babar, Tarzan, Superman, Mickey Mouse, Don Quixote, and other cultural icons from within and without the children's literature canon. This collage also illustrates the playful blending of high and low, adult and child cultures that has contributed to the integration of children's literature into the mainstream.

By questioning and erasing borders between the real, the fictional, and the fantastic, postmodern authors broach epistemological questions in a format that is understandable but challenging for children. Equally challenging are narratives told on various levels and from various perspectives (Peter Pohl, Tormod Haugen, for example). Books like these carry a fair amount of intellectual prestige—an important point for the status of children's literature today. Its new position has offered authors the full range of issues and topics addressed in adult fiction and a greater freedom to experiment, and it has offered readers and critics of children's literature a means to participate in the public debate.

NOTES

1. Gundel Mattenklott, *Zauberkreide: Kinderliteratur seit 1945* (Stuttgart: J. B. Metzler, 1989), pp. 14, 165.

2. Cited in James Krüss, *Naivität und Kunstverstand. Gedanken zur Kinderliteratur* (Weinheim and Basel: Beltz, 1992), p. 76.

3. Ibid., p. 88.

4. Peter Hunt, *Criticism, Theory, and Children's Literature* (Cambridge: Basil Blackwell, 1991), p. 54.

5. Alison Lurie, "William Mayne," in *Children and Their Books: A Collection of Essays to Celebrate the Work of Iona and Peter Opie*, ed. Gillian Avery and Julia Briggs (Oxford: Clarendon Press, 1989), p. 369.

6. Otto Gmelin, *Böses aus Kinderbüchern und ein roter Elefant* (Frankfurt: Haag und Herchen, 1977), pp. 186, 212.

7. Charles Newman, *The Post-Modern Aura. The Act of Fiction in an Age of Inflation* (Evanston, Ill.: Northwestern University Press, 1985), p. 51.

8. Ibid., p. 178.

REFERENCES

Dirx, Jörn-Peter. *Alles Rainer Zufall*. Ravensburg: Otto Maier, 1987.

Ende, Michael. *The Neverending Story*. Trans. Ralph Manheim. New York: Doubleday, 1983.

Ewers, Hans-Heino. "Zwischen Literaturanspruch und Leserbezug. Zum Normen- und Stilwandel der Kinder- und Jugendliteraturkritik seit den 70er Jahren." *Tausend und ein Buch* 4 (August 1993): 4–14.

Ewers, Hans-Heino, Maria Lypp, and Ulrich Nassen, eds. *Kinderliteratur und Moderne. Ästhetische Herausforderungen der Kinderliteratur im 20. Jahrhundert*. Weinheim and Munich: Juventa, 1990.

Gmelin, Otto. *Böses aus Kinderbüchern und ein roter Elefant*. Frankfurt: Haag und Herchen, 1977.

Haugen, Tormod. *Romanen om Merkel Hanssen og Donna Winter og Den store flukten*. Oslo: Gyldendal, 1986.

Hunt, Peter. *Criticism, Theory, and Children's Literature*. Cambridge: Basil Blackwell, 1991.

Krüss, James. *Naivität und Kunstverstand. Gedanken zur Kinderliteratur*. Weinheim and Basel: Beltz, 1992.

Lurie, Alison. "William Mayne." In *Children and Their Books: A Collection of Essays to Celebrate the Work of Iona and Peter Opie*. Ed. Gillian Avery and Julia Briggs. Oxford: Clarendon Press, 1989.

Mattenklott, Gundel. *Zauberkreide: Kinderliteratur seit 1945*. Stuttgart: J. B. Metzler, 1989.

Newman, Charles. *The Post-Modern Aura. The Act of Fiction in an Age of Inflation*. Evanston, Ill.: Northwestern University Press, 1985.

Scieszka, John. *The Stinky Cheese Man and Other Fairly Stupid Tales*. New York: Viking, 1992.

Zipes, Jack. "Down with Heidi, Down with Struwwelpeter, Three Cheers for the Revolution. Towards a New Socialist Children's Literature in West Germany." In *Children's Literature* 6 (1977): 162-179.

Part III

Experimental Writing and Postmodern Trends

From Grand Narrative to Small Stories: New Narrative Structures in Recent Scandinavian Children's Literature

Åsfrid Svensen

Traditionally the bildungsroman has had a strong position in children's literature. In a typical story of this kind, we follow the child through three stages of growth and maturation; the intermediate stage of estrangement, temptation, and chaotic experience prepares for the final stage of reconciliation and harmony. The aim and progress of the protagonist's life already seem predestined in the initial stage, but the challenges of the intermediate stage are necessary for him or her to become aware of the real values in life.

Astrid Lindgren's *Ronja rövardotter* (*Ronia, the Robber's Daughter*, 1981), is a modern version of the bildungsroman. We follow Ronja through the usual three stages, but in the final stage her father and his robbers, not Ronja, are forced to go through painful development and accept new ways of thinking.

Even so, *Ronja rövardotter* corresponds to a grand narrative in our culture: a narrative about a child's inborn, stable identity and a course of life the seeds of which may be found in the child at birth.

In the 1980s and 1990s, however, stable identities and predestined, linear, chronological courses of life are becoming gradually less obvious in children's literature. The intermediate breakup stage of the bildungsroman seems to have conquered the entire narrative field of some novels, with no final harmony to overcome the disorder. Instead of the single, chronological course of one character, we find parallel, simultaneous stories of two or several characters, representing a multitude of possibilities. The possibilities are not always *real* in the fictive world: some of the characters use their creative talents to play changing parts in a variety of constructed situations and imaginary stories. They stage their lives, often inspired by literature or modern mass media.

In novels by two outstanding Swedish authors, a character of this kind is drawn in contrast to a more traditional character with stable identity and social background. In Maria Gripe's *Shadow* tetralogy (1982–1988), the mysterious housemaid Carolin upsets and fascinates Berta and her conventional, bourgeois family. The strong and daring Carolin introduces new habits and fresh ideas into a world of rigid formality. But she refuses to give information about her background, and Berta is nearly driven to despair by Carolin's lack of constancy. Who is the real Carolin behind her always unpredictable attitudes and behavior? Is the core of her personality her passion for acting?

In Peter Pohl's *Janne, min vän* (*Johnny, My Friend*, 1985), Janne cycles on his fabulous bike into the life of the narrator Krille and rapidly becomes his closest friend. But Krille knows nothing about Janne and his background, and Janne gives no explanation of his long absences. Dark secrets are hinted at, and in the end Krille is forced to realize that the Janne he has known is a fictive character, played by a child whose social identity and position are unbearably painful.

There is no final harmony in this novel. Mysterious episodes are left unexplained, and the central mystery of Janne's identity is only partly solved. Janne is dead, Krille is in desperate grief, and the well-ordered life and society he has known seem only a stage set concealing chaos, brutality, and violence.

In spite of this, *Janne, min vän* is not a depressing book. The friendship between the two children is drawn with unusual emotional intensity, and the novel is thrilling, humorous, and full of surprises.

Carolin and Janne challenge our traditional concepts of identity. They cross normal borderlines between male and female, real and imagined, and seem to achieve their genuine potential in acting parts rather than in showing their "true" selves.

Likewise, several recent Norwegian novels let their characters display their creative resources through staged plots and through imagined events and situations. Tormod Haugen's *Skriket fra jungelen* (The Scream from the Jungle, 1989), is composed like a TV soap opera, with a large number of characters and interlinking plots. Rune Belsvik's *Den som kysser i vinden blæs ikkje bort aleine* (*Kissing in the Wind*, 1987), uses motifs and characters not only from TV but from one particular soap opera, *Dynasty*. The main star from *Dynasty* is invited to a tiny island in western Norway, on the pretext that she might find her roots there. Everyone, including the star, knows this to be an illusion, but everyone makes the most of it. The interaction between Hollywood and the small fishing village releases high comedy, but also gives new vitality to the local culture as well as to the actress.

We find counter-stories to traditional narrative patterns in many recent children's books. In children's literature of the nineteenth century, there are other grand narratives in addition to the bildungsroman; books for boys present imperialist stories about conquering European heroes in remote parts of the world, and in books for girls the heroine finds happiness through an all-absorbing love. For instance, Stig Ericsson and Stig Holmås have written counter-stories to James Fenimore Cooper and Edward Sylvester Ellis, taking the point of view of the Native Americans.

Mette Newth has written similar counter-stories to the imperialist narratives, in her case stories about the Danish–Norwegian conquest of Greenland. *Bortførelsen* (*The Abduction*, 1987), is a historical novel about two seventeeth-century adolescent Inuits taken by force from Greenland to Bergen and kept prisoners there.

Inserted in this sinister main plot there are contrasting stories about traditional Inuit life in Greenland that show deep respect for the totality of nature and the necessity of cooperation and solidarity between people. We follow the thoughts of the Inuit girl when she tries to forget the cruelty and pain inflicted on her in Bergen by dreaming of her past life in Greenland. Style and mode change frequently. We find lyric sensitivity in the descriptions of landscape, weather, her little brother helping an injured bird, and her grandparents, who have to die because they are too frail to go through the hardships of the coming winter. Dramatic intensity characterizes the story about two young men competing while hunting a polar bear. In a desperate fight, one of the young men is seriously maimed by the bear, and the other man succeeds in killing the beast. But quite as important are the rituals following this dramatic climax: the soul of the polar bear is set free through a solemn ceremony, and later the two young men go through ritual procedures of reconciliation. Rivalry and envy cannot be allowed to impair the solidarity among all members of the tribe.

A counter-story from 1994 is Jo Tenfjord's *Sally Sjørøverdatter* (Sally, the Pirate's Daughter). The narrator of this novel turns out to be the daughter of Long John Silver in Robert Louis Stevenson's *Treasure Island.* Stevenson's novel is hardly imperialist in its attitudes, and Tenfjord's text alludes to it with humorous and affectionate irreverence rather than with indignant rejection. But Sally is as tough and audacious as her pirate father. Jim Hawkins, hero and narrator of *Treasure Island,* made his fortune in cooperation with the squire and the doctor, and in the end was fully accepted as a young gentleman. Sally, illegitimate child and mulatto, tells us a different version, a female, lower-class, non-white version of partly the same events, partly new and surprising events not related in *Treasure Island.*

A European spirit of adventure and an exotic island are important motifs in one of Jostein Gaarder's novels as well, but the implications are different here. *Kabalmysteriet (The Solitaire Mystery,* 1990), presents a complicated set of stories within stories like nested Chinese boxes. In the main story, twelve-year-old Hans Thomas and his father travel by car from Norway to Athens, hoping to find their mother and wife; she left them eight years earlier, in an attempt at self-realization. On their way sout, Hans Thomas receives a mysterious gift: a microscopic book with strange stories covering nearly two centuries. The boy reads about past events, including families broken and family members lost, shipwrecks, estrangement on a remote tropical island or in a remote Swiss mountain village, and playing cards coming alive. The fantastic stories in the tiny book are incredible, but they still seem to interfere with Hans Thomas' own life in a disturbing way.

There also are striking similarities between his own situation and the circumstances he reads about. An important character in the tiny book is the joker, the card that does not belong to spades, hearts, diamonds, or clubs. Hans Thomas and his father both consider themselves to be jokers—single, unadjusted, odd persons with no fixed identities and no fixed attitudes or positions. Throughout European history, again and again, provocative, rebellious outsiders have questioned accepted ways of thinking and sometimes have caused upheaval in the established order. Hans Thomas' father is interested in philosophy and history, and on their way to Athens, he tells his son about some of these jokers, from Socrates to Napoleon. The stories of the tiny book present other jokers in the context of fantastic tales about the island and the living playing cards.

The interplay between the stories of the tiny book and Hans Thomas' own story helps the boy to gain a better understanding of his own life—and of restless, disturbed, disconnected modern Europe and its roots deep in Greek antiquity. Above all, reading the tiny book strengthens his sense of wonder, his ability to raise questions and never feel satisfied with conventional answers.

Kabalmysteriet has some postmodernist features, but I would not call it a postmodernist novel. The unifying elements are too strong, across the multitude of stories and the many gaps and fractures in the stories.

Some other recent novels have obvious postmodern characteristics that link them to dominant trends in adult fiction since the 1970s. In both cases these characteristics are connected to impressions of a rapidly altering modern world, unstable social relations, and the *virtual reality* of computers and mass media replacing cultural heritage.

Nevertheless, in traditional children's literature we also quite often find some of the formal features of the modern books I have commented upon. Intertextuality and stories within stories are no new inventions. For instance, the main characters of children's books from the nineteenth century sometimes act out the stories they have read in fairy tales or in books about Native Americans, and they live out their parts in vivid identification with Cinderella or the last Mohican. Still, the children are finally brought back to reality, often with some sort of moral message extracted from their play. And the border between the reality of the main fiction and the imagined realities of the stories within the story is always quite clear.

Not so in the modern books to which I have referred. There the borders of the normal ordering cognitive systems are blurred. Like postmodernist adult fiction, these children's books show their readers a reality that is far less easily surveyed, understood, and controlled than the fictional reality of traditional realistic novels. The traditional ending of the children's novel solves every mystery, binds up loose ends, and ensures that indecision, doubts, and conflicts give way to clarity and conciliation. The main character advances in understanding and maturity.

In the recent novels we often find an "open" ending, where questions are left unanswered and important decisions are not yet taken. Uncertainty is more or less accepted; the future is unpredictable. A unifying, harmonizing ending is not so easily achieved because the disintegration of the world of everyday life has gone too far. In the novels we see this disintegration in the multitude of stories, and also in the interplay (and sometimes the clash) between differing interpretations, differing views of life, differing cultural patterns. The plurality of manners and ideas sometimes results in bitter conflict, sometimes in fragmentation, disconnectedness, and loneliness; this is often the case in Tormod Haugen's books. But the disintegrated world can also be a world of numerous possibilities and incitements to creative imagination. The clearest example of this is Belsvik's *Den som kysser i vinden*.

But none of these books carry relativism to the extreme. Postmodern irony, skepticism, and sense of emptiness and absurdity are rarely found in children's books. In her ideas of a profound but often concealed individuality, Maria Gripe frequently alludes to Romantic or pre–Romantic ideas. In many of her books she goes quite far in rejecting social identity and conventional values, but she never rejects the importance of the search for identity and self-fulfillment. Mette Newth's novels convey firm values in their exposure of oppression and injustice.

In novels by other authors, we may find uncertainty and the quest for values rather than unambiguous conclusions. But they all have one traditional value in common: a strong sense of the importance of the child's integrity. Perhaps after all a remnant of the grand narrative still lingers.

REFERENCES

Belsvik, Rune. *Den som kysser i vinden blæs ikkje bort aleine*. Oslo: Det Norske Samlaget, 1987.

———. *Kissing in the Wind*. Toronto: Groundwood Books, 1989.

Gaarder, Jostein. *Kabalmysteriet*. Oslo: H. Aschehoug & Co., 1990.

———. *The Solitaire Mystery*. London: Orion Children's Books, 1996; New York: Farrar, Straus & Giroux, 1996.

Gripe, Maria. *Skuggan över stenbänken*. Stockholm: Bonniers Junior Förlag, 1982.

———. *. . . och de vita skuggorna i skogen*. Stockholm: Bonniers Junior Förlag, 1984.

———. *Skuggornas barn*. Stockholm: Bonniers Junior Förlag, 1986.

———. *Skugg-gömman*. Stockholm: Bonniers Junior Förlag, 1988.

Haugen, Tormod. *Skriket fra jungelen*. Oslo: Gyldendal Norsk Forlag, 1989.

Lindgren, Astrid. *Ronja rövardotter*. Stockholm: Rabén & Sjögren, 1981.

———. *The Robber's Daughter*. London: Methuen Children's Books, 1983.

———. *Ronia, the Robber's Daughter*. New York: Viking Penguin, 1983; Puffin ed., 1985.

Newth, Mette. *Bortførelsen*. Oslo: Tiden Norsk Forlag, 1987.

———. *The Abduction*. London: Simon & Schuster, 1989; New York: Farrar, Straus & Giroux, 1989.

Pohl, Peter. *Janne, min vän*. Stockholm: Almqvist & Wiksell, 1985.

———. *Johnny, My Friend*. Woodchester Stroud, U.K.: Turton & Chambers, 1991.

Stevenson, Robert Louis. *Treasure Island*. 1883. New York: C. Scribner's Sons, 1912.

Tenfjord, Jo. *Sally Sjøroverdatter*. Oslo: N. W. Damm & Søn, 1994.

8

The Status of Sequels in Children's Literature: *The Long Secret* and *Beyond the Chocolate War*

Bettina Kümmerling-Meibauer

In the famous Australian school story *Teens* (1890), written by Louise Mack, the two female protagonists discuss the pleasures of children's literature with sequels. Mabel, who has read neither *Little Women* nor its sequel, *Little Men*, asks her girlfriend:

"Are they all the same? I do love a lot of books about the same people. I never can get a book big enough, can you?"—"I think they always end them too soon. I would like them to go on, and on, and on. But *Little Women* goes on to when they get married, and *Little Men* goes on a long time after. But still it would have been nice if there could have been another afterwards. I think that if I were an author I would write a book that would go on to the very, very end."—"Till they all die, everyone of them."[1]

This dialogue emphasizes the satisfaction children get from a continuation of a story. They wish to read of further adventures of characters they have come to admire.[2] Furthermore, it is stressed that a book that ends with conventional formulas such as marriage or departure of the main figure(s) can be continued until the real end, which means the death of the protagonists.

On closer examination, one will notice that sequels are a common phenomenon in children's literature. Many popular children's books—even the children's classics—have sequels. The success of the first book demands a continuation of the story, often called for by the publisher, who reacts to the clamor of readers.[3] What—besides economic matters—are the reasons for writing sequels? Is the sequel a sheer imitation of the plot situation, structure, and thematic concern of the original work? Must the reader be well acquainted with the story of the first book in order to understand the events of the sequel? Why do children ostensibly enjoy reading sequels of popular books?

To avoid misunderstandings, the term "sequel" needs some explication. By "sequel" I mean every book written as a continuation of a first book. Though in "series book research" a "series" can be of any length, from two up to any number desired, I would like to keep to the term "sequel" in the following discussion in order not to blur the bonds between syndicate-generated series and sequels of books that were not originally intended to be continued. In addition, a sequel rouses certain expectations on the part of the reader that are shaped by the nature of the sequel itself. It touches on all elements: setting, characters, plot situation, theme, and narrator's voice. The popularity of sequels contradicts their marginal status in literary criticism.[4] They seem to be suspicious from a literary point of view, and many critics claim that the sequel is inferior to the original work.[5] However, exactly what constitutes the literary value of a sequel is not well understood. Even the newly established concept of "series book research,"[6] which focuses on the similarities of series books and concentrates on formula-written and syndicate-generated series books, largely neglects the question of what constitutes the difference between the original work and the sequel.[7] As yet, there is little theoretical research on the phenomenon of sequels in children's literature.[8] Scholars of children's literature have not recognized that the concise study of sequels will help to establish new insights into narrative problems as far as the plot construction, the ending, and the reopening of literary works are concerned.[9]

My approach is based on a detailed analysis of two modern American children's novels and their sequels: *The Chocolate War* (1974) and *Beyond the Chocolate War* (1985), by Robert Cormier, and *Harriet the Spy* (1964) and *The Long Secret* (1965), by Louise Fitzhugh. It is widely accepted that *Harriet the Spy* and *The Chocolate War* are milestones of children's literature that have paved the way for all those taboo-breaking children's books that were to appear in the 1970s.[10] In addition, these novels prove to be interesting examples because they are both followed by sequels praised by critics as being masterpieces on a par with the original works.

Before going into detail, I wish to outline my main points. First, I will concentrate on a study stressing the overriding thematic concern, the focus on a strong figure and the development of the protagonists. Second, I will explore the narrative elements that structure the novels and build a connection between the original work and the sequel. Fitzhugh and Cormier imagined their books to be complete, but they noticed that some open questions remained at the ends of their novels, and thus sequels appeared. However, in many ways the sequels subvert the meaning of the original work. In this way, it happens that new aspects are added to the original work that change the meaning of its components. Readers are encouraged to think of the new aspects as causes of events they did not at first acknowledge. In this regard, one must be aware that in the course of these novels, characters grow and develop along lines suggested by an overriding thematic concern. While Fitzhugh's books are concerned with the progression through time of an individual who is an artist in the making, Cormier's novels are dominated by the theme of evil, which is realized with increasing violence. What ties the novels together is the focus upon a strong character. The difference between original work and sequel is that in the sequels, both authors choose a neglected character from the first book with whom they sympathize as a protagonist of the sequel: Obie as opponent to Archie in *Beyond the Chocolate War*, and Beth Ellen as counterpart to Harriet in *The Long Secret*. By this choice the authors create a change in point of view.

In Cormier's novels, the protagonists are Archie Costello, who established a reign of terror at a Catholic college, and his antagonists Jerry Renault (in the first novel) and Obie (in the second novel). By the end of the first novel, Jerry is defeated and Archie can improve his power. It remains open whether Jerry will die because of his serious injuries. The pessimistic ending, unusual in children's literature, shocked many readers because the novel depicts adults and children in ways contrary to the norm. The hero with whom the reader might sympathize has not—against all expectations—overcome the obstacles. He seems to be the only character capable of development; the other figures remain obviously unchanged.

The sequel, *Beyond the Chocolate War*, is tied to the first novel by the same setting and the focus on the antihero Archie. It is interesting that Jerry Renault reappears, but he is not Archie's antagonist. He prepares for a new encounter with Emile Janza, whom he conquers symbolically with his passivity. Whereas Jerry plays a minor part, Obie is the focus of attention. He has succeeded in outwitting Archie twice (with the marble box and with the guillotine), but at last Archie emerges victorious. By the end of the second novel, Obie is, like Jerry at the end of the first novel, (symbolically) defeated by Archie's sound remark that, due to their cowardice, he and his schoolmates are jointly responsible for the evil and tyranny at the college.

In Fitzhugh's two novels, the protagonists are the developing writer, Harriet, and the developing artist, Beth Ellen, whose values are in direct conflict with those of their families and of society. The focus is on the difficulties that life poses for Harriet and Beth Ellen. As the story unfolds, so does the reader's awareness of the irony and complexity of the human condition, chiefly as it is reflected in Fitzhugh's characterization of Harriet. By the end of the novel, Harriet has begun to understand human interdependence and to empathize with others. She and her friends are back together, each accepting the other for who she/he is.

The sequel, *The Long Secret*, seems startlingly different because the reader most often sees the old protagonist Harriet from Beth Ellen's point of view.[11] The two girls are very nearly opposite in outlook and behavior. Harriet serves to provoke responses from Beth Ellen and to stimulate the reader's awareness of her. These results would never have been achieved had Harriet been absent. Indeed, had Harriet not criticized Beth Ellen's lack of ambition and dragged her around in pursuit of the note writer, neither girl would have grown as much as she has by the end of the novel. Beth Ellen arrives at the same balanced position Harriet reached at the end of the first book, but from an opposite direction.

In summary, *Beyond the Chocolate War* and *The Long Secret* are sequels to their respective original works for three reasons. First, they are continuations of the old protagonists' story and their confrontation with essential problems.[12] Second, they show the new protagonists' development occurring in many ways opposite to the development of the old protagonists. Third, they make the message of the original books more explicit.

As a matter of fact, one will notice that the plot situation progresses to climax situations within each of the works, and eventually to a full climax in the final work. The sequels point out the limitations of literary art. The fictional worlds extending before and after the novel are generally unavailable to the reader. The sequels work against that limitation by extending the scope of the author. The form of the sequel offers the reader a kind of vision into a character's growth that a single novel can rarely offer. This is possible because with a familiar character, readers are able to broaden their experience while remaining within a familiar frame of reference. Thus, the sequels make the situation more meaningful, so that one can look back and interpret the first book in terms of the meaning of the new one. The effect is that each novel seems complete in itself, yet also seems to give a slice of a much larger story. The suggestion of a world beyond the single novel and the assumption that readers have a knowledge of some of the history as they read the sequel is a partial answer to the question of what makes a sequel a sequel.

Apart from the thematic concern and the development of the main characters, other aspects that have thus far gone unnoticed must be taken into consideration: the narrative literary strategies that help to build a connection between original work and sequel. I have isolated three patterns that are central in these works: parallelism, open-endedness, and circularity.

When reading a sequel, one looks first for parallels with the original work; these parallels may occur in the title, characters, setting, or plot situation. I wish to call this phenomenon *parallelism*, which I consider to be the sequels' references to scenes and characters of the original work. This occurs in both sequels, but manifests itself in different ways in each. Cormier uses the strategy of informing the reader who is not familiar with the first story by means of a new voice: Obie explains what happened during the "Chocolate War" to the newcomer Ray Bannister.[13] In *The Long Secret*, one will not find a synopsis of the previous story of *Harriet the Spy*. Several remarks about Harriet's notebooks and her memories about her nurse Ol' Golly have the character of hints rather than of a recapitulation of the original story.[14] However, not even Obie's short summary can convey the emotions and menacing atmosphere of *The Chocolate War*; his summary is not the "real heart of the story." This insight leads to the important question of whether one needs to know the first novel in order to understand the story of the sequel. As mentioned above, *Beyond the Chocolate War* and *The Long Secret* can be read as independent novels. The reader does not necessarily have to have read the original novel in order to understand the sequel; nevertheless, I would argue that the background of the first novel enables the reader to have a better and a more thorough appreciation of the sequel.

What is more interesting from a narrative point of view is the question of how a seemingly finished story can be reopened and continued. This problem points to the apparent *open-endedness* of the novels. The importance of form and especially of ending in literature has been stressed by such scholars as Barbara Herrnstein-Smith, Frank Kermode, J. Hillis Miller, Victor Sklovsky, and Marianna Torgovnick.[15] However, they did not apply their ideas to sequels. The aporia of ending arises from the fact that it is impossible ever to tell whether a given narrative is complete or whether a story merely ends.[16] Closure in the text is seldom so definitive that it cannot be reopened in a subsequent text with the same characters.[17] If the ending is thought of as a tying up in a careful knot, this knot could always be untied by the narrator through the telling of further events.[18] A detailed analysis of the ending of the first novel will thus help to demonstrate the literary strategies necessary for writing a successful sequel.

The ending of Cormier's novel *The Chocolate War* is unexpected.[19] Conventionally, the hero wins, but Jerry Renault loses in a fight against Emile Janza. The novel's closure defies the expectations of many readers, which relate to the conventions of children's literature rather than to those of reality.[20] In fact, the essence of Cormier's novel is his evocation of elements of horror fiction and thriller that create a nightmarish atmosphere and an intense feeling of hopelessness. The open-endedness will convey doubt and an inability or refusal to make absolute and unqualified assertions.[21] Thus, the most interesting type of narrative fragment may be that which propels the reader into responsibility for the unwritten narrative conclusion. By leaving what follows to the reader's imagination, Cormier evokes the necessity to come to terms with the substance of the story and with the problem of social responsibility for the future.[22]

The ending of *Harriet the Spy* is effective because of its contrast with the inflected ending that earlier children's books lead us to expect. Harriet has reached a momentary balance between her self-love and her need for others, but she risks rejection nearly every time she writes notes and stories. Finally, the reader cannot know whether she will always be able to regain a satisfying balance between her need to be herself and her need for love. There are too many unknowns, and the book remains open-ended.[23] The reconciliation with her friends and their simultaneous departure could be described in a restricted sense as closural allusion.[24]

In summary, a new topic is established at the end of these novels. The cliff-hangers at the end of the books push readers to decide for themselves which future the protagonists will pursue. This phenomenon of anti-closure, which seems to be a characteristic feature of modern literature,[25] transgresses the usual demarcations separating children's literature from adult literature. The story "opens out" and creates an ambiguity of closure.

The noteworthy parallels between the closures of the first novel and of its sequel point to another phenomenon that I would like to call *circularity*. Besides the reciprocal reflection of endings, one will probably notice the close connections between the openings and the endings of the respective novels. A good example to illustrate this assumption is the beginning of *The Chocolate War*,[26] which is a symbolic anticipation of the ending when Jerry Renault is defeated by the bully Emile Janza in a murderous fight. The opening words, "They murdered him," recur with variations at the end of the same volume. His friend Goober refers back, with his comment "They murder you" (p. 187), to the first sentence of the novel and makes obvious the crucial connection between beginning and ending. The opening of the sequel starts—as does the original work—in medias res, with a mysterious allusion to Jerry's arrival at Monument and Bannister's construction of a guillotine.[27] This paragraph, which has the function of building up the suspense for the reader, who—contrary to the statement of the first sentence of the book—assumes a connection between the two events. Going on their knowledge of the structure of the first book, readers even expect that the beginning of the sequel refers to its ending. The opening, in fact, precipitates the crisis and the closure of the novel with Archie's feigned execution by Bannister's guillotine.[28]

Harriet the Spy opens with the description of a game with the name "Town," which was invented by Harriet.[29] This play demonstrates her wish to get "power" over other people in her neighborhood. Even if she has control over her play, she loses it when confronted with the real town and its inhabitants. She succeeds with her strategy in the beginning but fails when she is caught spying. Harriet has to learn to accept other people's hurt feelings when they read her sarcastic notes and to acknowledge that she cannot "play" with their emotions. The beginning of *The Long Secret* leads readers who are familiar with the first book along the wrong track.[30] Almost certainly the readers assume that the story is about Harriet and her notes until they realize that there is an anonymous notewriter who might indeed be someone other than Harriet. The secret of the mysterious notes is solved by the end, and thus the closure is a fulfillment of the intimated problem of the novel's first paragraph.

Looking back, the following points have been stressed: with regard to the thematic study, two differences between original work and sequel were discussed: the representation of the major characters of the first book from different points of view in the sequel, and the choice of a minor character in the original work as a new protagonist of the sequel. The sequels are more than a continuation of the first book insofar as they show the development of both the new and the old protagonists. Second, I explored the narrative elements that structure the novels of Cormier and Fitzhugh and build a connection between first book and sequel. In this regard, three patterns were isolated: parallelism, open-endedness, and circularity. Through a detailed study of these issues, one will be able to determine what makes a sequel a sequel, and thus carry the narratological analysis of sequels toward more fruitful directions.

NOTES

1. Louise Mack, *Teens: A Story of Australian School Girls* (1890; Sydney: Cornstalk Publishing, 1924), p. 96.

2. Studies in the field of empirical reader research and reading psychology stress the satisfaction readers get from a repetition of familiar formulaic narratives. See John G. Cawelti, *Adventure, Mystery, and Romance* (Chicago: University of Chicago Press, 1976); and Faye Riter Kensinger, *Children of the Series and How They Grew* (Bowling Green, Ohio: Bowling Green State University Popular Press, 1987).

3. As far as I know, it seems extremely rare that an author refuses to write a sequel. Ian Serraillier refused to write a sequel to his famous book *The Silver Sword* (1956). The French author Hector Malot, instead of writing a sequel to *Sans famille* (1878), wrote another famous book, *En famille* (1893), whose title certainly alludes to the first novel but consists of a new story with new protagonists.

4. Paul Deane, *Mirrors of American Culture: Children's Fiction Series in the Twentieth Century* (Metuchen, N.J., and London: Scarecrow Press, 1991), gives a synopsis of criticism and censorship of sequels and series in children's literature.

5. Even Roderick McGillis assumes (in his introduction to a special issue on "series books") that the sequel—after all—is inferior to the initial work. *Children's Literature Association Quarterly* 14 (1989): 162–195.

6. Fred Erisman, "The Stepchild in the Basement: Trends in Series Book Research," *Newsboy* 30 (1992): 12–16) differentiates between series books as books conceived, written, and produced as uniform series, and clusters of books that only gradually turn into a series.

7. Even Wallace Martin's excellent study, *Recent Theories of Narrative* (Ithaca, N.Y.: Cornell University Press, 1986), does not contain theoretical studies about sequels or series.

8. The special issue on "series books," *Children's Literature Association Quarterly* 14 (1989), is the exception to the rule. Even there, little attention is paid to narrative theory.

9. When critics suspect that there is little difference between the sequels, the books are obviously identified as formula fiction, and they acknowledge that it requires—because of its apparent sameness—no individual theory.

10. The history of these novels' reception is an interesting example of the process whereby a book becomes part of the literary canon. See Virginia Wolf, *Louise Fitzhugh* (New York: Twayne, 1991); and Patricia Campbell, *Presenting Robert Cormier* (New York: Twayne, 1985).

11. Several critics were puzzled by Harriet's seeming to be as irritating as she does in the book, and by Fitzhugh's failure to portray her as softened by her experiences in the first book.

12. One important difference between the two books is that Harriet is an insider in *The Long Secret,* with parents and close friendships.

13. See Robert Cormier, *The Chocolate War* (New York: Dell, 1986), pp. 32–33.

14. See Louise Fitzhugh, *Harriet the Spy* (London: Harper, 1992), pp. 25, 167.

15. See Barbara Herrnstein-Smith, *Poetic Closure: A Study of How Poems End* (Chicago and London: University of Chicago Press, 1968); Frank Kermode, *The Sense of an Ending: Studies in the Theory of Fiction* (New York: Oxford University Press, 1967); J. Hillis Miller, "The Problematic of Ending in Narrative," *Nineteenth-Century Fiction* 33 (1978): 3–7; Victor Sklovsky, *Théorie de la littérature* (Paris: Éditions du Seuil, 1965); Marianna Torgovnick, *Closure in the Novel* (Princeton: Princeton University Press, 1981).

16. This opinion is in contrast to the theoretical view of Peter Brooks, who draws attention to the fact that narratological studies miss the dynamics of temporality in plot as part of their ideology. As Brooks claims, in justifying the association he makes between the Freudian psychoanalytic concept of desire for death and the narrative notion of an ending: "The narrative must tend toward its end, seek illumination in its own death—yet this must be the right death, the correct end" (*Reading for the Plot: Design and Intention in Narrative* [New York: Knopf, 1984], p. 103). Brooks's concept of plot unity is an effective and far-reaching presupposition. It motivates the type of problems with which plot models are engaged. See Ruth Ronen, "Paradigm Shift in Plot Models: An Outline of the History of Narratology" (*Poetics Today* 11 [1990]: 817–842), which deals with narrative plot models and possible-worlds semantics.

17. See Torgovnick, *Closure in the Novel.*

18. J. Hillis Miller argues further that our inability to define beginnings and endings is not just a formal problem that might be solved by constructing a better theory: "No narrative can show either its beginning or its ending. It always begins and ends still in medias res, presupposing as a future anterior some parts of itself outside itself." "The Problematic of Ending in Narrative," p. 5.

19. "'Maybe the black box will work the next time, Archie,' Obie said. 'Or maybe another kid like Renault will come along.' The lights went off again. Archie and Obie sat there awhile not saying anything and then made their way out of the place in the darkness" (p. 191).

20. See Sylvia P. Iskander, "Readers, Realism and Robert Cormier," *Children's Literature* 15 (1987): 7–18. See also Cormier's comment: "As long as what I write is true and believable, why should I have to create happy endings? My books are an antidote to the TV view of life, where even in a suspenseful show you know before the last commercial that Starsky and Hutch will get their man. That's phony realism. Life just isn't like that." P. Janeczko, "In Their Own Words: An Interview with Robert Cormier," *English Journal* 66 (1977): 11.

21. Sarah Gilead, "Magic Abjured: Closure in Children's Fantasy Fiction," *PMLA* 106 (1991): 277–293; and Margaret R. Higonnet, "Narrative Fractures and Fragments," *Children's Literature* 15 (1987): 37–54, have drawn attention to the eminently important role of closure in fragmentary ending in modern children's fiction.

22. Peter Hunt has argued against what many critics have assumed to be the psychological necessity of linear structure and conventional closure in children's literature. He notes examples of final uncertainty in children's books that suggest the child's ability to adapt complicated clues and subtle structures from an early age. "Necessary Misreadings: Directions in Narrative Theory for Children's Literature," *Studies in the Literary Imagination* 18 (1985): 107–121.

23. Janie and Sport wait in silence until Harriet finishes writing in her notebook: "All three of them turned then and walked along the river" (p. 265).

24. Victor Sklovsky, *Théorie de la littérature*, identifies some of the methods used in the short story to evade traditional closure—for example, finishing a story with a description or a commonplace remark. He calls these "negative" or "degree zero" endings.

25. Barbara Hermstein-Smith explains the apparent anti-closure in modern poetry as a desire for the illusion of realism in her *Poetic Closure: A Study of How Poems End*.

26. "They murdered him. As he turned to take the ball, a dam burst against the side of his head and a hand grenade shattered in his stomach. Engulfed by nausea, he pitched toward the grass" (p. 7).

27. "Ray Bannister started to build the guillotine the day Jerry Renault returned to Monument. There was no connection between the two events." Robert Cormier, *Beyond the Chocolate War* (New York: Dell, 1986), p. 3.

28. While Archie remains unhurt, another person dies: at the same time as the execution, the pupil David Caroni commits suicide by jumping from a high bridge. Both scenes are intertwined to increase the reader's ignorance and suspense.

29. "Harriet was trying to explain to Sport how to play Town" (p. 5).

30. "The notes were appearing everywhere. Everyone was talking about it: The first time Harriet and Beth Ellen ever saw anyone get one was one day in July." Louise Fitzhugh, *The Long Secret* (London: Harper, 1990) p. 1.

REFERENCES

Bosmajian, Hamida. "Louise Fitzhugh's *Harriet the Spy*: Nonsense and Sense." In *Touchstones. Reflections on the Best in Children's Literature*. Ed. Perry Nodelman. Vol. 1. West Lafayette, Ind.: Children's Literature Association, 1985.

Brooks, Peter. *Reading for the Plot: Design and Intention in Narrative*. New York: Knopf, 1984.

Campbell, Patricia. *Presenting Robert Cormier*. New York: Twayne, 1985.

Cawelti, John G. *Adventure, Mystery, and Romance: Formula Stories as Art and Popular Culture*. Chicago: University of Chicago Press, 1976.

Cormier, Robert. *The Chocolate War*. 1974. New York: Dell, 1986.

———. *Beyond the Chocolate War*. 1985. New York: Dell, 1986.

Deane, Paul. *Mirrors of American Culture. Children's Fiction Series in the Twentieth Century*. Metuchen, N.J. and London: Scarecrow Press, 1991.

Erisman, Fred. "The Stepchild in the Basement: Trends in Series Book Research." *Newsboy* 30 (1992): 12–16.

Fitzhugh, Louise. *Harriet the Spy*. 1964. London: Harper, 1992.

———. *The Long Secret*. 1965. London: Harper, 1990.

Gilead, Sarah. "Magic Abjured: Closure in Children's Fantasy Fiction." *PMLA* 106 (1991): 277–293.

Hermnstein-Smith, Barbara. *Poetic Closure: A Study of How Poems End*. Chicago and London: University of Chicago Press, 1968.

Higonnet, Margaret R. "Narrative Fractures and Fragments." *Children's Literature* 15 (1987): 37–54.

Hunt, Peter. "Necessary Misreadings: Directions in Narrative Theory for Children's Literature." *Studies in the Literary Imagination* 18 (1985): 107–121.

Iskander, Sylvia P. "Readers, Realism and Robert Cormier." *Children's Literature* 15 (1987): 7–18.

Kensinger, Faye Riter. *Children of the Series and How They Grew; or, A Century of Heroines and Heroes, Romantic, Comic, Moral*. Bowling Green, Ohio: Bowling Green State University Popular Press, 1987.

Kermode, Frank. *The Sense of an Ending: Studies in the Theory of Fiction*. New York: Oxford University Press, 1967.

Mack, Louise. *Teens: A Story of Australian School Girls*. 1890. Sydney: Cornstalk Publishing, 1924.

Martin, Wallace. *Recent Theories of Narrative*. Ithaca, N.Y.: Cornell University Press, 1986.

McGillis, Roderick. "Series Books." *Children's Literature Association Quarterly* 14 (1989): 162–195.

Miller, J. Hillis. "Narrative and History." *ELH* 41 (1974): 455–473.

———. "The Problematic of Ending in Narrative." *Nineteenth-Century Fiction* 33 (1978): 3–7.

Nodelman, Perry. "Robert Cormier's *The Chocolate War*: Paranoia and Paradox." In *Stories and Society. Children's Literature in Its Social Context*. Ed. Dennis Butts. Basingstoke, U.K. and London: Macmillan, 1992.

Paul, Lissa. "The Feminist Writer as Heroine in *Harriet the Spy*." *The Lion and the Unicorn* 13 (1989): 67–73.

Ronen, Ruth. "Paradigm Shift in Plot Models: An Outline of the History of Narratology." *Poetics Today* 11 (1990): 817–842.

Schmidt, Gary D. "See How They Grow: Character Development in Children's Series Books." *Children's Literature in Education* 18 (1987): 34–43.

Sklovsky, Victor. *Théorie de la littérature*. Paris: Éditions du Seuil, 1965.

Torgovnick, Marianna. *Closure in the Novel*. Princeton: Princeton University Press, 1981.

Veglahn, Nancy. "The Bland Face of Evil in the Novels of Robert Cormier." *The Lion and the Unicorn* 12 (1988): 12–18.

Wolf, Virginia. *Louise Fitzhugh*. New York: Twayne, 1991.

9

Gillian Cross's *Wolf*:
An Exploration of Patterns and Polarities

Susan Clancy

Since 1945, our world has seen many changes. Children's literature is but one area in which these changes have been reflected. Today many children's authors recognize that the conventional subject matter of children's stories and its presentation in traditional forms is no longer always appropriate. Libby Gleeson, an Australian author, acknowledges that the "world has changed, the writing has changed and kids have changed." No longer can we only give children "the safe, warm, conservative story, the Pollyanna syndrome"[1] that for many of us was part of our own childhoods.

One of the agents of change has been technology. It has been used to put the world at the fingertips of many young readers, expanding their knowledge base and their world experience far beyond that of the 1940s. This has enabled them to become aware of issues relating to war, racism, dysfunctional families, gender identity, societal values, and political expediency—indeed, many of them have lived through such experiences. As well as extending the knowledge base, technology has broadened opportunities for the way we process story. It is no longer necessarily linear and sequential. The techniques used in video and film have opened the door to multiple story strands happening simultaneously, developing children's ability to follow quite complex methods of patterning stories.

When we align these changes with the developments in understandings of literary theory, we find that since 1945, the critical focus has moved from the text to the reader, to the transaction between them, until today, when we consider the text, the writer and the reader, and the culture and ideologies that create them. This, in turn, encourages recognition of dominant and resistant readings that foreground different sociocultural and/or political beliefs that impinge on the writer's construction of text and the reader's interpretation.[2]

Our need for story, however, has not changed. Story has always been an integral part of human existence. As long as 60,000 years ago, the Australian Aboriginal people, "along with every researched indigenous culture," told stories that "make reference to the primary polarities or complementations of opposites that are evident in the natural world." In this way, Aboriginal society was able to transfer "laws concerning marital patterns, familial respect, and responsibility codes."[3] Provided a balance between these polarities existed, stability was maintained. When the balance was disturbed, disharmony and destruction ensued. Stories that today sustain and nurture the reader make similar use of polarities and balance, allowing readers to develop a sense of continuity of human existence.

Herein lies the challenge for writers. How can they reflect these changes while retaining the basic elements of story? What can they write about that will be interesting and relevant to the children of today? How can they construct it, in order to capture and maintain reader interest? One of the more successful attempts to address this challenge has been made by Gillian Cross in *Wolf*. My purpose here is to consider her experimentation in producing a text that reflects a number of these changes, yet maintains the essence of ideas that are an integral part of human storying.

In *Wolf*, Cross addresses social, cultural, and political issues in a complex and highly structured piece of writing that invites readers to explore, question, and hypothesize in order to create multiple meanings from the literal and metaphorical polarities or complementations of opposites that she sets up in relation to characters, ideologies, and setting. When these are linked in a variety of story patterns, we find a technique that can be likened to a kaleidoscope, where many fragments of the plot are revealed, then structured and restructured by the viewer into an endless variety of configurations. Each can stand alone with its own sense of unity and identity, or become an integral part of the multifaceted nature of meaning that the text evokes.

Peter Hunt asserts that "most experimental fiction tends to replace the narrative of resolution with the plot of revelation," although he acknowledges that usually "children's books tend to favour the plot of resolution."[4] *Wolf* demonstrates a move away from the narrative of resolution and experiments with a plot of revelation. This occurs initially through the range of story patterns: conventional narrative interspersed with fairy tale, dream, nonfiction, myth and legend, and rhyme that emerge in the shape of a detective story with snippets of natural science, environmental concerns, and social history. An initial reading of this text invites readers to access the story from their own points of interest, understanding, or need. Subsequent readings reveal details that could easily be missed, or encourage the reader to foreground alternative information, so that different elements of the plot emerge.

At the most literal level, the text weaves the story of a thirteen-year-old girl, Cassy, caught up in an adventure with elements of mystery, excitement, and suspense, arranged in a conventional narrative pattern. However, running parallel with this is the *Little Red Riding Hood* fairy tale, seemingly caught within Cassy's dreams, that gives voice to a metaphorical extension of her fear and current predicament. There are as well tangential nonfiction components that highlight aspects of wolves as creatures of the wild and objects of human aggression. These opposing threads of fact and fiction, dreams and reality, polarize the symbol of the wolf as an aggressor and a social animal.

Meaning and interpretation of the many plot fragments are dependent on the access point(s) readers choose. For instance, the work of Bruno Bettelheim and his interpretations of fairy tales, based on a Freudian construction of the psyche, a belief that "only by struggling courageously against what seems like overwhelming odds can man succeed in wringing meaning out of his existence,"[5] provides one path to follow. It can be argued that Cassy does indeed "struggle courageously" to overcome the seemingly "overwhelming odds" that threaten to destroy life as she knows it, and that in the process she finds meaning for the way in which her life has been constructed.

Because some of the fairy-tale component of the narrative is explored through dreams, it is also possible to consider a Jungian perspective, where the patterning of dreams can be charted as a process of "individuation," a journey of psychic growth that involves the conscious coming to terms with one's own inner centre or Self.[6] Cassy's dreams, based on *Little Red Riding Hood*, allow her to work through her life until she must finally confront the truth about her father, and recognize her own feelings and beliefs so that she can begin to take control of her own life. The narrative reinforces this perspective for the reader by frequent and incomplete frames of a dreamed version of *Little Red Riding Hood*.

Alternatively, if we consider Jack Zipes' work with fairy tales, a sociocultural view emerges, one that highlights issues relating to the civilizing process in accordance with the social codes of the times.[7] In this text, Cassy's problem is to discover exactly where she fits within the world, despite the dysfunctional nature of her family; her gender identity, as it relates to both female and male characters within the text; and the struggle to come to terms with the range of societal and cultural values she faces.

Different versions of the *Little Red Riding Hood* story suggest different interpretations, through their depiction of the changes that have occurred, in accordance with societal and cultural beliefs. The most notable of these is from Charles Perrault's version, where Little Red Riding Hood is devoured by the wolf as a consequence of her actions.[8] Later versions have it that she is saved from the evil wolf by the brave male woodcutter. Each of these versions offers opportunities for readers to explore different sets of social and moral issues relating to family structures, social constraints, and the polarities of good and evil. If we pursue this tale to the present day, when research is indicating that children often have more to fear from those they know than from strangers, then the identification of Cassy's father as the wolf reveals a contemporary and disturbing layer of the text.

The evil nature of the wolf is further developed through the insertion of stories within the story. Although the main avenue for this is *Little Red Riding Hood*, the text is also laced with the werewolf legend, believed to have originated in a story told by Petronius in the first century A.D., and since then embroidered upon by later generations until we have the Hollywood versions of today.[9] The story Lyall chooses to tell again makes the suggestion that the werewolf is in fact the father figure, and is killed by his daughter.

"For an instant," murmured Lyall, still telling his story, "she saw the terrible face at the window. The grey muzzle, the pricked ears and the long murderous fangs. Shaking with terror, she pulled the pistol from under her pillow—and fired!"

"'And then?" breathed Goldie. Lyall's voice was soft now, every syllable crystal-clear.

"Then she opened the door and a body slumped across her feet. It was the body of her father, with a bullet hole in his left temple."[10]

This perception of the werewolf is then linked, through the performance Lyall is devising for schools, with the traditional rhyme from *The Three Little Pigs*. He has devised "a litany of accusations from history, myth and folk tales"[11] that highlights the most fearful aspects of the wolf, then builds the suspense by interspersing it with the rhyme, "Who's Afraid of the Big Bad Wolf?" By juxtaposing these elements, Cross is further exploiting a most terrifying view of the wolf while beginning to make explicit the nature of the fear that haunts Cassy.

The nonfiction strand of the text's structure reveals an opposing view of the wolf. It is depicted as a social animal, many species of which are now extinct because of their victimisation by humans. Cassy cannot reconcile this view of the wolf with the one that lurks in her dreams. The sensible side of her nature, instilled by her Nan, will not believe there is any connection between wolves and people—after all, "wolves are wolves and people are people." For Cassy, Robert's view that "the way we think about wolves is twisted up with the way we think about ourselves"[12] is initially complete nonsense.

Because this text is English, the symbol of the wolf becomes culturally significant. From the mythical Roman beginnings of the wolf that nurtured Romulus and Remus to the Kipling story of Mowgli and his life with the wolves, to the development within the Boy Scout movement of Cub groups under the leadership of Akela, there emerges a view of the wolf as a nurturer and protector, one that does not fit with Cassy's perception of a "nightmare shape, with gnashing yellow teeth and a long grey muzzle."[13] This polarization of the wolf as nurturer and stalker links the reader directly to fragments from each of the structural strands within the text.

We should also consider the evolutionary nature of the wolf from its beginnings as a component of myth to its place in literature today, and its relationship with the hero, in this case Cassy. In the literary sense, we could ask if this text is indicative of the domestication of myth, where the exploits of the hero become less part of a total pattern of life and death, and more important for their own sake.[14] Depending on the readers' perceptions about the place of the wolf in literature, it could be argued that Cross has set up the literary polarities of myth, founded on the deeds of gods and heroes and embodying ancient cultural beliefs, and the contemporary novel, grounded in realism and the role of the individual. Such a view then begins to reveal elements of story, encoded long ago by our ancient cultures.

Cross's opposing perspectives of the wolf—as werewolf, a manifestation of personal fears, and wolves in their natural world, as an example of a cooperative social unit, provide both psychological and socially constructed entry points for her readers. The group of Lyall, Goldie, Robert, and Cassy form the metaphorical wolf pack of which Lyall, as leader, is in control. He is fiercely territorial, reacting aggressively to infringement by outsiders. While he is prepared to accept Cassy, as a female cub, into his pack, he will fight to the death to protect her and his territory from Mick Phelan, the lone wolf, the renegade, the werewolf. Goldie, as the she-wolf, is playful and submissive to Lyall, but also prepared to protect her own, as Robert explains to Cassy: "When she heard where you'd gone she went berserk. Got the explosive, dragged us all off to the police and bullied them into setting up a trap!"[15]

However, if the metaphorical construction is removed, we are left with two males in positions of power over the female characters. This power highlights the sexual, protective, and predatory nature of the male psyche. The highly structured social unit in which they find themselves also reinforces gender stereotypes. Goldie is cast to fit the male perception of blondes—beautiful—as she sits "in one corner, as still and upright as a doll in a glass case. A black fringed shawl round her shoulders and her long golden hair combed over the silk, straight and gleaming," but with little intelligence: "You're good at turning your brain off, aren't you, Goldie?"[16] The female characters of Goldie and Cassy's Nan set up similar polarizations of the female psyche. Goldie is represented as playful, sexual, beautiful, and creative, but disorganized and unable to really care for herself or her child in a conventional manner. Nan is practical, sensible, and with no time for the lighter side of life. Goldie's existence is seemingly aimless, without shape or purpose. Nan's is rigorous and demanding. Cassy is caught between them as she attempts to be the person Nan wants her to be: "'Of course Cassy never dreams,' Nan always said. 'She has more sense to be sure. Her head touches the pillow and she's off, just like any other sensible person. There's been no trouble with dreams, not since she was a baby.'"[17] The irony is that the reader knows there are things in Cassy's life she can't control. Like Goldie, she has parts of her life that she fears to remember.

The technique of employing opposites to explore the characters is further extended to consider other sociopolitical contexts. Cassy's alternative home situations are the squat, associated with a particular lifestyle and a consequence of social inequalities and political ineptitude, and the small, crampled existence in Nan's home, which, although socially acceptable, is barren in terms of any richness of imaginative experience. Within this same context, Lyall and Mick Phelan are again set apart. Both are driven by ambition and the political climate, but Lyall's aim is personal, in that he is seeking to have a home and the money to feed and care for his group. Phelan is driven by his political beliefs about Northern Ireland—beliefs that he considers set him apart from any social restrictions. He is at war, unafraid to kill, and prepared to use his mother, daughter, and wife to win his war. He is driven by the need to destroy whereas Lyall works to construct a harmonious unit.

Within this structure, Cross sets out to achieve balance. Cassy moderates the views of the female psyche, and Robert serves a similar purpose with the male characters. The final view of the wolf, as achieved in the performance piece, is a balanced depiction. In this way, Cross maintains the order within society that is necessary to achieve harmony.

Through these complex linkings of patterns and motifs, Cross slowly reveals her plot, leaving readers with impressions, pictures, feelings, and a need to make their own meaning.

If we are prepared to accept that "the reading process is selective,"[18] then the ebb and flow set up through the structure in this text, gives readers a choice. They can simply follow one story pattern through, or they can access other revelations as the text unfolds, forming links across the stories until they are satisfied with their personal meaning.

As a reader, I am reminded of Ed Young's *Seven Blind Mice*, based on the ancient fable "The Blind Men and the Elephant." Each mouse ventures out and examines a small section of an unknown object. He fills the gaps with his own understanding and reports his finding to the whole group. Only the last mouse takes the time to explore the whole thing, and place each of the smaller discoveries into context.[19] Perhaps *Wolf* is a little like this. Each interpretation can bring satisfaction, but when all the fragments are put together, we find a story with richness and depth that move well beyond those of many traditionally based narratives.

Cross's experimentation in developing a "plot of revelation,"[20] using patterns and polarities, demonstrates how one children's author has met the challenge of constructing a text that reflects changes in contemporary society. In so doing, she displays an understanding of the way in which readers access and interpret texts, and a recognition of the need for story to nurture and sustain human existence.

NOTES

1. Libby Gleeson, "Are There Books Children Should Not Be Reading?," in *At Least They're Reading! Proceedings of the First National Conference of the Children's Book Council of Australia* (Port Melbourne: D. W. Thorpe, 1992), p. 8.

2. Bronwyn Mellor, Annette Patterson, and Marnie O'Neill, *Reading Fictions* (Scarborough: Chalkface Press, 1991), p. 4.

3. Johanna Lambert, "Introduction," in *Wise Women of the Dreamtime: Aboriginal Tales of the Ancestral Powers*, ed. Johanna Lambert (Vermont: Inner Traditions International, 1993), pp. 2, 9.

4. Peter Hunt, *Criticism, Theory, and Children's Literature* (Oxford: Basil Blackwell, 1991), p. 118.

5. Bruno Bettelheim, *The Uses of Enchantment* (London: Penguin, 1991), p. 8.

6. M. L. von Franz, "The Process of Individuation," in *Man and His Symbols*, ed. C. G. Jung (London: Arkana, 1990), p. 166.

7. Jack Zipes, *Fairy Tales and the Art of Subversion* (New York: Routledge, 1983).

8. Charles Perrault, "Little Red Riding Hood," in *The Trials and Tribulations of Little Red Riding Hood*, ed. Jack Zipes (New York: Routledge, 1993), pp. 91–93.

9. Adam Douglas, *The Beast Within: Man, Myths and Werewolves* (London: Orion, 1992), pp. 41–44.

10. Gillian Cross, *Wolf* (Oxford: Oxford University Press, 1990), p. 65.

11. Ibid., p. 90.

12. Ibid., p. 38.

13. Ibid., p. 110.

14. Hugh Crago, "Terra Incognita, Cognita," in *Children's Literature: The Power of Story*, ed. Rhonda Bunbury (Melbourne: Deakin University, 1980), p. 12.

15. Cross, *Wolf*, p. 139.

16. Ibid., pp. 15, 31.

17. Ibid., p. 2.

18. Wolfgang Iser, "The Reading Process: A Phenomenological Approach," in *Reader-Response Criticism: From Formalism to Post-Structuralism*, ed. J. Tompkins (Baltimore: John Hopkins University Press, 1990), p. 55.

19. Ed Young, *Seven Blind Mice* (London: Andersen Press, 1994).

20. Hunt, *Criticism*, p. 118.

REFERENCES

Bettelheim, Bruno. *The Uses of Enchantment*. London: Penguin, 1991.

Crago, Hugh. "Terra Incognita, Cognita." In *Children's Literature: The Power of Story*. Ed. Rhonda Bunbury. Melbourne: Deakin University, 1980.

Cross, Gillian. *Wolf*. Oxford: Oxford University Press, 1990.

Douglas, Adam. *The Beast Within: Man, Myths and Werewolves*. London: Orion, 1992.

Franz, M. L. von. "The Process of Individuation." In *Man and His Symbols*. Ed. C. G. Jung. London: Arkana, 1990.

Gleeson, Libby. "Are There Books Children Should Not Be Reading?" In *At Least They're Reading! Proceedings of the First National Conference of the Children's Book Council of Australia*. Port Melbourne: D. W. Thorpe, 1992.

Hunt, Peter. *Criticism, Theory, and Children's Literature*. Oxford: Basil Blackwell, 1991.

Iser, Wolfgang. "The Reading Process: A Phenomenological Approach." In *Reader-Response Criticism: From Formalism to Post-Structuralism*. Ed. J. Tomkins. Baltimore: John Hopkins University Press, 1990.

Lambert, Johanna, ed. *Wise Women of the Dreamtime: Aboriginal Tales of the Ancestral Powers*. Vt.: Inner Traditions International, 1993.

Mellor, Bronwyn, Annette Patterson, and Marnie O'Neill. *Reading Fictions*. Scarborough: Chalkface Press, 1991.

Perrault, Charles. "Little Red Riding Hood." In *The Trials and Tribulations of Little Red Riding Hood*. Ed. Jack Zipes. New York: Routledge, 1993.

Young, Ed. *Seven Blind Mice*. London: Andersen Press, 1994.

Zipes, Jack. *Fairy Tales and the Art of Subversion*. New York: Routledge, 1983.

Part IV

Paradigm Shifts

Reflections of Change
in Children's Book Titles

Maria Nikolajeva

There is an aspect of children's literature that, as far as I know, has never been investigated before. Contemplating the recent history of children's literature, we notice an interesting evolution in the titles of children's books. My point of departure here is the thesis, which I have pursued in another study,[1] that contemporary children's literature is generally developing from plot-oriented texts toward character-oriented texts, to use Tzvetan Todorov's terminology.[2] We can also apply the model that I find extremely useful in children's literature research, namely, Mikhail Bakhtin's theory of the polyphonic novel,[3] and say that children's literature today is rapidly developing from epic to polyphonic.

Paradoxically enough, the most traditional titles of children's books consist of the main character's name. Paradoxically, since, as I mentioned, the focus in contemporary children's books tends to shift from action toward character. However, most classical children's book titles have the protagonist's name—Heidi, *Winnie-the-Pooh, Mary Poppins*—as is true of many classical mainstream titles, such as *Jane Eyre, Moll Flanders, David Copperfield*—or *Oedipus Rex*. Let us call these titles *nominal*.

Another common pattern of a traditional title is a combination of a name and an epithet—*Anne of Green Gables, Emily of New Moon, Tistou of the Green Thumbs, Peter Rabbit, Harriet the Spy, Tarka the Otter, Ramona the Pest, Babar the Little Elephant, Karlson on the Roof*—or an adjective—*The Happy Lion, Curious George.* The adjective "little" seems to be a special favorite with children's writers: *Little Lord Fauntleroy, The Little Princess, Little Black Sambo, The Little Prince, The Little Witch,* and so on. Nominal titles also may contain only an epithet: *The Treasure Seekers, The Pirates of the Deep Green Sea, A Traveller in Time.* From these titles, we get quite a good idea of the kind of book we are dealing with, unless we have a slightly mysterious epithet, such as *The Borrowers.*

A character's name can be combined with a place: *Five on a Treasure Island, Alice in Wonderland, The Wizard of Oz, The Wizard of Earthsea*—it is also common in mainstream literature, for instance, *Iphigenia in Tauris.* A name can also appear with an object (*James and the Giant Peach*). Finally, a title may consist of a character's name with another name, preferably that of an antagonist, thus creating a conflict: *Emil and the Detectives*. Another extremely popular combination is *The Adventures of . . .* : Pinocchio, Tom Sawyer, and so on.

It is common in children's literature for books to have sequels. Sequels of novels with nominal titles sometimes add another name: if the first title was *Josephine*, the sequel will be *Hugo and Josephine*. The sequel may stress the character's new situation, for instance, *Emily Climbs* or *Anna Keeps Her Promise*. Often the sequel is titled *New* [or *Further*] *Adventures of . . .* or *More About . . .* or *Mary Poppins Comes Back*. When we have read *The Borrowers*, we have no problems with *The Borrowers Afloat* or *The Borrowers Aloft*.

The practice of having the protagonist's name in the title is, at least in children's literature, a didactic narrative device, giving the young reader direct and honest information about the contents of the book. The novel *Heidi* is about a girl called Heidi, and *Winnie-the-Pooh* is about a teddy bear called Winnie-the-Pooh. Cover illustrations support the apprehension of the protagonist. Such titles can also give some idea about the genre and the audience of the book: a girl's name will probably be associated with a book for girls; a boy's name, with a book for boys, and hence with action and adventure. Consider *Just William* or *Emil's Pranks*.

We often teach our students of children's literature to identify the title character with the main character of the story. But is this always so? *Pippi Longstocking* can also be scrutinized from my viewpoint: Is the novel about Pippi Longstocking? Is she not rather a catalyst who initiates the story and brings excitement (or sometimes conflict) into the lives of the real protagonists, Tommy and Annika? There seems to be a tendency to have titles with the name of a character who is not the protagonist, for instance, *Sarah, Plain and Tall*.

There have been many funny incidents concerning title characters of children's books. According to the author, many adult coreaders were puzzled by the title *Jacob Have I Loved* because there is no character in the book named Jacob.[4]

It is very common in children's literature to have a collective protagonist, who is mentioned in the title. This is true not only of trivial literature, like *The Famous Five* or *The Secret Seven*, but also of titles such as *Eight Children and a Truck*, *The Children of the Noisy Village*, and *The Children of Green Knowe*. A collective protagonist is a typical narrative device of traditional children's literature, aimed at supplying an object of identification to readers of both genders and of different ages, and also to represent different aspects of human nature more palpably. As children's literature evolves toward greater psychological charge and a single, but complicated, "round" protagonist becomes more common, collective title characters give rise to questions. Who is the protagonist of *The Brothers Lionheart*? Rusky, the narrator of the story, starts by saying that he is going to tell us about his brother Jonathan. On closer examination, however, Jonathan has a subordinate part in the novel, and Rusky himself is obviously the protagonist.

It is here that we have use for contemporary narrative theory with its notions of point of view, narrative voice, and so on. It is illuminating, for instance, to compare two seemingly identically constructed titles, *Mio, My Son* and *Johnny, My Friend*. In the first novel, the point of view lies with the title character (the statement "Mio, my son" is the narrator's interpretation of his own situation). In the second novel, the title leads us to believe that the story is about Johnny, whereas, at least in some interpretations, Johnny is a catalyst who starts the emotional maturation of the protagonist/narrator.

Consider also the title that at first glance is of the type person + object: *The Lion, the Witch and the Wardrobe*. Compared with *Charlie and the Chocolate Factory*, it is much more complicated. Neither the lion nor the witch is the protagonist of the story (even though we might venture such an interpretation of Aslan).

In a similar way, there is an essential difference between the titles *Curious George* and *The Great Gilly Hopkins*. George is unquestionably curious, whereas Gilly is great only in her own eyes, so the title becomes bitterly ironical. Irony, traditionally believed to be beyond the young readers' grasp, has today become a significant feature of children's literature. Another example of a more ambivalent nominal title is *Tuck Everlasting*.

Further, in contemporary children's novels, titles consisting solely of a character's name mystify rather than clarify the genre, mode, or audience. Who or what is *Momo*? Who or what is *Borrobil*? Consider also the title *Journey*: Can you guess from the title that it is the character's name?

Although nominal titles do allow a certain degree of ambivalence and sophistication, as demonstrated, I would argue that they are basically plot-oriented. As in the folktale, the characters of traditional children's literature are subordinate to the plot; they perform actions, but there is little room for psychological characterization.

Among nominal titles we can also distinguish those that focus the readers' attention on the central object of the plot: *The Cuckoo Clock, The Phantom Tollbooth, The Weirdstone of Brisingamen, The Root Cellar*. Especially in fantasy, the adjective "magic" can compete with "little": *The Magic Bed-knob, The Magic Finger, The Magic City, The Magic Tunnel, The Magic Walking-stick*. Obviously these titles, too, are plot-oriented.

We have, further, a group of what may be called geographical titles, signifying a specific place that is essential to the plot: *Where the Wild Things Are, The Land of Green Ginger, The Land Beyond*. If a particular place is important, it may be accentuated in the sequels: *The Children of Green Knowe, The Chimneys of Green Knowe, The River at Green Knowe, An Enemy at Green Knowe*, and so on. In this group, too, mystifying titles are common: *Elidor* and *Westmark*. If "little" and "magic" are popular adjectives, the champion of settings is the island: *Treasure Island, The Coral Island, The Secret Island, Island of the Blue Dolphins*. However, the very recent title *The Island* is ingenious in its austere simplicity. This is what I would call a true postmodern title.

Another traditional type of title may be called *narrative*, that is, a title that in some way sums up the essence of the story. Naturally, nominal titles of the pattern *The Adventures of . . .* contain some form of narrative or action. Action-oriented or narrative titles are very common: *When Hitler Stole Pink Rabbit, Jacob Two-two*

Meets the Hooded Fang, Betsy's First Day at the Day-care Center. They also may be rather enticing or mystifying, such as *The Spring When Everything Happened.* Such titles were, at least in Sweden, extremely popular in the 1960s and early 1970s, during the period of extensive social realism in children's literature, resulting in books titled *Lasse's Grandfather Is Dead, My Daddy Says Your Daddy Is in Prison, Malena Starts School,* and so on. But also in other countries and much later we encounter titles like *Heather Has Two Mommies,* which immediately declare their contents and message.

However, narrative titles in contemporary literature acquire more symbolical and ambivalent meaning, for instance, *The Dark Is Rising, The Ice Is Coming,* or *Looking for Alibrandi.*

I have suggested that most nominal and narrative titles, with the reservations I have made, are plot-oriented, or epic. The polyphony (many-voicedness) or ambivalence of contemporary children's literature makes itself manifest in many ways. Of course, we can go as far back as the nineteenth century to find a *programmatic* title like *Sans Famille* (by programmatic I mean a title that gives a clue to the interpretation of the whole story). However, I am speaking about tendencies, and we can notice a remarkable increase in programmatic children's books titles since 1945: titles like *The Last Battle, The Real Elvis, Instead of a Dad, A Room of Her Own, Homecoming, Breaktime.* We can also regard these titles as *symbolical, metaphorical,* or *allegorical.* Children's books titles grow more and more ambivalent; *Red Shift* is probably the best example. This ambivalence can, however, be both humorous and serious. While titles such as *Magic by the Lake, The Time Garden* and *The Well-Wishers* are based on puns, *Unclaimed Treasures* contains several sophisticated levels of meaning, both literal and metaphorical.

The growing intertextuality of children's literature is today manifest in titles like *Neverland* (alluding to *Peter Pan*), *Friday and Robinson,* and *The Wonderful Adventures,* which is a modern rewriting of *The Wonderful Adventures of Nils.* These allusions are, however, more or less evident, whereas the title *Wolf* is ambivalent, symbolical, and intertextual on a deeper level. *Park's Quest* never explicitly mentions Percival, but the whole story is constructed as an anagram of the myth, and the similarity of names gives an additional clue. We can also discover paratextual titles, such as *Jacob Have I Loved, Midnight Is a Place, Admission to the Feast,* and *I Am the Cheese.* A title such as *In Search of Nancy Drew* is a direct allusion. As is often the case with intertextuality, the links to an earlier text sometimes function only on the adult coreader's level. I do not think that many contemporary children really appreciate the title *Centerberg Tales,* but the adult coreader is certainly amused. I have already mentioned some readers' difficulties with *Jacob Have I Loved,* although the quotation is explained in the novel. Like all postmodern artistic devices, intertextual titles put greater demands on the reader, and can be confusing and even intimidating. Naturally, the title *From the Mixed-up Files of Mrs. Basil E. Frankweiler* is more enticing and less ambivalent than *I Am the Cheese.*

Modern titles are often metapoetical: *The Facts and Fictions of Minna Pratt* or *A Pack of Lies.* Today, if we encounter titles with places or objects in them, they will most probably be symbolical, representing the character's state of mind, and thus apparently character-oriented and polyphone, like *The Toll Bridge* or *Strange Objects*. The title *The First Two Lives of Lukas-Kasha* evokes at least two diverse interpretations of the story.

I regard polyphony, ambivalence, intertextuality, and metafiction as typical traits of contemporary literature for young readers. These traits have been discussed in many studies, and I find it significant that they are also reflected in the titles. This corresponds to the general trend in children's literature toward texts that engage the young reader and supply material for contemplation rather than pure entertainment. It is sometimes sufficient to regard one author's works to see clearly the line of evolution—for instance, from the action-oriented *Comet in Moominland* to the existential *Moominland in November*, where November is less the name of a month than a symbol for the passing of time.

In conclusion, I would like to dwell briefly on some curious cases of changes when children's books are translated into other languages. As often as not, a changed title reflects the translator's—or probably the publisher's—interpretation of the text. One of the major American classics, *Charlotte's Web*, is titled "Fantastic Wilbur" in Swedish, that is, the focus has been shifted from the female character to the male, which naturally governs the readers' understanding of the story.

Zeppelin, a very poetic, existential Norwegian novel, is called *Keeping Secrets* in English. Now, the zeppelin of the story is not an object, nor even a symbol; it is a magic word, an incantation, much like "Sesame, open!" The dictionary meaning of the word is never revealed in the novel, so it is as mysterious for young readers as for the young protagonists of the novel. The enigmatic *Elidor* has acquired, in Swedish, an explanation in the title "Elidor, the Golden Country." *Unclaimed Treasures* has been published in Swedish as "Willa's Great Love," which to me sounds much like a soap opera. The ambivalent and symbolical *The Kingdom by the Sea* has been changed, in Sweden, into the sentimental "A Friend in Need." The list of similar examples is endless.

Translations of children's books, to an even greater extent than original publications, are manipulated by the adult coreaders' prejudices concerning young readers' mental capacity. I think we see this clearly in the tendency to change titles in translations, making them less ambivalent and thus—in my mind—less effective.

NOTES

1. See. Maria Nikolajeva, *Children's Literature Comes of Age: Toward a New Aesthetics*, (New York and London: Garland, 1995).

2. Tzvetan Todorov. *La Poétique de la prose* (Paris: Seuil, 1971).

3. Mikhail Bakhtin, *Problems of Dostoyevsky's Poetics*. Trans. Caryl Emerson. (Minneapolis: University of Minnesota Press, 1984).

4. Katherine Paterson, *The Spying Heart: More Thoughts on Reading and Writing Books for Children* (New York: Dutton, 1988).

11

High and Wild Magic, the Moral Universe, and the Electronic Superhighway: Reflections of Change in Susan Cooper's Fantasy Literature

Carole Scott

Susan Cooper's book *The Boggart*, published in 1993, offers a wonderful tongue-in-cheek commentary upon her own earlier work. This lighthearted modern fantasy once again invokes the Celtic tradition and the powerful Wild Magic that she used to such effect in her serious and demanding five-work series, The Dark Is Rising (1965–1978). But in a postmodernist, metafictive vein she reframes her material so that the solemnity of the earlier epic fantasies becomes a humorous romp. Whereas her earlier works evoke an "atmosphere [that] resonates with mythic themes and symbols"[1] and accord the deepest respect to magic, *The Boggart* approaches the legendary past and supernatural phenomena with an attitude of ironic familiarity. The striking changes in Cooper's work—which include the breaking of traditional boundaries, the redefinition of accepted modes of perception, and the stimulation of new insights into the nature and significance of magical power—provide a revealing window into the evolution of fantasy during the past few decades, a period that has involved rapidly accelerating innovation in so many fields.

Maria Nikolajeva, in *The Magic Code*, suggests that "the history of fantasy for children is the history of innovations and transformations, of creative reconstruction of old variables." She notes especially the increasing metaphorical sophistication in relationships between the ordinary and fantasy worlds, including temporal, spatial, and human dimensions; she also points out the increasing ambivalence of otherworlds no "longer . . . described exclusively in terms of good and evil, light and dark."[2] Sheila Egoff, in *Worlds Within*, similarly identifies fantasy's altered concept, asserting that, particularly since the 1960s, fantasy has attracted writers "who explore new territory or who discover new vistas in old territory," and that they are "experimenting with fantasy's inner core, breaking many of its conventions and so changing its purpose and values."[3]

The year 1945 marked the end of the Second World War, a war whose advanced technology redefined the borders of the battleground, first with the bombers and the V-2s that carried destruction to the civilian population, and later with the atomic bomb, whose devastation reached out to impact not only those well outside its target but also, through genetic spoliation, future generations. Technological sophistication also permitted the efficient extermination of "undesirable" citizens by their own countries, extending the focus of warfare to the enemy within. This real and conceptual shifting of boundaries, the intrusion of terror into the ordinary world, and the impact of unimagined powers are recurrent themes in Cooper's work; they are her legacy of a wartime childhood truncated by the premature awareness of human evil and of hovering menace expressed so graphically in her early, realistic, and somewhat autobiographical book, *Dawn of Fear*.

The development of Cooper's fantasy works clearly exemplifies the patterns that critics identify; those patterns accelerate as her oeuvre evolves. In her first fantasy sequence, The Dark Is Rising, Cooper increasingly manipulates myth and legend to her own purpose. The ongoing battle between the Light and the Dark takes place in a rather traditional, somewhat Miltonic universe with which are merged the landscape and figures of the Arthurian legends, including elements of Grail myths. The pastiche she makes of inherited beliefs, myths, and legends has been criticized for its inaccuracy regarding its sources, and for the unsystematic, even haphazard selection of elements and their reconstruction into a highly charged but somewhat dissonant moral landscape.

This conservative viewpoint is inattentive to Cooper's innovative refashioning or "creative reconstruction" of the sources. In the delineation of her universe, she melds a cosmology whose graphic design is inspired by *Paradise Lost* and whose underlying philosophy, founded on the power of Love and Justice, is basically Christian, with an operating system based on the incontrovertible laws of High (Moral) and Wild (Natural) Magic. From Celtic tales and a variety of legends Cooper borrows figures and objects such as Herne the Hunter and the Grail, adding new figurative personae such as the Walker and the Rider, and new characters such as King Arthur's son Bran, who is magically transported through time to grow up in the twentieth century. Into this universe she introduces both her contemporary characters and her Old Ones, whose lives straddle human and supernatural existences.

While Cooper's vision and design are clearly much more than a collage or found art, they do share some of their characteristics. The Grail, for example, while retaining a mystical dimension, does not have its original religious context. Divested of its religious connotations, it maintains its aura of power because of the message it carries, and illustrates the way that aspects of the past brought into the present are usually reshaped to fit into their new setting or are translated into a contemporary mode. Thus the ancient ritual of the Greenwitch, which brings luck to the village, is shown to involve the neglected spirit of Wild Magic, pictured as emotion unacknowledged and disregarded, and tied into a feminist perceptual context; and the power of evil is presented in modern dress through a bigoted Englishman's outburst of racial prejudice directed against an immigrant of color. The structural complexity of Cooper's many-layered world, with its amalgam of legend created from the dissolution of time and space boundaries, is repeated at many levels, including the creation of a contemporary moral and social philosophy, and of characters unbound by the traditional limits of time.

To add to the complexity of the dynamic, Cooper sets up a fluctuating universe of force fields that define the true nature of her reality. The relativity of human perception and the power of human emotion provide the energy that drives her world. She focuses increasingly upon the mutability of human perception and subsequent analysis, beginning with the Drew family's awakening to alternative ways of seeing as they reappraise the indicators leading to the Grail, and continuing with the exploration of negative/positive poles that serve as the lodestones of moral perception and relativity. Perception is strongly tied to emotional states of mind, as evidenced in the twisted vision of Hawkins, driven by jealousy and spite, or the frozen depressive state of Gwyddno Garanhir, which extends to control the world in which he exists.

The increasing metaphorical sophistication in relationships between the ordinary and fantasy worlds, including the temporal, spatial, and human dimensions that Nikolajeva identifies are clearly relevant in the five books of the series as Cooper develops subtle yet powerful relationships between the real and the fantastic worlds, including coexistent temporal and spatial overlays. The seriously flawed characters, such as Hawkins of *The Dark Is Rising* and Caradog Lewis of *The Grey King* and *Silver on the Tree*, serve as energy points or channels for the intrusion of evil into human affairs; the power of human perception, feeling, and desire pierces times and planes of existence with unimaginable force, breaking through the walls that divide worlds and states of being in a new kind of magic. Will Stanton uses this power to travel through time in much the same way that Bran uses traditional magical words and talismans. Thus perception and emotion are tied to magic as powerful forces that interact and interrelate as they impact human destiny.

In the deeply philosophical *Seaward*, which follows the quintet and is set almost entirely in a fantasy otherworld, Cooper renounces the clear distinction between good and evil, dark and light that had previously obsessed her vision of human endeavor, and embraces an increasing ambivalence. Poised between life and death, whose struggle is expressed in episodes such as the chess game, the battle for the tower, and the trek across the desert, the characters' involvement in the shifting balance between life and death is further complicated by the ambivalence of the deathly Lady Taranis with her two faces, one terrifyingly cruel, the other caring and beautiful. The revelation at the end of the book that the life and death forces, Lugan and Taranis, are not foes but brother and sister—two aspects of the same ongoing creative process—is the ultimate rejection of polarized perception. Embracing this holistic view of the universe is a giant step forward from the quintet, which expresses the battle between good and evil with such intensity and at so many levels.

As *Seaward* brings together so many disparate entities with their faint echoes of many traditions, Cooper reflects the modern world and looks toward a future where people representing a rainbow of heritages—history, culture, values, worldview—must weave their lives together to create a new moral universe in which all have a place and a part to play. The sources from which the characters are drawn increasingly represent a potpourri of world civilizations and literary genres. The child protagonists

Calliope and Westerley, come from different parts of the world, are of different races, and have different cultural histories. Ryan's selkie powers (like Cally's) emerge from Celtic mythology, and Stonecutter and the gigantic Stone People who come to life only in daylight also are drawn from traditional Western sources. But Peth, with his insect-like body, has stepped out of a science-fiction world, and Snake, the enfolding dreamworld presence who brings both peace and terror, is very different from the characters in the quintet, whose provenance is clear.

In *Seaward*, myth and magic are still highly significant, though becoming more fragmented and more innovative, as Cooper, accused by a contemporary critic of "gratuitous and overpowering" allusion and "helter-skelter"[4] events and symbolism, continues to move away from the more recognizable patterns that underlie the earlier work, toward an increasingly eclectic accumulation drawn from a variety of cultural traditions. Though the children may enter the fantasy world by very conventional means—an ornate mirror and a hidden door (though, unlike Carroll's and C. S. Lewis' worlds, these children are driven not by curiosity but by death and danger)—magic soon stretches to encompass a wide spectrum of powers. Many of these are connected in some way with the natural rather than the created environment: Ryan keeps death away by means of designs drawn with plants on the stone floor; the white bones that are West's heritage control the weather, as does the handkerchief of winds that Lugan gives; Peth's cocoon, which hides the children from their pursuers, is clearly related to a spider's web; and the magical effect of sunlight upon the Stone People has already been mentioned. But Cooper's eclectic imagination does not hesitate to delve into the psychic magic that also characterizes several sequences in the quintet. The rooms that materialize the children's desires are smaller versions of the entire otherworld that Peth identifies as "a waking dream." Magic and emotion are aspects of the same phenomena.

In *The Boggart*, Cooper has moved onto a different plane; unlike the other books discussed, it takes place entirely in the ordinary world, and may be characterized as enchanted realism rather than epic fantasy, with a shift in diction from the intensity of the earlier works to a light, informal discourse with an essentially humorous presentation. Here the Boggart himself, a creature of the Celtic myths and of the powerful Wild Magic so revered in Cooper's earlier sequence, is reduced to a Puck-like being whose sole pleasure, apart from stealing delicious tidbits, is to cause mischief. Transported in error to Canada from a lonely castle in his native Scotland, he is a complete anachronism in the world of electronic miracles belonging to the two children, Emily and Jessup. This kaleidoscopic shift in the approach to magic and archetype creates a new pattern from the elements of the earlier work, and is characterized by a self-consciousness and ambivalence in describing the intrusion of magic into everyday life.

The ironic humor that pervades the book is illustrated in the clash between the Boggart and Dr. Stigmore, the psychiatrist and parapsychologist who identifies Emily's disturbed adolescent rage as the source of the poltergeist-like effects of the Boggart's power. Here the Wild Magic and modern science meet in that realm of emotion and magic that Cooper has depicted with such innovation and subtlety in all her fantasy works. It is a particularly portentous battlefield to choose, since the increasing proximity between emotion and magic is hailed by Nikolajeva as an evolution in fantasy that gives it psychological depth, and that Egoff condemns as a destructive direction that weakens the genre. In *The Boggart*, Dr. Stigmore is the villain of the piece, sacrificing Emily's privacy for his own self-aggrandizement; he is described in Cooper's most derogatory terms as looking "a little like Adolf Hitler, without the mustache."[5]

In his *Critical Essays on American Postmodernism*, Stanley Trachtenberg summarizes some trends in metafiction and postmodernism, pointing out that "contemporary metafiction . . . emerged out of a climate in which advances in technology and information theory rendered obsolete conventional literary codes,"[6] and reminding us of John Barth's assertion:

it did happen . . . Freud and Einstein and two world wars and the Russian and sexual revolutions and automobiles and airplanes and telephones and radios and movies and urbanization, and now nuclear weaponry and television and microchip technology and the new feminism and the rest, and there's no going back to Tolstoy and Dickens & Co. except on nostalgia trips.[7]

Cooper's humorous reformulation of her earlier sources echoes Barth's sentiments as she foregrounds the present rather than the past, and brings North America, her own home for many years, into her sphere of vision. But although the weight of the past with its heavy morality has been shrugged off, and the legendary magical figure has dwindled to a sleepy anachronism, the Wild Magic is not to be underestimated; it has simply metamorphosed into another dimension. The early pranks of the Boggart involving peanut butter and Halloween games soon escalate into more serious dimensions, for he is uncontrollable, an Old Thing "outside the rules."[8] His merging with the theater's light board displays the depth and force of his inherent aesthetic and emotional power; his involvement in the electricity that runs the streetcars exhibits his destructive capabilities; and Emily contemplates with horror the extent of the destruction if the Boggart should find his way into a nuclear power plant.

Although sophisticated modern machinery, and electrical and nuclear power play a part in the book, Cooper focuses primarily upon the electronic power represented by Jessup's computer and his Black Hole game. In a clear ironic parallel, the galaxy as perceived through this game mirrors the vision of the night sky in the fourth book of The Dark Is Rising sequence. Just as Will and Bran employ High Magic to enter into the realm of the Grey King, so the Boggart uses the computer game as a doorway to return home. Merging with the computer's electronic impulses, a kind of Wild Magic that he understands, the Boggart is transcribed onto a computer disk, so that he can be mailed home to his "own country." While the Boggart revels in the computer's electronic mysteries, the children, Emily and Jessup in Canada and Tommy in Scotland, undergo the terror of the journey into the simulated black hole, the descent into nothingness over which they lose control as the computer, dominated by the Boggart, takes over. Though it is the death of the Boggart rather than their own that they fear, the reality of extinction is real and frightening.

By tying the Wild Magic of the Boggart to the technological magic of the modern world, Cooper has reframed it, once again revealing her theme of the power humankind might command, and the terrible consequences that can result from irresponsibility or the lack of control over destructive emotions. Good and evil are not pictured as organized forces that structure the universe within which humankind lives; rather, they are rendered as aspects and outcomes of human emotion and behavior. This sophisticated use of fantasy balances the perceived world with the inner world and pursues the ultimate arena of fantasy, the exploration of the relationship between inner and outer worlds, and the shifting dynamic between them. "Truth is a matter of imagination," Ursula Le Guin tells us. "You get the facts from outside. The truth you get from inside."[9]

Susan Cooper's fantasy works reflect the evolution of modern-day thinking, from the initial breaking of traditional boundaries experienced in the 1940s, to the current situation, where innovations unbelievable in the recent past have revolutionized human communication and the concept of the universe. As fantasy prefigures reality, the line between ordinary life and magic blurs, requiring a concurrent shift in fantasy literature. The self-irony and sense of parody reflected in Cooper's latest work reveal not only her understanding of the ways that reality and fantasy have converged, but also her humor at the arrogance of those who believe cience will one day explain not only human emotion but also magic itself.

NOTES

1. Sheila Egoff, *Worlds Within* (Chicago: American Library Association, 1988), p. 7.

2. Maria Nikolajeva, *The Magic Code* (Goteborg: Almqvist & Wiksell International, 1988), p. 116.

3. Egoff, *Worlds Within*, p. ix.

4. Ibid., pp. 219, 294.

5. Susan Cooper, *The Boggart* (New York: Macmillan, 1993), p. 184.

6. Stanley Trachtenberg, ed., *Critical Essays on American Postmodernism* (New York: G. K. Hall, 1995), p. 7.

7. John Barth, "The Literature of Replenishment," *Atlantic Monthly*, January 1980, p. 70.

8. Cooper, *The Boggart*, p. 134.

9. Ursula K. Le Guin, *The Language of the Night: Essays on Fantasy and Science Fiction* (New York: G. P. Putnam's Sons, 1985), pp. 125, 157.

REFERENCES

Attebury, Brian. *The Fantasy Tradition in American Literature: From Irving to LeGuin.* Bloomington: Indiana University Press, 1980.
Barth, John. "The Literature of Replenishment." *Atlantic Monthly*, January 1980, pp. 65–71.
Cooper, Susan. *Over Sea, Under Stone.* New York: Harcourt Brace Jovanovich, 1965.
———. *The Dark Is Rising.* New York: Atheneum, 1974.
———. *Greenwitch.* New York: Atheneum, 1977.
———. *Silver on the Tree.* New York: Atheneum, 1977.

————. *The Grey King.* New York: Atheneum, 1978.

————. *Seaward.* New York: Atheneum, 1983.

————. *The Boggart.* New York: Macmillan, 1993.

Egoff, Sheila A. *Worlds Within.* Chicago: American Library Association, 1988.

Kuznets, Lois R. "'High Fantasy' in America: A Study of Lloyd Alexander, Ursula Le Guin, and Susan Cooper." *The Lion and the Unicorn* 9 (1985): 19–35.

Le Guin, Ursula K. *The Language of the Night: Essays on Fantasy and Science Fiction.* New York: G. P. Putnam's Sons, 1985.

Manlove, Colin Nicholas. *Fantasy: Five Studies.* Cambridge: Cambridge University Press, 1975.

Nikolajeva, Maria. *The Magic Code.* Goteborg: Almqvist & Wiksell International, 1988.

Todorov, Tsvetan. *The Fantastic: A Structural Approach to a Literary Genre.* Trans. Richard Howard. Cleveland: Case Western Reserve Uiversity Press, 1973.

Trachtenberg, Stanley, ed. *Critical Essays on American Postmodernism.* New York: G. K. Hall, 1995.

12

"Terror is Her Constant Companion": The Cult of Fear in Recent Books for Teenagers

Roderick McGillis

I begin with a quotation from *Silent Stalker* (1993), a novel by Richie Tankersley Cusick, one of many contemporary authors writing novels of terror for young readers. The passage I have selected deals with a young girl named Jenny and a boy named Derrick, who claims to be protecting her from his mad twin brother, Malcolm. In actual fact, however, Malcolm and Derrick have another brother, Edwyn. The brothers are triplets, and Edwyn is the insane one. In the passage, Jenny and Derrick are in the depths below a typically European Gothic castle somewhere in the United States. As we might expect, Europe stands for decadence, perversion, torture, and even madness in the North American imagination. As Derrick, who in reality is Edwyn, leads Jenny deeper into the dungeons of the castle, he speaks of Malcolm:

His grip tightened, and he pressed Jenny tenderly against him.

"He fell in love with you, you know," Derrick said quietly. "That very first night. That very first time . . . he touched you—"

"Please don't," Jenny murmured. "Derrick, what are we going to do?"

"Ssh . . . you're safe now. Safe with me. . .

And then another dark place, darker even than before, Jenny could sense it and see it all at the same time, and she was being lowered down, down by her arms, down onto a cold wet floor, and it smelled of mildew and damp, and she could hear . . . *water*?

The rain . . . it's the rain I hear—the terrible storm—

Yet in the back of her mind she knew it wasn't the storm—no thunder—no lightning—just the thick, restless slurp of water. . . .

"Where are we?" she asked, and she was even colder now, something prickling along her skin . . . up her spine . . . filling her heart with sudden fear—"Derrick, where *are* we?"

Groggily she looked up. She could see the spurt of a candle, and she could see Derrick's face, but it seemed so far above her, everything miles and miles above her. . . .

Derrick looked down and smiled. The candlelight cast nervous shadows over his calm, calm face.

"We're in a secret place," he murmured. "Our secret. Yours and mine."
"Derrick—"
"In fact, it's so secret, nobody ever leaves here. Did I forget to tell you that?"[1]

Many aspects of this passage are typical of similar books for teenage readers. A forced inconsistency in the writing amounts to overwriting: Derrick tightens his grip, yet he holds Jenny tenderly; water "slurps" rather than laps or flows or some other less indelicate descriptor. A young female finds herself the object of another's domination and manipulation: here Jenny is manipulated by Derrick (Edwyn, remember), who lowers her onto a wet floor. The female victim appears consistently in these books. Jenny's clarity and grogginess, tightness and tenderness are examples not only of inconsistent writing, but also of paradox to create tension. Also intensifying the situation are the italicized thoughts of one of the characters, here Jenny. Despite these attempts to create fear, the author asserts the feelings of fear as much as she shows them ("filling her heart with sudden fear"). And finally, the situation is familiar: a young girl finds herself in danger, separated from family and unsure of who near her might be a friend and who might be an enemy. The girl is a victim, and her victimization includes a frisson that is clearly sexual, in this case unpleasantly so.

Often the girls in these books find themselves cut off from familiar spaces: in dark forests, on strange and exotic islands, alone in large houses, alone in empty buildings, alone at the beach, alone in the gym, alone at the lake, alone in a country phone booth, alone just about anywhere once the sun goes down, or alone in sinister Gothic castles, as in *Silent Stalker*. Often they are helpless; they require the assistance of a comforting and capable male. And because the male is comforting as well as capable, a titillation seeps into these books. Truly something creepy this way comes. For me, the most telling moment in the passage above occurs when Jenny sees "the spurt of a candle." Readers of Bram Stoker's *Dracula* (1894) might recall the moment in that book when three strong men violate the coffin of Lucy Westenra. As they force open the coffin, their candles drip "semen" onto the lid, reminding us just what is actually taking place here. Violation is common to books that draw on the sex–death instinct. Something in these books speaks to the instinct Freud discerned in all of us that turns toward sex and death. What could be more transgressive than vicariously experiencing this deeply disturbing and disturbed conflation of death and sex?

In case you doubt my reading of "the spurt of a candle," take a glance at several other suggestive passages in the book: "She could feel his body, tall and strong against her back" (p. 12), "Malcolm's heart was beating beneath her cheek, warm and solid" (p. 17), "eyes creeping over her" (p. 19), "raked Jenny from head to foot with his eyes" (p. 20), "so careful with her, so gentle with her" (p. 180). One of the characters in the book is an abused female named Nan (perhaps alluding to Oliver Twist) who remarks about the man she loves: "I take care of him. Even when he hurts me. Even when I know that someday he'll—" (p. 136). And yes, she dies at the hand of the murderer. Female characters are constantly the object of someone's gaze, someone hiding in the shadows, sometimes breathing audibly, watching. The repeated line in R. L. Stine's Babysitter books (so far there are four of these in print) says it all: "Hi, Babes. Are you all alone? Company's coming." Jenny, in *Silent Stalker*, experiences unspeakable torture in the fantastic Gothic structure to which her father has brought her, and nothing should be worse than enduring the probing, prying eyes of the stalker of the title. In fact, however, one character remarks to her that she "might be surprised how enjoyable some tortures could be" (p. 14). It might be horrific to be the object of someone's gaze, but it is also fascinating.

Silent Stalker might be an extreme example of a kind of writing adolescents find remarkably appealing, but it is by no means unique. In fact, horror books for adolescent readers have proven so popular that versions of the horror story are now appearing for readers from seven to eleven. Any number of series for young readers now exist: Fear Street, The Power, Blood and Lace, Goosebumps, Shadow Zone, and House of Horrors are some of them. It seems the torture of being watched and the sensation of being scared must be enjoyable, at least to readers who return again and again to these books. The books written specifically for teenage readers consistently put females in places where they can be, and are, watched. The female is a target.

I am speaking of the relatively recent phenomenon of teen horror books, books by writers such as Cusick, Christopher Pike, R. L. Stine, Carol Ellis, A. Bates, Jesse Harris, Joseph Locke, Diane Hoh, and others. In some cases the writer's name is significantly androgynous, and the books themselves pander to a rather familiar stereotype of the passive female/aggressive male that represents a throwback to an earlier era when questions of gender identity were clear and patriarchal. These books clearly derive from the work of such popular authors as Stephen King, Peter Straub, Anne Rice, and perhaps preeminently V. C. Andrews. Andrews' *Flowers in the Attic* (1979) is, and was, a hot read for teenagers. For those of you who haven't read this book, I will briefly fill you in on the plot. Four young children lose their father in a car accident, and they and their mother return to live with the mother's parents in a great country house. The catch is that the grandfather has never forgiven his daughter for marrying the man she married, her cousin, and in order for him to accept his daughter in his home, she must hide her children in the upper rooms of the house. In this act of duplicity she has the compliance of her mother, a stern and witchlike woman who appears to hate the children. To make what is a very long story short, enforced confinement over several years leads to the two older children's commiting incest, and one of the younger children's dying. The grandmother proves to be the witch she seems, and she both physically and emotionally brutalizes the children. The whole thing is nasty in the extreme, full of transgressions and the most unpleasant experiences. The book absolutely gloats over its readers, tantalizing them or her with bursts of violence and promises of perverse behavior.

Flowers in the Attic is an unpleasant read, but young people appear to like it. And publishers are clear on one thing: what the reader likes, the reader will get. If they read it, more will follow. And more books that delight in transgressing the bounds of good taste have followed. In 1993, 8 million copies of Christopher Pike's horror novels for teens and 7.5 million copies of Stine's Fear Street series were in print.[2] And Cosette Kies reports that in 1988, "182 horror novels/anthologies were published." This, she says, marks "an increase of 90% over 1987." The appeal of such books, Kies goes on to say, is "fun." Whether one likes it or not is, she argues, "all a matter of taste."[3]

They say that you cannot judge a book by its cover, but I'm not so certain this holds true for teen Gothic fiction. Cover after cover of these books shows a single figure, more often than not a female, framed, or what my colleague Mavis Reimer refers to as "targeted," in some way. An ugly knife blade contains the reflection of a blond-haired girl who appears terrified (Stine's *Broken Date*, 1988); a blond-haired young girl stands inside a phone booth, looking out at a threatening shadow visible at the bottom of the picture (Ellis' *My Secret Admirer*, 1989); a young blond girl screams, and we see her framed within the lens of a camera (Pike's *Die Softly*, 1991); a blond-haired young girl lies in bed, clutching a blanket to her bosom, as she watches a cocky young male materialize in front of her (Stine's *Haunted*, 1990); a young girl is visible in the window of a high school (A. Bates's *Final Exam*, 1990); a young girl with auburn hair stands with her back to us, framed in an iris with flames behind her (Jesse Harris' *The Possession*, 1992); a young auburn-haired girl sits on a bench while an older male figure watches from a window behind her (Stine's *College Weekend*, 1995); a young blond-haired girl, a look of horror on her face, crawls away from rats and toward a looming figure in a hoodlike mask (Cusick's *Silent Stalker*, 1993). The message the reader derives from these covers, and others like them, is that these books offer the secret and socially denied delights of female violation, abuse, and domination.

I refer to the hair of the females depicted not only to suggest the stereotypical nature of the characters depicted in these novels, but also to capture a sense of the novels' collective interest in such outward trappings of appearance. Hair and clothes are nearly always a main feature, sometimes the only feature, of character description. Here's a character named Tyler from Cusick's *The Locker* (1994): "He was wearing an overcoat way too big for him—a long flowing black thing buttoned right down over his black hightops. He was also wearing a black baseball cap, turned around backward." Black serves a dual purpose here: it's the fashionable color (or was in 1994), and it invokes mystery, danger, the brooding Gothic hero, here wearing the badge of every young boy these days, a baseball cap. The narrator of this book is a teenager named Marlee. She goes on to describe Tyler as "really cute," with soft hair. In short, he is "incredibly sexy."[4] Sabrina van Fleet, in Joseph Locke's *Deadly Relations* (Book 2 of Blood and Lace, 1994), is typically beautiful:

Her skin was so pale, it was nearly translucent, smooth as velvet and without a single blemish. Her eyes were large and a brilliant green with thick, dark lashes that needed no mascara. Her beautiful, heart-shaped face was framed by full, waving, shining blond hair that cascaded over her shoulders and ended just above her full breasts in front and just past her shoulder blades in back.[5]

In R. L. Stine's books we constantly learn what characters wear: "sleeveless blue T-shirt and very Hawaiian-looking baggy trunks," "501 jeans and a pressed button-down, blue workshirt," "tan chinos and a white pullover shirt with the little black Polo pony on the breast";[6] "a faded Bart Simpson T-shirt over jean cut-offs," "black denim jeans and a red-and-black Aerosmith T-shirt," "a green T-shirt over an orange sleeveless T-shirt over white tennis shorts";[7] "blue Ralph Lauren sweater over designer jeans," "her big, expensive, fur-lined coat";[8] "tight, pink bicycle shorts and white midriff tops," "a small gold bikini," "yellow-and-white-striped Giorgio beach bag," "gray sweatpants over a faded Hard Rock Cafe T-shirt."[9] But nothing illustrates the absurdity of this obsession with clothes better than the following passage from Stine's *Beach Party*. You should know that Karen is just about to find her friend Renee murdered in a kitchen:

> Then her [Karen's] eyes wandered down to the floor, and she saw two bare feet, the toes pointing up. Her breath caught in her throat.
> She walked closer.
> "Renee?"
> She peered around the island and saw a girl lying on her back, her mouth open in a frozen O of horror, her eyes wide, unmoving, staring up at the ceiling.
> "Renee?"
> She was wearing shorty pajamas.
> "Renee?"[10]

As you might guess, along with this focus on beauty and fashion, the books present characters who are very much middle-class. The chinos and Giorgio bags are only a slight indication of the books' emphasis on wealth. Characters drive hot and expensive cars: a "navy-blue Mustang convertible,"[11] a "1960 Thunderbird" fully restored,[12] "a Ferrari,"[13] "a souped-up Trans Am,"[14] an "old gray Mustang,"[15] "a shiny blue Pontiac Firebird,"[16] a "black 1968 Mustang convertible,"[17] a BMW,[18] "a brand-new silver Jaguar,"[19] and so on. They like expensive and trendy things. Consumerism looks good in the pages of these books.

A few of these books rely on a certain intertextuality to give them some semblance of substance. References to some of the more obvious aspects of popular culture turn up: people read Stephen King novels, references to the *Nightmare on Elm Street* films occur, as do references to the *Psycho* movies, *The Wolfman*, *Ghostbusters*, *Night of the Living Dead*, and of course *Dracula*. Plots take their form from such recent films as John Carpenter's *Halloween* (Stine's Babysitter books), Adrian Lyne's *Fatal Attraction* (Stine's *The Girlfriend*), Jerry Zucker's *Ghost* (Stine's *Haunted*), Sean S. Cunningham's *Friday the 13th* (Ellis' *Camp Fear*), John Landis' *American Werewolf in London* (Stine's *The Boyfriend*). Characters sometimes have obviously allusive names: Sabrina van Fleet, Lilith Caine, Helen Demeter. Most often, however, names are anonymous, akin to names of soap opera characters: Jenny Fowler, Herb Trasker, Karen Mandell, Katrina Phillips, Rachel Owens, Mark James, Marlee Fleming, Pete Goodwin, William Drewe, and my favorite, Pearce Cronan. Often references to popular culture figures occur: Def Leppard, Tom Cruise, Christie Brinkley, the Ninja Turtles, Matt Dillon, Tom Hanks, and so on. The attempt is to remain familiar and yet to fill the familiar with uncanny happenings. The message is: The familiar world we live in is dangerous, and you'd best get used to it.

The Victorians had books they referred to as "sensation" novels, and these modern Gothic horror books are versions of this kind of book, only marketed directly for the young. As well as stereotypical characters, they offer a racially homogeneous world. Everyone in these books is white, and everyone is acutely conscious of money and status. When characters are "dark," as in *Vampire Twins: A Trilogy*, by Janice Harell (1994), their swarthiness is a mark of their attraction, their mysterious association with things transgressive. The books are interesting in their cynicism. They set out to draw young readers in, using tired formulas that, in effect, make the reading experience predictable and comfortable. Here is titillation without apparent consequences. Here are books that confirm what the young readers already think of the world, and that confirm their interest in fashionable and marketable things. What these books say about their authors' view of young people is sad. The implied readers of these books hate or fear or are distant from their parents; are masses of seething libido; have brutal instincts; are obsessed with fashion and the material objects our consumer society offers; accept the "beauty myth"; use the language of cliché; and accept a view of the world in which violence and victimization are natural.

The villains of these books vary. Sometimes adults, such as an unassuming father (*Babysitter*) or a psychiatrist's receptionist (*Babysitter II*) or a stepparent (*Nightmare Matinee*) are psychopathic. Sometimes female friends are the culprits (*The Immortal, Camp Fear*), but more often than not the stalker or slasher or prowler or murderer is a male member of a group of friends. The motive for murder is usually revenge. In every case, the villain is deranged, and his or her derangement is the result of some psychic scar caused by an unfortunate love affair, a broken family, a humiliation, the mistreatment of a sibling, jealousy. The message, however, remains the same: the prowlers and murderers are among us, members of our own groups and families. The disturbing thing for me about this is the way these books assume that normalcy consists in this condition of threat. Everyone, but mostly young (and blonde) girls, is a target for some act of brutality. The world we live in is a world under siege. Rather than decry this situation or depict it as uncivilized, these books suggest that violence is natural and that the human community will always have its crazed members. It's as if Jack the Ripper has become domesticated in some way, normalized, rendered a familiar part of our human community rather than an unacceptable aberration. These books strike me as typical of our postmodern condition; they reflect a world gone crazy, and yet this craziness has somehow become accepted as normal.

In other words, these books reflect a society numbed to the very forces that erode safety and community. Speaking of family, these books depict a world in which no one has a family, no one has security. The individual, especially if that individual is a young, attractive female, finds no security in society; the world we inhabit is dark and ugly. Darkness has truly drawn down; the center has completely fallen apart. The beast has slouched its way here, and walks among and within us. The short rhyme Jenny receives from her friends at the end of *Silent Stalker* says it all:

Don't try to run
Don't try to hide
You won't get far
We're right outside[20]

NOTES

1. Richard Tankersley Cusick, *Silent Stalker* (New York: Archway Paperback, 1993), pp. 182–183.

2. Paul Gray, "Carnage: An Open Book," *Time*, August 2, 1993, p. 54.

3. Cosette Kies, *Young Adult Horror Fiction* (New York: Twayne, 1992), pp. 2, 9.

4. Richie Tankersley Cusick, *The Locker* (New York: Archway Paperback, 1994), pp. 6, 7.

5. Joseph Locke, *Deadly Relations*, Book 2 of Blood and Lace (New York: Bantam Books, 1994), p. 16.

6. R. L. Stine, *Haunted*, Fear Street series (New York: Archway Paperback, 1990), pp. 84, 59, 19.

7. R. L. Stine, *The Babysitter II* (New York: Scholastic, 1991), pp. 15, 43, 72.

8. R. L. Stine, *The Boyfriend* (New York: Scholastic, 1990), pp. 68–69.

9. R. L. Stine, *Beach Party* (New York: Scholastic, 1990), pp. 29, 30, 33, 76.

10. Ibid., p. 113.

11. Ibid., p. 1.

12. A. Bates, *Final Exam* (New York: Scholastic, 1990), p. 7.

13. Christopher Pike, *Remember Me* (New York: Archway Paperback, 1989), p. 14.

14. Jesse Harris, *The Possession*, Book 2 of The Power (New York: Borzoi Sprinters/ Alfred A. Knopf, 1992), p. 61.

15. Cusick, *The Locker*, p. 51.

16. Stine, *Haunted*, p. 12.

17. G. G. Garth, *Nightmare Matinee* (New York: Bantam Books, 1994), p. 13.

18. Stine, *Beach Party*, p. 27.

19. Stine, *The Boyfriend*, p. 51.

20. Cusick, *Silent Stalker*, p. 214.

REFERENCES

Andrews, V. C. *Flowers in the Attic*. New York: Pocket Books, 1979.

Bates, A. *Final Exam*. New York: Scholastic, 1990.

Cusick, Richie Tankersley. *Silent Stalker*. New York: Archway Paperback, 1993.

———. *The Locker*. New York: Archway Paperback, 1994.

Ellis, Carol. *My Secret Admirer*. New York: Scholastic, 1989.

———. *Camp Fear*. New York: Scholastic, 1993.

Garth, G. G. *Nightmare Matinee*. New York: Bantam Books, 1994.

Gray, Paul. "Carnage: An Open Book." *Time*, August 2, 1993, p. 54.

Harrell, Janice. *Bloodlines*. Vol 1. of *Vampire Twins: A Trilogy*. New York: Harper, 1994.

Harris, Jesse. *The Possession*. Book 2 of The Power. New York: Borzoi Sprinters (Alfred A. Knopf), 1992.

Kies, Cosette. *Young Adult Horror Fiction*. New York: Twayne, 1992.

Locke, Joseph. *Deadly Relations*. Book 2 of Blood and Lace. New York: Bantam Books, 1994.

Pike, Christopher. *Remember Me*. New York: Archway Paperback, 1989.

———. *Die Softly*. New York: Archway Paperback, 1991.

————. *The Immortal*. New York: Archway Paperback, 1993.

Stine, R. L. *Broken Date*. New York: Archway Paperback, 1988.

————. *Beach Party*. New York: Scholastic, 1990.

————. *The Boyfriend*. New York: Scholastic, 1990.

————. *Haunted*. Fear Street series. New York: Archway Paperback, 1990.

————. *The Babysitter II*. New York: Scholastic, 1991.

————. *The Girlfriend*. New York: Scholastic, 1991.

————. *College Weekend*. New York: Archway Paperback, 1995.

Stoker, Bram. *Dracula*. New York: Signet, 1969.

13

Suburban Scenarios in Simon French's *All We Know*: The Emergence of the Suburbs as the Spatial Framework for Australian Children's Fiction

Beverley Pennell

S etting is one of the components of narrative that writers may choose to foreground as an important signifying element in their fiction. In constructing settings, authors may choose to represent the external and material world, or spatiality, as the bearer of several possible kinds of significance. It may express inherent meaning, in which case its influence may be either malevolent or benign, or it may be in itself unsignifying, conveying such meanings as are subjectively attributed to it by the protagonists within the text. In recent Australian children's fiction, there has been a clear paradigm shift involving the representation of a wider variety of settings and altering the significances attributed to the traditional rural and pseudorural settings. For a century, Australian children's fiction has been dominated by rural settings that show the colonial landscape as either inherently idyllic and awaiting appropriation, or inherently hostile and offering threat and challenge to the personal agency of the principal protagonists. Representations of Australian spatiality as threat are evident in the titles of some of the most acclaimed fictions for children, such as Lilith Norman's *Climb a Lonely Hill*, Ivan Southall's *Ash Road*, and Colin Thiele's *Storm Boy*. In these titles the words "lonely," "ash," and "storm," each with its penumbra of negative connotations, contextually carry the burden of signification.

Only recently have Australian children's writers constructed positive representations of suburban settings as a part of the framework for the protagonists' emerging subjectivity. This paradigm shift is exemplified in Simon French's symptomatic and watershed novel *All We Know*,[1] which mostly takes place in suburban spaces that are predominantly represented as benign. Here the meanings attributed to suburban places are determined by the values and attitudes ascribed to them by human subjectivity: tensions may arise between protagonists as a result of their valuing places in significantly different ways. The narrative suggests that, with spatiality and temporality closely intertwined, every place can be invested with joys, sorrows, and secrets by those who have known it in the past, or who know it at present. Thus the significances of a place may alter over time because every place, like every person, is subject to change. Mutability is a central issue in the text as it maps moments of encounter within spatial frameworks that allow the main protagonist, twelve-year-old Arkie Gerhardt, continually to reassesss and reinterpret her everyday experiences. Her subjectivity evolves as she senses spaces of wholeness as well as engages with the inevitability of constant transformation within and without.

To represent the Australian landscape as benign, as French does, is to construct a counterdiscourse to the colonizing European discourses that have represented the Australian landscape as alienating and inhospitable to the white invaders. Bruce Clunies-Ross described the situation this way: "Remoteness, desolation, uselessness and a sense of being on the edge of the unknown have been latent in the idea of Australia and they contribute to that quality of indifference with which the environment is supposed to confront its white inhabitants."[2] Australia's Eurocentric spatial history has been constructed in terms of appropriation by imperial voices who named and labeled, followed by its ongoing representation in the patriarchal discourses of high culture as a site of indefatigable combat of humanity against an indomitable landscape. Graeme Turner's study of Australian narratives and artistic representations in film and literature led him to a further refinement of the ideological decoding of "the Australian context, both natural and social" that was offered by earlier commentators on the representations of spatiotemporal frameworks. Turner finds that

the customary opposition between the country and the city is denied, in favour of a more unitary view of the Australian context which uses the harshness of our natural environment as an alibi for the powerlessness of the individual within the social environment . . . there is an ideological proposition that negates the value of individual action and legitimates powerlessness and subjection.[3]

Turner is revealing here the tendency for the powerful imperial discourse of the center so to disempower colonial voices that they self-reflexively construct their own subjugation. If Helen Tiffin is correct to say that "Decolonisation is a process, not arrival,"[4] then the writing of Simon French is a part of the decolonization of spatiotemporal frameworks in Australian children's literature. It seems that French is working outside the traditional paradigm because his main protagonist is constructed to demonstrate increasing agency as focalization presents her "feeling almost as though she might be able to make it absolutely anywhere in the space of an afternoon."[5]

The discourse very precisely uses the idiomatic expression "the space of. . . " which so completely combines spatiality and temporality. The character is represented as exulting in a sense of power and purpose as she moves through this space. Throughout the text, Arkie is represented as encountering new spaces with enthusiasm, then unraveling the complexity and variety of their meanings as she experiences or imagines everyday life in these different settings.

The lack of the suburbs as a positively represented spatial framework in Australian children's fiction remains an extraordinary phenomenon when we consider that the European invaders have always dwelt predominantly in the urban areas that are mainly on the east coast of the continent. In 1947 the official government census figures showed 75 percent of the population living in urban areas, and 50 percent living in the suburbs of the capital cities. By 1981, 85 percent of the population were urban dwellers and 60 percent were attached to the capital cities.[6] After 1950, the suburbs so predominated in the urban landscape that they could not be ignored in any analysis of Australian life, but that did not mean that they received approval. The vast "urban sprawl" and "ribbon development" of the bungalows on quarter-acre lots were the bane of town planners' lives and the focus of vitriolic aesthetic disdain after 1950 from Australian architects like Robin Boyd, who wrote a famous work (*The Australian Ugliness*) denigrating the urban landscape.

To understand the suppression of the contemporary suburb as the spatial framework for Australian children's fiction, there are two contending artistic voices within Australian culture whose dialectic must be explained. This explanation will show how important a change resulted from the writing of Simon French, leading children's literature away from representations of childhood either as a rural/outback adventure in the 1950s and 1960s or as misery in historicized urban slums, as depicted in texts during the 1960s and 1970s.

In the 1890s in Australia, the voice of the colonized emerged in poetry and short stories to create what is known as the Bush Tradition in Australian literary history.[7] The writers of this tradition were attached to a particularly nationalistic periodical called *The Bulletin*, which reached a wide popular audience. The writers constructed a patriarchal discourse of working-class mateship and rustic simplicity that they used to combat the hegemonic Anglocentric voice of the urban-dwelling middle class of superior political and socioeconomic status. These writers saw themselves as interpreters of the "true" Australian landscape which was "other" to the feminized sophistication of Anglocentric urban environments. They reveled in difference, as is shown by the closing lines of Henry Lawson's short story, "The Bush Undertaker": "And the sun sank again on the grand Australian bush—the nurse and tutor of eccentric minds, the home of the weird, and of much that is different from things in other lands.[8]

The Bush Tradition is one extreme voice in the battle for Australian cultural identity. The other extreme voice emerged in the mid-twentieth century when this popular and working class nationalist mythology underwent a dramatic paradigm shift. The Bush Tradition was appropriated for high culture by writers like Patrick White, whose audience was intentionally international rather than parochial. The elevation of wild, or bush, landscape by high culture meant that the bush became the spatial framework where archetypal myths were enacted in a landscape that was represented as infernal.

The unfortunate corollary of the elevation of the bush was the denigration of the suburban landscape. During the early decades of the twentieth century, a tradition was being constructed that represented the city and the bush as binary opposites. Suburbia and the suburbs were "the middle landscape" or "the place forever in between,"[9] and as such, they were not yet written into being. In Hugh Stretton's book, *Ideas for Australian Cities* (1970), he claimed that Australians preferred to live in the suburbs, yet in 1971 he wrote:

> Thus grew the conformity of the background of life to a norm so inflexible that it might almost have been ordained by law. This background continues to grow, and who could expect a vital race of individualists to grow in its warm shallows?
>
> Now consider the characteristic Australian neighbourhood with its wire-strung streets and serried rows of similar houses getting more similar every year, in comparison with its antithesis. That antithesis is not hard to find; it is the standard domestic condition of Europe and many other parts of the world, and has been so since Roman times. The antithesis to the Australian domestic style is people living inside instead of outside their cities.[10]

Stretton's essay does not, in fact, privilege the European domestic housing option. What he was staunchly promoting was choice of housing styles. Nevertheless, his judgment about the quality of human subjectivity formed within "stultifying" suburban conformity stands unqualified, softened only by its being framed in his discourse as a rhetorical question. Stretton is suggesting that spatial frameworks can form human subjectivity. This belief of the Anglocentric dominant culture is represented in *All We Know* by the character of Arkie's grandmother, Nan, who speaks disparagingly of "beachside suburbs" and of "home units" using the names of spaces to signal that everything within those places is, for her, "other" and outside the approved world order.

In 1994, more than twenty years after Stretton's book, an important new book of essays, *Beasts of Suburbia*, was published. In it a variety of scholars and artists began a resignification of the Australian suburbs as a cultural site. One of the editors offers a redefinition of "suburbia" that is a recuperation of the term, freed from hegemonic discourse of the aesthetics of European high culture:

> Real suburbs are never as they were remembered but are always in a state of transformation. In some ways suburbia does not have a geographical location. Suburbia has been a way of identifying traces which are not, perhaps never were, really present. Thus suburbia has been a way of talking about other things; about change, family, community, childhood, and the tenuous habits we sometimes name as tradition. Suburbia names an imagined place which can hold together and enunciate a sometimes attenuated sense of self in the world.[11]

The publication of *All We Know* preceded this redefinition, winning the Children's Book Council of Australia's Award for older readers in 1987. The "suburbia" represented by this text foregrounds the ideas outlined by *Beasts of Suburbia*, as the text constructs a dialogue about the meaning of social concepts like family, community, and childhood. Change is certainly the predominant issue in the life of the main focalizing protagonist.

In *All We Know*, French represents the plurality of the Australian suburbs, which is a long way from Stretton's "conformity." The reader sees the representation of what Chris McAuliffe calls "a fascination with the 'minor languages' of suburbia."[12] There is the "weekender" bungalow with its backyard and garden in the beachside suburb that Arkie shares with her brother, Jo, their mother, Susan, and Susan's partner, Michael; there is Nan's very upper-middle-class, dignified, and elegant North Shore home with its library and tennis court; there are the home units and flats where Arkie's school friends and their families live. French's positive representation of the urban landscape details the ambient sights, sounds, and smells of the suburbs. His depiction of Ramsay Street, where Arkie and her family live, is full of warmth; the suburban street has a culturally diverse population who undertake their routines of work and leisure freely, impinging upon one another's lives as need or desire determines. Far from depicting suburban alienation, French evokes a strong sense of community in his detailing of the soccer games in the street, bike riding in the vacant lot or Michael's backyard; in the children's informally visiting one another's homes; and in the sharing of interests, skills, and resources, such as we see with Michael and the mechanics at the local garage. Jo and Ian love the computer games in the take-out food shop, and the video shop is considered essential to leisure and entertainment by Kylie and her mother. Arkie and her peers can go roller-skating or surfing, see films, and go to the zoo. This suburb is clearly an O.K. place in which to be living.

French's vibrant depiction of streetscapes is captured in the representation of the business area of the suburb, which is equally alive with interest and constant sensory impact that vary according to the time of day. The descriptions of the nighttime suburb when Arkie and her family are walking home from the restaurant contrast strongly with the sensory impressions of Arkie's early Sunday morning walk to the newsdealer. The suburb offers leisure activities for children and adults to share or to enjoy separately—walking the dog, jogging, going to the pub or the markets, eating out in a variety of restaurants. French describes a Moroccan restaurant in a building that had once been a milk bar:

The restaurant was fifteen minutes' walk from home, a converted shop in a tiny side street between the main road and the beach.

Someone in the kitchen had classical music playing on a tape deck, and the aroma of spicy food filled the room where tables of people joked and conversed.[13]

French's discourse makes this place seem like a special, secret hideaway where sensory pleasure and positive experiences are guaranteed. The fact that suburban settings can be transformed—in this case the former "surfies" milk bar becomes a Moroccan restaurant—is seen as surprising by Arkie but delightful, even though it may prompt moments of nostalgia in those, like Michael, who lived through the period of transformation.

For the narrator of *All We Know*, and Arkie, all places have qualities to be savored and any place can be viewed positively or negatively, depending upon the values and attitudes of the perceiver. For instance, as Arkie and her former best friend, Kylie, settle down on the balcony of Kylie's home unit, Arkie sees "a view of the beach and ocean, and when Arkie glanced in the other direction, her own house was visible beyond the other blocks of home units and the vacant block." On the other hand, Kylie sees "the view through the iron railings" of dirt and garbage and plants dying from car pollution:

"It always smells around here. Cars and trucks, other people's garbage."

"The sea smells nice. At night, when there's a breeze, I can smell the salt air from my bedroom."

"Yuk, you're kidding. All the sea smells of is dead seaweed."[14]

The dialogue here offers readers two points of view that require active readers to establish views of their own. The reader sees in the dialogue between Arkie and Kylie, and in other parts of *All We Know*, French's very serious attempt to represent spatiality as ideologically benign and to demonstrate how the meaning ascribed to a place will vary from person to person.

Finally, I want to show how *All We Know* rejects the dominant Anglocentric culture of old Australia. This is represented in the text by the spatial framework of Arkie's grandmother's impressive home with its large rooms, its lounge lined with oak bookshelves, and the tennis court to one side. Nan's home is constructed as an ostentatious showpiece that speaks of order and decorum. Arkie focalizes the italicized words, and the narrator expands what Arkie would not articulate: "*This must have been an amazing place to have grown up in.* Arkie breathed in the odours of furniture polish and aerosol air freshener that seemed to permeate each grandly furnished room of the stately house."[15] Arkie's thoughts here turn out to be ironic because her mother, Susan, did not enjoy her childhood here. The framed portrait of Susan in her school uniform, sitting at a piano, symbolizes Susan's childhood entrapment in this space. Susan was expected to become a decorous ornament to the stately house. She has failed this expectation altogether: she is divorced, in a de facto relationship, living in an unfashionable suburb, and, in Nan's view, not taking sufficient control of Arkie's life.[16]

Arkie realizes that Nan's power resides in the discourse she uses: "*Sometimes she* [Nan] *really reminds me of mum. Sometimes I think they look exactly the same, but when Nan speaks she says everything so differently.*"[17] Nan uses this discourse of power to control everything she considers hers to dominate. She effectively uses it to keep her daughter's partner, Michael, distanced. Arkie notes that Nan "often spoke to Michael as though meeting him for the first time."[18] Michael sits in Nan's lounge, enduring the disapproval of his de facto relationship with Susan offered by her wedding photographs, which show Susan with her "legitimate" partner.

Nan's language even has the power to transform Arkie's normally casual home in Ramsay Street, with "the house becoming quieter, restrained and bound by unshakeable order" whenever Nan is baby-sitting. This serves to demonstrate once again the text's ideological stance that the values a place holds are bestowed upon it by human subjectivity and are not invested in the place itself. The text is unequivocal in its rejection of Nan's worldview. While she continues to presume power, her daughter and granddaughter remove themselves to spaces far from her site of authority, a site where spatiality is constructed by dominant cultural practices like "Family tradition," seeking to turn each of them "into a particular kind of person."[19]

All We Know uses the representations of place as part of the process of signification in its discourse. If French's book is a marker, albeit an exemplary one, of how the Australian suburbs have become an increasingly foregrounded site for representing environments in which Australian children grow up and where their cultural and ideological subjectivity is framed, then suburbia may well have "come of age" in Australian children's fiction. The recuperation of the concept of "suburbia" has involved asserting the possibilities for personal cultural growth that are provided by such a diverse grouping of people as one finds on a suburban street, and a sense of an available community that is not intrusive but can be an invaluable source of support when needed. Conformity as an essence of suburbia is clearly rejected, and while alienation is certainly present, it is represented as a problem to do with human relationships, not places and spaces. Some places disappear from the map, just as people disappear from our lives. *All We Know* is one marker that Australian cultural identity can now be constructed as pluralistic, and that new myths of identity will allow for a broader range of places to be represented in our literature as spatial frameworks for fulfilled and creative lives. As Chris McAuliffe says of those who are involved in the rewriting of the ideological significance of Australian spatiality: "The artists seemed to understand themselves not as mythic Australians nor as citizens of the world but rather, to use the suburban term, as locals."[20] This is exactly the perspective assumed by the implied author of *All We Know* in constructing the spatial framework for his text.

NOTES

1. Simon French, *All We Know* (Ringwood: Puffin/Penguin Books, 1988).

2. Bruce Clunies-Ross, "Landscape and the Australian Imagination," in *Mapped but Not Known*, ed. P. R. Eaden and F. H. Meares (Adelaide: Wakefield Press, 1986), p. 227.

3. Graeme Turner, *National Fictions: Literature, Film and the Construction of Australian Narrative*, 2nd ed. (St. Leonards: Allen & Unwin, 1993), p. 9.

4. Helen Tiffin's comment is in her essay "Post-Colonial Literatures and Counter-Discourse," *Kunapipi* 9, no. 3 (1987): 17.

5. French, *All We Know*, p. 150.

6. J. C. R. Camm, and John McQuilton, *Australians: A Historic Atlas* (North Sydney: Fairfax, Syme and Weldon, 1987), p. 33.

7. Definitions of "bush" as an Australian term are found in G. A. Wilkes, *A Dictionary of Australian Colloquialisms* (Sydney: Sydney University Press, 1978). The first reference appeared in 1803, in the colony's newspaper *Sydney Gazette*. The later definition from Wilkes's *Australia Revisited* (1853), pp. 65–66, suggests that "bush" now was "indiscriminately applied to all descriptions of uncleared land, or to any spot away from a settlement."

8. Henry Lawson, "The Bush Undertaker," in *A Literary Heritage: Henry Lawson* (Sydney: Weldon, 1988), p. 42.

9. Brenda Niall's definitive study of the history and development of Australian children's literature, *Australia Through the Looking Glass: Children's Fiction 1830–1980* (Brunswick: Melbourne University Press, 1984), confirms that the same tendencies in mainstream art were strongly evidenced in children's fiction, as in other areas of art, at midcentury. She writes that in children's fiction after 1945, leading writers "share a strong feeling for the natural world and an unequivocal rejection of urban Australia" (p. 216). This seems to confirm the idea that the national myths that inform our unconscious minds are reinscribed in the texts of children's

writers because the writers are imbued with this implicit ideology.

John Stephens found the situation persisting in recent Australian picture books. In "Representations of Place in Australian Children's Picture Books," he concludes "that with few exceptions Australian picture book landscapes body forth a social ideology which is conservative and traditional." In *Voices from Far Away: Current Trends in International Children's Literature Research* 24, ed. Marie Nikolajeva (Stockholm: Stockholm Centrum för Barnkulturforskning vid Stockholms Universitet, 1995), p. 112 .

10. Hugh Stretton, "The City," in *Living and Partly Living: Housing in Australia*, ed. Ian Mackay et al. (Melbourne: Thomas Nelson, 1971), pp. 35–36.

11. Sarah Ferber et al., *Beasts of Suburbia: Reinterpreting Cultures in Australian Suburbs* (Melbourne: Melbourne University Press, 1994), p. xvii.

12. Chris McAuliffe, "Don't Fence Me In: Artists and Suburbia in the 1960s," in Sarah Ferber et al., *Beasts of Suburbia* (Melbourne: Melbourne University Press, 1994).

13. French, *All We Know*, p. 65.

14. Ibid., pp. 56–57.

15. Ibid, p. 117.

16. Ibid., p. 119.

17. Ibid., p. 92.

18. Ibid., p. 118.

19. Ibid., p. 250.

20. McAuliffe, "Don't Fence Me In," p. 110.

REFERENCES

Bennett, Bruce. *An Australian Compass: Essays on Place and Direction in Australian Literature*. South Fremantle: Fremantle Arts Centre Press, 1991.

Camm, J. C. R., and John McQuilton. *Australians: A Historic Atlas*. North Sydney: Fairfax, Syme and Weldon, 1987.

Eaden, P. R., and F. H. Meares, eds. *Mapped but Not Known*. Adelaide: Wakefield Press, 1986.

French, Simon. *All We Know*. Ringwood: Puffin Books, 1986.

MacKay, Ian, Robin Boyd, Hugh Stretton, and John Mant. *Living and Partly Living*. Melbourne: Thomas Nelson, 1971.

Niall, Brenda. *Australia Through the Looking Glass: Children's Fiction 1830–1980*. Brunswick: Melbourne University Press, 1984.

Stephens, John. *Language and Ideology in Children's Fiction*. London and New York: Longman, 1992.

———. "Representations of Place in Australian Children's Picture Books." In *Voices from Far Away: Current Trends in International Children's Literature Research* 24. Ed. Maria Nikolajeva. Stockholm: Stockholm Centrum för Barnkulturforskning vid Stockholms Universitet, 1995.

Turner, Graeme. *National Fictions: Literature, Film and the Construction of Australian Narrative*. 2nd ed. St. Leonards: Allen & Unwin, 1993.

Wilkes, G. A. *A Dictionary of Australian Colloquialisms*. Sydney: Sydney University Press, 1978.

14

Reading Children's Literature Multiculturally

Daniel D. Hade

It has been over thirty years since Nancy Larrick wrote in public what most scholars of children's literature knew but could never say: that in American children's books, persons of color rarely appeared. For a few years, publishers seemed to respond to this gap by producing books about African Americans and other minority groups. By the 1980s there was a very small but significant core of "multicultural" books available. Then Rudine Sims's *Shadow and Substance* appeared. In that book, Sims argued that just because a book had an African American character in it, it didn't mean that book described an authentic African American experience. Sims's argument was quickly reduced to a now familiar dictate: Only persons from a particular cultural group may write about that group. This dictate has come to dominate thinking about American children's books to such an extent that some white authors are astonished to discover that publishers won't accept manuscripts if the main characters are persons from groups other than that of the author.[1]

The responses to Larrick's and Sims's works are good examples of what David Theo Goldberg calls "managed" multiculturalism. A managed multiculturalism takes itself to be committed to the celebration of cultural difference. This celebration of difference is often conducted in such a way as to fix boundaries between groups, the effect of which is to leave groups constituted as givens. In the case of the response to Larrick, both publishers and scholars took the appearance of persons other than white males to be a "good" and "honest" representations of their particular group. The question that Larrick raised, and the response it prompted, centered on a belief that stories are vital to the formation of children's identities, and that the presence or absence of certain people has an impact on children's understandings of themselves. What was left out of this discussion was the importance of misrecognition of others and how this misrecognition can inflict harm.[2] In the case of the response to Sims, the children's book world accepted that the identity of the author matters in the authenticity of the story. What happened here was that groups and authors became "essentialized"—that is, their identifies became fixed around certain characteristics and experiences. What goes unchallenged in managed multiculturalism is the meaning or value a society places on differences of race, class, and gender, and how society distributes power, resources, and status among different groups. To take up this challenge is to move toward a critical multiculturalism.

Critical multiculturalism has three aspects. First, critical multiculturalism is a systematic critique of the ideology of westernness. This means challenging the domination of assumptions held by Western culture. Second, critical multiculturalism is the challenge of living with each other in a world of difference. Multiculturalism means searching for ways to affirm and celebrate difference while also seeking ways to cooperate and collaborate across different groups of people. Third, critical multiculturalism is a reform movement based upon equity and justice. Goods and privileges are concentrated with white, wealthy males; they are not distributed justly across race, class, and gender. Critical multiculturalism is about naming this injustice and struggling toward social change and social justice. In the words of Hazel Carby, critical multiculturalism is "to make visible what is rendered invisible when viewed as the normative state of existence."[3]

Toni Morrison has argued brilliantly, in her book *Playing in the Dark: Whiteness and the Literary Imagination*, that Americans live in a *racialized* society. "Racialized" does not mean the same as "racist," though they are not incompatible terms. "Racialized" means that race matters in how we think about one another. "Race" is a category into which Americans slot people, and that category has meaning. However, it is considered graceful and generous to ignore race as having any meaning—that is, for most whites, an unracialized society is their reality. Extending this argument to other markers, culture in the United States has taught Americans that there is meaning in the identity of someone as black or white, male or female, rich or poor, but acknowledging these meanings publicly is considered to be bad form. By examining how race, class, and gender mean in our stories, we begin to understand how we live our lives according to these meanings. Race, class, and gender are social semiotics—they mean—they are signs to be interpreted. By denying that race, class, and gender are not signs to be interpreted, we also deny what is obvious: that literature is a cultural product and that race, class, and gender do matter in our lives.

How do race, class, and gender, as *signs* to be interpreted, mean in the stories we put before children? I am using "sign" in the sense that the semiotician C. S. Peirce used it. A sign is comprised of an indivisible and triadic relationship of symbol (what appears on the page), referent (the object that is represented by the symbol), and an interpretant (the meaning brought *to* the sign that mediates between the symbol and the referent). This means that we do not think to get meaning; rather, we use meaning to think. Interpretation is the means by which we understand text. I want to focus, then, upon "interpretation," in the sense that Tony Watkins describes as the generation and circulation of meanings in children's books, by attending to "what is said or represented by a symbolic form"[4] and how these meanings misrecognize and essentialize people.

Native Americans have long been identified romantically by the dominant culture as having lived in perfect harmony with their environment. This view can still be seen in recent children's books. For example, *Brother Eagle, Sister Sky*, by Susan Jeffers, spent many weeks on the *New York Times* Best-Seller List and has sold over 300,000 copies, an extraordinary print run for a book in the United States. The book, an illustrated version of a speech made by Chief Seattle, was much praised for its detailed illustrations and for its message of environmental responsibility by journals such as *The Horn Book Magazine* and *School Library Journal*, and earned the top prize from the American Booksellers Association. The book was also severely criticized for depicting the Suquamish people of the Pacific Northwest and the plants and animals of that area inaccurately, and for attributing the words of the text to Chief Seattle when no evidence existed that Seattle had ever spoken those words. The controversy became so heated that it made the front page of the *New York Times*, an unheard-of "accomplishment" for a children's book.

Lost in the controversy about the accuracy of Jeffers' book was discussion of how she used Native Americans as a sign to convey meaning. The cover of *Brother Eagle, Sister Sky* provides some clues. We see on the cover a Native American chief, presumably Chief Seattle, in traditional dress (though not necessarily the traditional dress of the Suquamish people), hands placed upon the shoulders of a contemporary, blue-eyed, Anglo boy. The boy is gazing at a dragonfly, seemingly unaware of Seattle's presence. We can see the colors of the boy's shirt through Seattle's hands, suggesting that Seattle's presence is spiritual, not physical. Seattle's headdress and body blend into clouds and mountains, suggesting that he is connected to the natural world. He seems to be there to guide the boy into an appreciation of the natural world.

Inside the book, Jeffers continues this theme. As we read the words attributed to Chief Seattle, Jeffers shows Native Americans living in an unspoiled environment. However, the Native Americans illustrated by Jeffers are clearly not Suquamish. They are shown with the wrong clothing (in fact the clothing matches that of no known Native American people) and the wrong canoe, and as riding horses, though the Suquamish didn't ride horses. Even the words attributed to Seattle are suspect—a filmmaker claims to have written them in the 1970s for an Earth Day celebration. At the end of the book Jeffers shows a forest that has been clear-cut, a family of European Americans planting trees, and a mystical Native American family watching approvingly. Seattle's words become a prophecy spoken on behalf of all Native Americans to European Americans: respect the land or you will lose it.

If *Brother Eagle, Sister Sky* is viewed as a book about Seattle and the Suquamish people, it is a failure. Rather, Jeffers uses the association of Native Americans with living environmentally responsible lives to send a message to European Americans.

The appearance of Native Americans in a book about the environment means something, and it has little to do with the particulars of a Native American culture. Jeffers borrows from dominant American culture its image of Native Americans as a sign of environmental responsibility. What is stated implicitly in *Brother Eagle, Sister Sky* is that Native American responsibility should be juxtaposed with European American irresponsibility. In the views of many, this may be a flattering, albeit romantic, image of Native Americans. But the book isn't really about Native American culture. The meanings implied for the images of Native Americans in these two books are white meanings—that is, the signs are used as the dominant culture would normally use them. White America has appropriated Native Americans as a sign that white America will use to convey meaning about environmental responsibility. This, in effect, turns Native American subjectivity into white American objectivity.

Race is sometimes used by authors as a literary device, a way of setting characters apart from each other. *The Moves Make the Man*, by Bruce Brooks, who is white, is the story of two teenage boys, one black and one white, living in North Carolina in the 1960s. The story is narrated by Jerome Foxworthy, an African American boy, who desegregates the white high school and later is denied a place on the basketball team even though he is clearly the best player in the school. Brooks raises these two serious and important racial issues in the book and then ignores them. It is bewildering that a story narrated by a character who is the first black student in a North Carolina high school and is unjustly kept off the basketball team wouldn't be dominated by these events. That is, it is shocking if you are expecting Brooks's story to be about a black character's life. If we hold that Jerome's race matters, then Jerome's race, in the story Brooks chose to tell, serves a much different function than to comment on racial issues.   Why is Jerome black if Brooks isn't going to explore issues of race seriously? Brooks needs the character of Jerome to offset Bix Rivers, a messed-up white boy. Jerome may be the narrator, but the story is Bix's. Both Jerome and Bix are outcasts and loners—Bix, because he is mentally unstable; Jerome, because he is the only African American in the school. The characters need each other, and in the process Jerome serves as a foil for Bix. Although as outcast and as alone as Bix (though for different reasons), unlike Bix, Jerome is totally sane. It is Jerome's ability to use fakes and deception on the basketball court that serves as a comment on Bix's revulsion against anything false, including a basketball move. Jerome's blackness and saneness contrast sharply with Bix's whiteness and mental instability. This "salt and pepper" theme of crazy white paired with sane black is common throughout American film, television, and literature. Brooks's book, which was a Newbery Honor winner, is an example of how a white imagination uses race in an attempt to be unracialized.

The identification of certain races as victims also has been used by authors as a literary device enhancing themes. Few books in the United States have raised as much controversy as Ouida Sebestyen's *Words by Heart*, which won numerous awards and earned great praise from some of the mainstream of the children's book world (International Reading Association, *School Library Journal, Booklist*), and drew great wrath, primarily from African American critics. The book tells of the Sills family, who have moved from an all-black community to a place where they are the only black family. Immediately the family is threatened with violence, but Ben Sills, the Bible-quoting father, urges his family to remain calm and not rush the white folks. Eventually, Ben is fatally wounded by a white boy angry at Ben for taking a job that had once been his father's. Incredibly, the dying Ben begs his daughter Lena not to press charges against his murderer but to forgive him. This story reportedly comes from Sebestyen's (who happens to be white) family history. Interestingly, Sebestyen changes the race of her characters from white to black, to great effect. Her story is one of forgiveness and plays to the Christian tradition of Christ as the suffering servant. Ben Sills is put into the Christ-like role, suffering the racism of the town with patience and an understanding that his tormentors cannot act otherwise. The act of forgiving a murderer is accentuated by the races of those involved, the victim being African American and the perpetrator being white. Sebestyen has played upon the sign of African Americans as victims to make her point about forgiving one's enemies. To a white American reader, what greater act of forgiveness could there be than an African American family forgiving the white boy who has killed their father?

Though this is a powerful use of race, this use nonetheless objectifies—that is, it makes the African American characters objects rather than subjects. Real issues of race, class, and gender are ignored when the sign is appropriated for other reasons by dominant groups. However, we are rarely taught to read in such a fashion. I've had more than one white colleague defend *Words by Heart* as brilliant and as accurate. "Surely there were black families like that and surely there were men like Ben Sills," they argue. But defending a book's verisimilitude doesn't quite work in this case. When I reply that I've yet to have an African American student read that book and find it anything but abhorrent, my colleagues seem stunned. This is a stark difference in how race is read by different readers.

So far, I've looked at how race can mean in certain American children's books. But along with race, class and gender also are used by authors in misrecognizing and essentializing ways to construct meaning. *Santa Calls*, by William Joyce, was received well by critics when it appeared in 1993. On the surface, *Santa Calls* would seem to be a pleasant Christmas story about a brother discovering that he truly likes his younger sister. A closer look, though, shows that how Joyce uses race, class, and gender is vital to the story he tells. He uses race as a symbol of mystery and evil, class as hyperbole, and gender as stereotype. Art Atchinson Aimesworth is the protagonist of *Santa Calls*. An orphan raised by his aunt and uncle, his name and his dress (sweater and tie) suggest that he belongs or aspires to the upper class. His best friend is a "young Comanche brave" named Spaulding Littlefeets, a hyperbolic mix of names that suggests the language of a young child, an upper-class white background, and Native American roots. Art also has a little sister, Esther, to whom he is often mean. One day a large crate is delivered to Art from Santa Claus, who invites Art to assemble the contents and come north. A flying machine is assembled. The basket for passengers arrived broken, so Spaulding lends his "beloved canoe to the cause."[5] The illustrations show Spaulding dressed in attire similar to Art's except for a leather headband and a long, braided ponytail. Art, Spaulding, and his sister Esther climb aboard the canoe and fly north.

At the North Pole they meet Ali Aku, captain of the Santarian Guards. Ali Aku, dark-skinned and dressed in exotic high hat, flowing cape, and scimitar, brings to the story a sense of Oriental mystery reminiscent of Edward Said's argument that orientalism is a sign of mysteriousness to the Western mind. The children help Ali Aku fight the Dark Elves and their evil Queen. The Dark Elves are, of course, dark-skinned, signifying evil. Interestingly, the Dark Queen is light-skinned, perhaps suggesting that the dark-skinned elves are incapable of providing leadership. During the fight, the evil Queen abducts Esther, and Art must rescue his little sister. When the adventure is over, the children are returned to their home in Abilene, Texas, and Art wonders why Santa called him in the first place. At the end of the book, we are shown two letters, one from Esther to Santa, asking for her brother to be nicer to her, and a response from Santa, saying he is happy the adventure has done the trick.

Much of the humor of the book comes from the positioning of "exotic" (to the white reader) elements: non-Western names and artifacts in places where a white audience would not expect them. The story is resolved through the worn-out trick of the adventurous boy rescuing the hapless girl, albeit through being tricked by his sister and Santa Claus. This book is brilliant in many ways, but its use of race and gender belie a white male imagination at work. The book works because readers are willing to accept persons of color as objects; the existence of the poor, albeit offstage, which makes the pretentiousness of Art humorous; and the idea that boys can appreciate girls best if girls give boys the opportunity to be strong.

So far, I have looked at books written or illustrated by white authors in ways that Tony Watkins might describe as revealing how meaning or signification serves to sustain relations of domination. This domination is sustained through misrecognizing or essentializing characters. There is another twist to this. Authors who do not resort to misrecognition or essentialism can use the signs of race, class, and gender to subvert relations of domination, shattering stereotypes in the process.

In *Flossie and the Fox*, Patricia McKissack uses race, class, and gender to produce political satire of the powerful. Flossie is poor, black, and female. She speaks the black dialect of rural Tennessee. Flossie is sent by her grandmother to deliver a basket of eggs and is told to beware of the fox, who will surely try to steal the eggs. Flossie tells her grandmother she doesn't know what a fox looks like. Shortly after entering the forest, the fox appears.

> Slowly the animal circled round Flossie. "I am a fox," he announced, all the time eyeing the basket of eggs. He stopped in front of Flossie, smiled as best a fox can, and bowed. "At your service."
>
> Flossie rocked back on her heels then up on her toes, back and forward, back and forward . . . carefully studying the creature who was claiming to be a fox.
>
> "Nope," she said at last. "I just purely don't believe it."
>
> "You don't believe what?" Fox asked, looking way from the basket of eggs for the first time.
>
> "I don't believe you a fox, that's what."
>
> Fox's eyes flashed anger. Then he chuckled softly. "My dear child," he said, sounding right disgusted, "of course I'm a fox. A little girl like you should be simply terrified of me. Whatever do they teach children these days?"
>
> Flossie tossed her head in the air. "Well, whatever you are, you sho' think a heap of yo'self," she said and skipped away.[6]

The fox is male, and his use of "King's English" suggests he is also white and rich. When Flossie shows no fear of the fox, stating that she doesn't know what a fox looks like, so why should she be frightened of him, the fox insists that she be afraid of him. Flossie replies that she will not be afraid of him until he can prove he is a fox. This bold statement disarms the fox, and their positions become reversed—Flossie is in control, and the fox becomes more and more desperate as he is unable to respond to the challenge to his authority. Flossie, using her cunning, outsmarts the fox and, at the end of the story, admits that she knew he was a fox. She refuses to grant the white, rich, male fox the privileges the fox believes are his birthright.

At the beginning of the story McKissack, introduces Flossie, who is poor, black, and female, three signs of weakness. Flossie is a potential victim. The fox, by virtue of being male and talking like a rich white man, is powerful, the kind of character who takes from victims. These are conventional signs of domination, the signs that Joyce exploits in *Santa Calls*. McKissack, unlike Joyce, *subverts* these signs, lifting Flossie from victim to agent and deflating the rich, white, male fox.

Accounting for how race, class, and gender mean in children's stories cannot be a task just for the critic. I share with Peter Hollindale the view that the task of adults is to teach children how to read, so that to the limits of each child's capacity, children will not be at the mercy of what they read. Perhaps if children can read the ideology in their books, they will be able to read it in other areas of their lives.[7]

NOTES

1. Kathryn Lasky, "To Stingo with Love: An Author's Perspective on Writing Outside One's Culture," *The New Advocate* 9 (1996): 1–7.

2. Charles Taylor, "The Politics of Recognition," in *Multiculturalism: A Critical Reader*, ed. David Theo Goldberg (Cambridge, Mass.: Blackwell, 1994).

3. Hazel Carby, "The Multicultural Wars," in *Black Popular Culture*, ed. Gina Dent (Seattle: Bay Press, 1992), pp. 193–194.

4. Tony Watkins, "Cultural Studies, New Historicism and Children's Literature," in *Literature for Children: Contemporary Criticism*, ed. Peter Hunt (London: Routledge, 1993), p. 179.

5. William Joyce, *Santa Calls* (New York: HarperCollins, 1993), unpaged.

6. Patricia C. McKissack, *Flossie and the Fox* (New York: Dial, 1986), unpaged.

7. See Peter Hollindale, "Ideology and the Children's Book," *Signal* 55 (1988): 3–22.

REFERENCES

Brooks, Bruce. *The Moves Make the Man*. New York: Harper & Row, 1984.

Carby, Hazel. "The Multicultural Wars." In *Black Popular Culture*. Ed. Gina Dent. Seattle: Bay Press, 1992.

Goldberg, David Theo. *Multiculturalism: A Critical Reader*. Cambridge, Mass.: Blackwell, 1994.

Hollindale, Peter. "Ideology and the Children's Book." *Signal* 55 (1988): 3–22.

Jeffers, Susan. *Brother Eagle, Sister Sky*. New York: Dial, 1991.

Joyce, William. *Santa Calls*. New York: HarperCollins, 1993.

Larrick, Nancy. "The All-White World of Children's Books." *Saturday Review*, September 11, 1965, pp. 63–85.

Lasky, Katherine. "To Stingo with Love: An Author's Perspective on Writing Outside One's Culture." *The New Advocate* 9 (1996): 1–7.

McKissack, Patricia. C. *Flossie and the Fox*. New York: Dial, 1986.

Morrison, Toni. *Playing in the Dark: Whiteness and the Literary Imagination*. New York: Vintage, 1992.

Peirce, C. S. *Collected Papers*.6 vols. Ed. P. Weiss and C. Hartshorne. Cambridge, Mass.:
    Harvard University Press, 1931–1935.
Said, Edward. *Orientalism*. New York: Vintage, 1978.
Sebestyen, Ouida. *Words by Heart*. Boston: Little, Brown, 1979.
Sims, Rudine. *Shadow and Substance: Afro-American Experience in Contemporary
    Children's Fiction*. Urbana, Ill.: National Council of Teachers of English, 1982.
Taylor, Charles. "The Politics of Recognition." In *Multiculturalism: A Critical Reader*. Ed.
    David Theo Goldberg. Cambridge, Mass.: Blackwell, 1994.
Watkins, Tony. "Cultural Studies, New Historicism and Children's Literature." In *Literature
    for Children: Contemporary Criticism*. Ed. Peter Hunt. London: Routledge, 1993.

Part V

National Literatures

The Journey Inward: Adolescent Literature in America, 1945–1995

Anne Scott MacLeod

T he end of the Second World War brought the United States a prosperity that for two decades reached nearly every level of American society. It also opened a half-century that would give adolescents greater freedom, greater economic power, and more adult attention, both approving and otherwise,than at any other time in American history. The juncture between adolescence and economics was not at all coincidental; puberty is biological, but the nature, length, burdens, and hazards of adolescent experience are shaped by economic and social realities. In the Depression and the war years, American youngsters moved quickly through adolescence into adult responsibilities. After 1945, as prosperity made the earnings of teenagers less necessary to their families, society could, and did, mandate a longer period of education. By 1960, high school attendance became nearly universal in the United States, stretching young adult dependency at least through four years of secondary school. The same period saw adolescents become a prime consumer market. Since many teenagers worked part-time, and since family incomes often allowed them to keep their wages, adolescents became avid consumers of carefully targeted leisure products, including films, recordings, magazines, and, of course, books.

Adolescent fiction has continued as a major subset of children's literature. The novels evolved over five decades as society, demographics, and a changing economy altered the experience and the expectations of the young. Stated broadly, and ignoring variations that inevitably exist in so large a literature, the path of American adolescent novels has been from outward to inward; from concern with the young adult's relationship to the larger community to a nearly exclusive emphasis on the adolescent's inner feelings. Over the same period, the social distance between adults and adolescents has diminished. The contemporary fictional adolescent is less firmly attached to traditional family structures, more autonomous, on more nearly equal terms with adults than were the fictional youngsters of earlier literature.

From 1945 to about 1965, adolescent novels sang of intact families, affection between parents and children, and an accepted hierarchy of adult over child. Apart from their contemporary language, the stories would have seemed quite familiar to readers of the nineteenth century, committed as they were to proving the rightness of home-taught values. Patricia Spack, in her study of adult fiction about adolescents, notes that eighteenth- and nineteenth-century moralistic texts offered fantasies of ideal adolescents who combined "the rationality of the adult with the compliance of the child."[1] So, too, did the teen novels of the first two postwar decades. In the work of mainstream authors like Beverly Cleary, Lenore Weber, and Madeleine L'Engle, girls complied with conventional expectations and were rewarded with the affection of family and friends, and the attentions of a truly nice boy. Boys' stories taught similar lessons, though against tougher odds. Henry Felsen's stories about car-crazy high school boys rang with adult concern over the explosive mix of youth and gasoline. The stakes were high, and Felsen's instructive plots hit harder than the mild tales written for girls. In the end, however, even reckless boys learned to heed adult counsel and to conform to conventional social mores. While the postwar era had its share of anxiety over adolescents, the literature on the whole conveyed confidence that community values would prevail.

The social revolutions of the 1960s and 1970s, however, transformed literature for the young. The literary model for most teen novels became J. D. Salinger's *The Catcher in the Rye*, so much so that by the 1970s the first-person narratives of an alienated adolescent commenting on and rejecting the tainted mores of adult society were a cliché of adolescent fiction. *Catcher*, however, is neo-Romantic: the protagonist is idealistic and kind-hearted, a better person than any of the adults who fail and betray him. Adolescent literature adopted the alienation of the Salinger model, and the rejection of conventional values, but not the Romanticism that gilded its hero. Protagonists of the new teen novels were rarely romanticized; they were just lost and unhappy and remarkably passive in their distress. They were not idealistic but cynical. To these fictional adolescents, their alcoholic mothers and deserting fathers justified their scorn of adult values, but remarkably few of them thought about other, more satisfactory ways to live. In fact, they seldom envisioned a future in which they actually did anything other than survive.

While this literature was clearly shaped by social and political events, the books read less like social criticism than like private psychotherapy sessions. Authors said little directly about society's flaws, but much about adolescents as victims of society and especially of their families; they took a therapeutic approach to their protagonists, suggesting that they look inward for the emotional strength they needed, since the adult world could not—or would not—help them. They shifted the focus of adolescent development from adaptation to a larger world to contemplation of the inner self, a contemplation that was neither spiritual nor intellectual, but psychological. The task for adolescents in these books had less to do with finding a place in society than with achieving a tolerable level of emotional comfort. John Donovan's 1969 novel says a good deal in its title alone: *I'll Get There. It Better Be Worth the Trip*. "There" is undefined, but the implied goal here, as in most of the literature, is little more than simple survival—getting through the teen years to the equally undefined territory beyond.

The inwardness of these novels is striking; so is the nearly universal hostility toward adults in general and families in particular. The first-person voice offers no moderating commentary on the thesis—again all but universal in the fiction—that adults are unhappy, ineffectual beings who have nothing to teach the young. Few 1970s authors tried to defend either the family as an institution or the values of the adult society.

Since 1980, the bleakness of the literature has modified, but the basic landscape is in many respects unchanged. Fictional adolescents still struggle with a dysfunctional society, still deal with adults who are mostly unable to offer much help, and still contend with a staggering range of personal problems. Two differences stand out, however. First, fewer authors insist on the total isolation of their protagonists. Though some repeat the formulas of the 1970s, most 1980s and 1990s novels acknowledge that human beings need other human beings. Family, defined broadly as people who care about one another, whether related or not, is understood to be important. Second, fictional adolescents are less passive now than they were in the 1970s. They are still largely on their own, but in many novels they have the resources, in the form of friends, emotional maturity, and an occasional helpful adult, to deal with serious problems and even to arrive at an outlook that accommodates the pain of experience without blighting all hope.

One contemporary novelist brings together a number of the elements that seem to me to distinguish current adolescent literature from that of the 1970s. Chris Crutcher has published six novels since 1983, and while his work is not prototypical, his sense of the middle-class adolescent's world, and of the relations between adults and adolescents, has many echoes in contemporary young adult novels.

Crutcher's characters are high schoolers on the brink of adulthood. Unlike the adolescents of 1970s fiction, they are not isolated but living—not always peacefully—within a web of relationships with friends, teammates, coaches, teachers, and school life. Their lives are as riddled with problems as any in the sixties-seventies era: these teenagers contend with sexual and physical abuse, tragic death, crippling accidents—but the stories and the moral judgments are more complex.

What emerges from Crutcher's books is a general picture of adult–adolescent relationships in a new age. The affection and respect between generations, so taken for granted in the 1940s and 1950s and so thoroughly repudiated in the 1960s and 1970s, are reinstated, but with profound differences. Neither is automatic; they must be earned, as they are between adults. Parental authority, insofar as it exists, is influence, and is granted by the child. Crutcher's protagonists are on generally easy terms with their parents, though scarcely in the 1950s mode. They are casually knowledgeable about adult sexuality, even in connection with parents and teachers—unthinkable in the past but emblematic of the shrinking social distance between generations in adolescent fiction.

Yet teenagers are not adults, as they well know. A recurrent figure in Crutcher novels is a coach or a trainer who functions as a guru. He or she challenges students to stretch their physical limits, inducing the Zen experience of dissolving boundaries between action and actor, and—sooner or late—supplies tough-minded wisdom. It is to these gurus that protagonists turn when troubles pile up, and it is they, rather than parents, who voice the philosophy that Crutcher offers to the young.

The advice is therapeutic—personal and limited. There are no universal moral systems invoked, no absolute codes of behavior, no comprehensive attempts at explaining the evil in the world (and there is evil in these books). Adolescents are counseled to accept what is, and to take responsibility for their own actions. Their attention is directed to their own behavior, and to that alone, as one coach says:

All you have in this world, really, are your responses to it. Responses to your feelings and responses to what comes in from outside. . . . That's all responsibility is, responding to the world, owning your responses. It isn't about taking blame or finding out if something's your fault. . . . You have no control over the world. You have no control over anyone except you.[2]

This advice, like the trauma that brought it about, is a far cry from the mild dilemmas and comfortable messages of teen fiction in the 1950s. Today's adolescent literature reflects fundamental revisions in American social attitudes and in the structural arrangements of American families. Ironically, the revisions had their roots in the 1950s, though authors of adolescent novels, like most other Americans in that complacent era, hardly noticed. The agent of change was the same affluence that made Americans sure that they lived in the best of worlds. As prosperity extended adolescence, promoted consumerism, and gave adolescents unprecedented freedom via cars and spending money; as growing numbers of women began to work outside the home; as government assumed greater responsibility for the welfare of the old and the poor, family expectations, for parents and children alike, began to change. The reciprocal obligations of kinship diminished, and the autonomy of both adults and children increased.

The 1960s and 1970s are now synonymous with social upheavals, including the remaking of the family. Adolescent fiction responded not with an accurate picture of the new social landscape, but with the highly ambivalent adult reaction to it. It was an oddly unsympathetic literature. As harshly as authors criticized adult society for failing children, they rarely conveyed much warmth toward the alienated young who were its victims. Like most other adults, authors had mixed feelings about rebellious teenagers, and little counsel to offer. They understood no better than the young what had gone wrong or how it was to be mended. If fitting into the existing society and accepting its values was no longer the definition of growing up, it was not at all clear what was.

Nor is it now. Some Americans hope to restore 1950s calm by reconstructing the traditional family. But the realities of a postindustrial economy argue against such simplicities. In the 1990s, not affluence but a society with little need for unskilled labor dictates extended education and therefore years of semidependence for young adults. Together with high divorce rates, greater fluidity in working careers, and long life expectancy, the need to support children well past legal majority has altered the relations between men and women as well as between adults and children. It is hard to imagine families returning wholesale to the man-as-breadwinner, woman-at-home pattern of the past. The autonomy of today's young adults is not, as in the past, the independence of full-time workers. Autonomy now is emotional, not economic, a product of new family arrangements and of the earlier exposure of children to adult life, in reality and on television. In spite of political agitation, these developments are not likely to reverse.

Contemporary mainstream adolescent literature has absorbed most of these changes. The fiction as a whole accepts nontraditional models of family, concedes the sexual knowingness of the young, and acknowledges a more equal standing of adolescents with adults. The definition of maturity is still unclear, but where it comes through—as in Crutcher's work—it is personal rather than social. Very little in contemporary adolescent fiction suggests that maturity requires or even involves taking a stand on social needs, problems, prospects, or failures. There are many implied and explicit *values* in the literature—kindness, tolerance, antiracism—but little critique of a social system that often ignores these. It is even rare for modern protagonists to come to any conclusions about their future role in the world, as earlier fictional adolescents so often did. The late twentieth century has granted adolescents a level of personal freedom undreamed of in the 1940s, 1950s, and 1960s, yet the literature seldom suggests that adolescents can or even want to translate that freedom into the power to change a society that manifestly fails them.

NOTES

1. Patricia Meyer Spacks, *The Adolescent Idea: Myths of Youth and the Adult Imagination* (New York: Basic Books, 1981), pp. 25, 26.

2. Chris Crutcher, *Chinese Handcuffs* (NewYork: Dell, 1983), pp. 122, 123.

REFERENCES

Crutcher, Chris. *Chinese Handcuffs*. NewYork: Dell, 1983.
Donovan, John. *I'll Get There. It Better Be Worth the Trip*. New York: Harper & Row, 1969.
Salinger, J.D. *The Catcher in the Rye*. Boston: Little, Brown, 1951.
Spacks, Patricia Meyer. *The Adolescent Idea: Myths of Youth and the Adult Imagination*. New York: Basic Books, 1981.

16

The Novel for Adolescents in Quebec: Stereotypes and New Conventions

Danielle Thaler

One of the significant phenomena in the publishing industry since 1970 has been the development of series for adolescents. True, this is not a new phenomenon; at least as far back as the eighteenth century,[1] there have been books aimed at adolescents or, let us say, books that were highly recommended to adolescents. Long before the last quarter of the twentieth century, publishers recognized adolescents as budding consumers and offered them specialized series. Furthermore, there have always been novels recounting the psychological and sentimental development of young heroes who are swept up in social upheaval (the bildungsroman). Suffice it to say, modern young people's literature did not invent the character of the adolescent (or that of the child, for that matter). The phenomenon has, however, seen a period of particularly intense growth, both in Quebec and elsewhere.[2] Indeed, novels are attempting, for the first time, not only to speak about adolescence but also to speak to the youth of today's liberal consumer society in terms that allow them to recognize themselves in the images that the literature projects. This, in any case, is the claim of those novelists who have chosen to promote this "new" genre of novel.[3]

Thus, a first look at this evolution reveals that it involves less the emergence of new themes than the institutionalization of a new reader, one whose needs are considered with understanding. It is a matter of responding to an expectation, of developing a complicity with the reader. In fact, many writers working in this genre have said that their novels never would have seen the light of day had they not been tuned in to today's youth.

This being the case, what, exactly, has changed in the representation of adolescence to explain the development of a (new) literature for adolescents? Indeed, ever since it developed into its own genre, literature for adolescents has constantly had to be preoccupied with its reader. From its inception, then, it has survived through trying to reflect, as carefully as possible, the reader's own image. Therefore, the history of literature for youth is also—*especially*, perhaps—the history of the representation of its reader.

I will thus endeavor to define the image of the adolescent in today's series for young people in Quebec, all the while inquiring into a possible evolution in this representation.

I thought it would be worthwhile to draw upon the recent novels of Dominique Demers, which clearly illustrate what has been happening in the Québécois series for adolescents. Her trilogy about an adolescent girl (*Un Hiver de tourmente*, 1992; *Les Grands Sapins ne meurent pas*, 1993; *Ils dansent dans la tempête*, 1994) was a huge succes among young Quebecers, and her publishers, La Courte Échelle and Québec/Amérique, are well integrated into the Quebec market. Demers is all the more interesting because, as a critic and teacher, she also has studied the novel for adolescents. And since it is impossible to speak of evolution without a point of comparison, I will compare Demers's work with another trilogy: Lucy Maud Montgomery's series, written in the 1920s, about Emily of New Moon. Both authors have admitted that the trilogies have a somewhat biographical foundation. Each trilogy follows its heroine into adulthood.

However, whereas Montgomery's series, like all of the Prince Edward Island native's other novels, is in keeping with the tradition of nineteenth-century young people's literature, Demers's novels have aspired to be innovative in their presentation *of* adolescents *to* adolescents.

ADOLESCENCE: PROBLEMS AND REPRESENTATION, FROM THE BILDUNGSROMAN TO THE MODERN NOVEL FOR ADOLESCENTS

In her novels, Dominique Demers poses a problem that she considers essential: the existence of a specific, recognized literature for adolescents. Under what conditions is such a literature possible? Without taking up the problem in such explicit terms, she nevertheless attempts to provide a response when she speaks of the representation of adolescence for adolescents.[4] She defines two priorities as being essential conditions: the themes and the reader. She thus advocates a literature for adolescents that both speaks about and to adolescents, and that reflects the most faithful image possible of the reader. In this sense, the novel becomes a mirror, rediscovering a function that writers of the nineteenth century assigned it. But now, it no longer reflects the complexities of an entire society; instead, it offers to a narrowly targeted audience that audience's own image, giving it a reason to continue reading and to buy the book. While it may be an exaggeration to say that this concept necessarily leads to complacency, it is nevertheless legitimate to wonder if the image reflected can be faithful and objective. More generally, can any literary form that emphasizes the reader's response above all else avoid this dilemma?

As said before, there is nothing new about the theme of adolescence. Narrative literature is brimming with young people. Indeed, virtually since the inception of the novel, the youth has been one of the most familiar figures in the genre. Moreover, it became the favorite character of the nineteenth-century bildungsroman, because it allowed the author to explore the theme of the individual's integration into society—which has always been a good way of presenting a portrait of that society.

What distinguishes *Le Grand Meaulnes*, say, from the Marie-Lune series, lies primarily in the domain of authorial intention. The major difference between Alain-Fournier and Demers is the latter's choice of young people as target readers. This choice reflects an awareness of the distance that separates today's young people from those of the past. It is true that the heroes of those old novels belonged to the aristocracy or other privileged bourgeois families, whereas Demers creates middle-class heroes who are, let us say, socially unexceptional, probably in order that they more closely resemble today's typical adolescent. Marie-Lune's mother owns a hair-styling salon in surburban Montreal, and her father is a sports reporter for a local newspaper. The family name (Dumoulin, which one could translate as "from the mill") is chosen expressly to convey the family's unexceptional status. Demers shows a desire to erase any question of class difference and to favor a uniformity of social standing among her main characters.

On the other hand, Montgomery's heroine, Emily of New Moon, belongs to a privileged society, and the farming family that takes her in, the Murrays, lives a life of great comfort. Moreover, Emily is an outsider by nature; she has nothing in common with the students she meets at the village school. Demers's Marie-Lune is not an outsider. This difference between two characters who thus seem to have nothing in common permits us to inquire into the development of the literary status of the child/adolescent as heroine. Emily is molded in the tradition of the exceptional heroine, a descendant of the long line of impertinent and rebellious heroes whose principal figures are to be found in Victor Hugo's Gavroche and Mark Twain's Huckleberry Finn. She fully accepts her position as a heroine of the sort extolled by children's literature until very recently, a legacy of nineteenth-century traditions. Marie-Lune, on the other hand, belongs to the new race of antihero that has so densely populated European literature since the First World War. As a result, Marie-Lune's daily life is one of banality, whereas Emily's is transfigured by her vision of the world.

A CHARACTERISTIC OF THE ADOLESCENT/HERO IN THE NOVEL FOR ADOLESCENTS: FROM SOLITUDE TO ALIENATION

Whereas Emily the outsider opens up to the world more and more, her counterpart's isolation intensifies, becoming increasingly burdensome. Isolation: this is perhaps one of the themes that, in the portrayal of contemporary adolescence, contrasts sharply with previous portrayals in the bildungsroman, which has always depicted the adolescent's discovery of the world (albeit a rather limited world). An entire class of narrative literature for adolescents has established this solitude as a common theme. We see it in Judy Blume's heroines, for example, and in the characters of Janni Howker.

This solitude first becomes evident through the narration. An emptiness gradually envelops Marie-Lune, whose narrative trajectory takes a turn that is perhaps unexpected but that hardly favors her entry into society or into any well-defined social group. Marie-Lune's mother dies in the middle of the series' first volume; her father, barely present up to this point, slowly disappears completely thereafter. Pregnant, she gives up her baby for adoption; and Antoine, her first lover, kills himself. The climax of this progressive stripping away of society, the final plunge into infernal night before Marie-Lune's redemption and return to society, is her retreat—at first imposed but later voluntary—to a convent.

Even from the beginning, however, Marie-Lune's life unfolds in isolation. At first, this isolation is geographic. The heroine's taste for open, snowbound areas that are isolated and lost, and for great expanses of fir, becomes an essential element of her psychology. The solitude of these great landscapes reflects the solitude of an adolescent who believes she has been abandoned.

Moreover, the trait that most characterizes Demers's heroine is the narrowness of her horizons. Whereas Montgomery's Emily, come what may, persists in opening her eyes wide to the world around her, Demers's Marie-Lune closes in upon herself, becoming preoccupied exclusively with her adolescent problems. We may say that without actually entering the convent, Marie-Lune nevertheless renounces the world. Not happiness, but the world—unless we consider the world to be the cramped, narrow happiness that she finds in the arms of Jean. The male characters have no real depth. They are little more than a pair of arms in which the heroine may let herself go.[5] This pattern reaches its apex in the final volume of the trilogy. After a two-year absence, Jean, the modern Prince Charming, arrives in time to save the heroine, who, respecting the model of her literary forebears, has only to throw herself into the hero's arms and retreat from the world. In any case, the outside world does not really exist; it has depth only to the extent that, adhering to a Romantic concept of landscape, it reflects the adolescent's inner state of being.

To what extent does the choice of a first-person narration contribute to the narrowing of the character's horizons? The question is all the more important given that we are dealing with the narrative choice of fashion in today's novel for adolescents.[6] It owes its dominance to the fact that it gives the novel a falsely autobiographical appearance that nevertheless favors the play of secrecy and identification at the edge of the personal and intimate. However, this is an ancient literary recipe, one of the oldest narrative traps, that still manages to ensnare the reader's ego. It is the great mythical pledge of authenticity, and thus the most magnificent of narrative deceptions wherein three egos—the author's, the reader's, and the character's—end up merging into a narrative Holy Trinity. While this triple identification remains capable of producing a salutary sublimation in the adolescent, it nevertheless testifies to a withdrawal into the self that excludes any true critical distance.[7]

Is it consequently a matter of portraying the condition of adolescents (or individuals, even) at the end of the century—individuals doomed to a solitude they cannot escape because in some way this solitude, as shaped by liberal consumer societies, is the very essence of the condition of modern adults and of modern adolescents? This is a strange paradox at century's end, where "communication" is the prevailing buzzword. The final volume of Demers's trilogy thus appears to carry a certain symbolic value: the convent represents both modern humanity's ineptitude for communication and the failure of language, rendered useless in any attempt at real communcation. But words—or, at least, the written word—have not completely lost their magic power. Indeed, letters play an essential role in the three volumes: letters from her mother to Marie-Lune, from Marie-Lune to her baby, from Sister Elisabeth to Marie-Lune. Letters often close the volumes. But each letter is a means of communicating with a distant figure. It is as though the only true conversation can be a deferred one; the only real encounter, one that is outside daily life, either above it or below, on the verge of unending silence. The mother's letters arrive only after her death; while alive, her relations with Marie-Lune were strained. Marie-Lune's letters to her baby are written before it is born, as she is deciding whether to put it up for adoption. She receives the letter from Elisabeth at a time when Elisabeth is taking a vow of perpetual silence, another form of death. These particular exchanges serve as a possible explanation for the vocation that takes shape toward the end of the third volume: writing as a means to salvation.

Curiously, writing as a vocation has spread like a virus among the characters in novels for adolescents. This is a theme that runs through Lucy Maud Montgomery's entire trilogy, one difference being that Emily of New Moon's writing opens up to the world. Emily cuts a narrative path that runs in the opposite direction to Marie-Lune's: starting from the solitude into which she descends following the death of her father, with whom she maintains a one-way correspondence, she develops a life where friendships and relationships proliferate. From this opposition emerge two antithetical concepts of writing: writing in order to name, grasp, and conquer the world in all its facets (the vision of Emily and Montgomery); and writing in order to withdraw more completely into oneself and capture the trembling of the endangered ego (which seems to be the vision of Marie-Lune and of Demers).

INITIATION IN THE NOVEL FOR ADOLESCENTS:
DEATH, SEXUALITY, AND THE SACRED

Each volume of the Marie-Lune trilogy corresponds more or less to one of the pivotal experiences that mark the heroine's adolescence and hallmark her passage from childhood to adulthood. The first volume deals with her first sexual discoveries and, at the same time, with the event that will turn her childhood upside down: her mother's death. The two experiences are inextricably linked. But one must inevitably conclude that all the modern therapies, family planning programs, and psychological aids are not enough to calm the anguish and despair of a young woman faced with the dual experience of death and motherhood; the final volume leads to the threshold of religion. Demers offers us a heroine who crumbles in the face of a simultaneous confrontation with death and sexuality before starting to put herself back together after her (at first antagonistic) encounter with the sacred.

According to Mircea Eliade, among the most important researchers of initiation rites: "In general, initiation comprises a triple revelation: the revelation of the sacred, death, and sexuality."[8] One might think that there is little in common between contemporary representations of adolescence and this so-called primitive mode of thought. In fact, the differences between the two are less striking than the consistencies. The image of the adolescent conveyed by literature for adolescents, and particularly by Demers's novels, has few differences from that reflected by the bildungsroman. It is as though generations of writers have been constantly reworking the image of an eternal adolescent affected by the triple experience of death, sexuality, and the sacred. Thus the paradox in Demers's trilogy is that novels aspiring to present a new image of the adolescent end up offering a representation of the adolescent in her most eternal aspects. Marie-Lune is certainly a possible representation of the eternal adolescent, incarnate in a young woman of the 1990s.[9] What changes is the manner in which the writer tackles the trilogy of death, sexuality, and the sacred, her manner of privileging one over the others. It may also be the manner in which the adolescent hero experiences the triple discovery socially—that is, at a given moment in the history of society.

Demers thus belongs to that generation of writers who, following most notably the example of the American Judy Blume, have chosen to speak openly to adolescents about sexuality, as well as about AIDS, suicide, and such. If an evolution has actually occurred, it is probably in this area.[10] Few novels for adolescents today neglect to describe the first sexual experience and its accompanying anguish. In some novels, one has to wonder whether this first experience does not become the essential goal of the young hero's quest.

Forbidden fruit varies with the seasons, and yesterday's taboos become today's morals. Thus, in the North American society of the 1990s, neither sexuality nor abortion is a taboo subject in the novel for adolescents. Quite the contrary. This is one reason why it seems that the novel for contemporary adolescents has very quickly created new stereotypes and imposed new conventions. Susie Morgenstern has written:

I am both worried and relieved when I read the books mentioned above. Relieved because they are good. . . . Worried because they all say the same thing. I can find analogies among practically all of my colleagues. We go ahead, rush in, rack our brains, do our best, hope and, without fail, say exactly what has already been said before. We can only conclude, along with the old wise man, that "There is nothing new under the sun."[11]

Therefore, the essence of Demers's originality does not lie in her depiction of what used to be taboo. Perhaps the value of her text lies in understanding that her heroine can escape despair and self-absorption only by confronting the spiritual. One of Judy Blume's heroines says that the teen years are, first and foremost, a story of pimples.[12] If that is so, then pimples will no longer do for Dominique Demers. The quest for the spiritual, this rupture, is the subject of *Ils dansent dans la tempête*. Although we may say (granting a few exceptions) that one of the new conventions of the novel for young people is the banishment of the religious and of religious morals, Demers seems to have guessed that a liberal consumer society and its egocentric materialism can never save her heroine. The salvation both of the author and of the work is as at stake.

Dominique Demers broaches the religious through the theme of death. Death is another stereotype in the novel for adolescents—death of the other, as well as the encounter with one's own death. Suicide is not a new idea. It has haunted the young heroes of literature since René and Werther. Marie-Lune, too, almost naturally, considers letting herself die.[13] This desire persists right up to the final chapters of the third volume.[14] But the religious is introduced through Sister Elisabeth, who cures

Marie-Lune of her sickness, as though only the emergence of the sacred could triumph over the dead, over death. Although the trilogy closes with this cure and the indication of conjugal happiness, it would nonetheless be untrue to say that Marie-Lune lives life to the fullest.

In her acceptance, Marie-Lune is still renouncing something. From this viewpoint, the novels seem quite ambiguous. Is Demers advocating a return to the moral values of a former time, the religious values that have been repudiated by writers for young people for quite some time? Oddly, the only truly positive character in the entire story—the only one to provide Marie-Lune with hope and an example to follow—is Elisabeth, she who embodies another world, living outside our society in a vow of silence and representing the moral and spiritual values of another age.

Are we therefore obliged to believe that parental models have failed, deserving only of rejection and disavowal? Strangely, this is not the case in Demers's novels, for it would be untrue to claim that Marie-Lune maligns her parents' way of life. The respective worldviews of Marie-Lune and the adults are not so different. The conflicts that emerge are far less intense and profound than those in which Montgomery's protagonist was involved. Marie-Lune never offers her own vision of the world or philosophy of existence in response to those of her parents and other adults. Hers in fact is indistinct from theirs. Her quest for happiness resembles that of her mother; the roles are virutally interchangeable. Marie-Lune quickly becomes her dead mother's reincarnation.

Emily, it seems, made more dangerous demands because she had dreams to realize. She was portrayed by the author as possessing the will to be her true self, without submitting to the Murray family's, and society's, vision of what kind of child she should be. She had the desire to fulfill her dream of becoming a writer, despite her Aunt Elisabeth's opposition. The conflicts between Emily and many of the adults in the trilogy were, in reality, conflicts between worldviews, among completely incompatible philosophies of existence. Furthermore, seen in the context of their time, Emily's demands were not far removed from those of the first feminists.

So it seems that in terms of worldviews and demands, a character like Emily is much more subversive than a Marie-Lune. But we must not overstate this difference, because Montgomery's novels do not take society to task in every aspect of life. Morals are respected, and the feminist demands of someone like Emily are only barely tolerated. Our heroine, as in the heyday of the bildungsroman, ends up rejoining the ranks and integrating perfectly into society. Thus does rebellion give way to submission.

CONCLUSION

Obviously, literature for young people has always projected values that society has wanted to see endure or evolve, and thus transmit. This is as true today as it was in the past, even though it seems less obvious. Now, as then, adults are the ones who create that literature. Whatever one may say, it is always an adult's representation of themselves that adolescents receive in the literature that is aimed at them. It is a vision of adolescence that the author chooses to assume and, through the author, the vision that society or part of society has assumed. A truly adolescent representation of adolescence would necessarily be written by young people. As well, it would have to avoid the clichés and commonplaces that often weigh it down despite the author's best intentions. Can this literature, caught between a moral and social vocation, on the one hand, and the need to please a targeted audience, on the other, be truly challenging? This remains to be seen.

Without denying that there has been an evolution in the novel for adolescents, we must realize that it is not as clear-cut as might be expected. Moreover, when we are dealing with series, the representation of adolescence has a tendency to produce a system of conventions and themes that quickly become stereotypes. The writing itself is not spared, what with fashion imposing a youthful and familiar style, one based on short sentences and parataxis. Indeed, everything is short in this novelistic genre: sentences, paragraphs, chapters, volumes. A large part of the current literary production for adolescents is running the risk of never exceeding the level or the shelf life of mass-market fiction. The mass-consumption novel cannot help but be reductive; what has been gained in terms of representation of the adolescent has been lost at the poetic, imaginative, and interpretive levels. Nevertheless, these series do fulfill a function because they relate intimately to the anguish and curiosity of their readers, and they are understood at the first reading. Hence their success.

The question that arises, then, concerns the representation of adolescence for adolescents. Do Marie-Lune's solitude, despair, and lack of vision signify that it is no longer possible to dream, to rebel? That the horizon has darkened to the point where the adolescent hero is condemned only to passivity or to withdrawal into the self?

If series of Québécois novels for adolescents follow U. S. trends, as has happened in the past, we are likely to see (as Anne Scott MacLeod has shown[15]) that the bleakness will be somewhat modified, stories will become more complex, protagonists will be less passive, and relationships between adults and adolescents will be reinstated on a new mode as boundaries between adults and youth evolve. This is good news, for young people should have access to as wide a range of representations of themselves as possible, and be encouraged to look for it in a great variety of texts and images.

NOTES

I gratefully acknowledge David Clarke's work on the translation.

1. In 1790, Madame Leprince de Beaumont published *Le Magasin des adolescents*. Starting in 1784, Arnaud Berquin edited a periodical, *L'Ami des adolescents*. See François Caradec, *Histoire de littérature enfantine en France* (Paris, Albin Michel, 1977), p. 23.

2. An examination of the series for adolescents in Quebec shows that many were established at the end of the 1980s: Boréal Inter (1989); novels for adolescents from Coïncidence Jeunesse (1989); Roman Plus from Courte Échelle; Échos from Héritage (1991).

3. It has often been said that *Le Dernier des raisins*, by Raymond Plante, was the first Québécois novel to speak about adolescents to adolescents. It was published by Québec/Amérique in 1986.

4. Dominique Demers, "Représentation et mythification de l'enfance dans la littérature jeunesse," (Ph.D. diss., Université de Sherbrooke, 1993), p. 343.

5. "Il m'a entourée de ses grands bras, et tout est redevenu comme avant" (*Un Hiver de tourmente*, p. 40); "On s'est embrassés longtemps. Et on est restés enlacés plus longtemps encore" (p. 57); "Je me suis blotti contre son corps. Il m'a serrée très fort" (p. 70); "Je ne l'ai pas laissée parler. Je l'ai embrassé. J'avais envie de me noyer dans ses bras" (p. 101).These are only a few examples.

6. John Row Townsend said, "The number of sub-Holden Caulfields who speak in the first person with the same tone defies calculation." Quoted in Susie Morgenstern, "400 milliards de Holden Caulfields," *Littérature pour la jeunesse—le roman, L'École des lettres* 1, no. 9 (May 1989): 81.

7. Judy Blume's novels are not without humor and irony, which helps us tolerate the navel-gazing attitude of most of her heroines. But does the *I* risk causing confusion, in the sense that we do not know whom we should credit for the irony: the character or her creator? Robert Cormier, on the other hand, makes more subtle choices, for he does not coddle his characters. And he can hardly be accused of being complacent toward his adolescent heroes. Sympathetic, perhaps, but never complacent.

8. Mircea Eliade, *Le Sacré et le profane* (Paris: Gallimard, 1965), p. 159.

9. The author openly admits this. While insisting upon the autobiographical dimension of the first volume, *Un Hiver de tourmente*, she speaks of the transposition of a story of her adolescence into the 1990s. When she discusses in her dissertation the series of novels by Plante that opens with *Le Dernier des raisins*, she calls our attention both to the autobiographical character of the novels and to the transposition from one context to another of a story which could have been set in a different era. In this regard, she lets us in on a confidence of Plante: "The adolescents of the 1980s were much like the adolescent I had been: the same fears, the same lack of self-assurance, the same desire to love and the fear of not being loved in return" ("Représentation et mythification," p. 281).

10. However, is the problem really one of knowing whether certain taboos are thus being broken and some prohibitions flouted? The way had been cleared by the media—television, radio, and the press—and novelists for adolescents simply responded to a demand, knowing full well that any scandal would entail no serious repercussions.

11. Morgenstern, "400 milliards de Holden Caulfields," p. 83.

12. Margaret, in *Dieu, tu es là? C'est moi, Margaret*: "Si vous voulez savoir, être adolescent, c'est tout à fait dégoûtant . . . entre les boutons et la peur de sentir mauvais" (p. 3). "Je me suis réveillée ce matin avec un bébé bouton éléphantesque sous le nez. Les boutons, c'est comme les embryons. Ça enfle tranquillement. Au début, notre face ne sait pas qu'elle est enceinte. Dans mon cas l'accouchement ne devrait pas tarder" (*Un Hiver de tourmente*, p. 31).

13. See chapter 12.

14. "Je veux mourir," she tells Sister Elisabeth in chapter 7 of the novel.

15. Anne Scott MacLeod, "The Journey Inward: Adolescent Literature in America, 1945–1995," in this volume.

REFERENCES

Belaval, Annie-France. "Pourquoi les adolescents devraient-ils lire?" *Lire avec les adolescents—L'École des lettres* 12–13 (June 1994): 9–19.

Caradec, François. *Histoire de la littérature enfantine en France*. Paris: Albin Michel, 1977.

Cowan, Ann S. "Canadian Writers: Lucy Maud and Emily Bird." In *L. M. Montgomery: An Assessment*. Ed. John Robert Sorfleet. Guelph, Ont.: Canadian Children's Press, 1976.

Demers, Dominique. *Un Hiver de tourmente*. Montreal: La Courte Échelle, 1992.

————. *Les Grands Sapins ne meurent pas*. Montreal: Éditions Québec/Amérique, 1993.

————. "Représentation et mythification de l'enfance dans la littérature jeunesse," Ph.D. diss., Université de Sherbrooke, 1993.

————. *Ils dansent dans la tempête*. Montreal: Editions Québec/Amérique, 1994.

Egoff, Sheila. "The Problem Novel." In *Only Connect: Readings on Children's Literature*. Ed. S. Egoff, G. T. Stubbs, and L. F. Ashley. 2nd ed. Toronto: Oxford University Press, 1980.

Eliade, Mircea. *Le Sacré et le profane*. Paris: Gallimard, 1965.

Labarrère, André. "Manuels à l'intention des parents et ouvrages à l'usage de la jeunesse au XIXe siècle." *Littérature pour la jeunesse—le roman, L'École des lettres* 1, no. 11 (May 1989): 15–24.

MacLulich, T. D. "L. M. Montgomery and the Literary Heroine: Jo, Rebecca, Anne, and Emily." *Canadian Children's Literature* 37 (1985): 5–17.

Madore, Edith. *La littérature pour la jeunesse au Québec*. Montreal: Éditions Boréal, 1994.

Martinoir, Francine de. "Livres pour enfants, littérature pour adolescents de Montaigne à nos jours. *Littérature pour la jeunesse—le roman, L'École des lettres* 1, no. 11 (May 1989): 25–35.

Merlet, Marie-Isabelle. "Les Collections pour adolescents." *Dossiers des actes de lecture*, no. 1: *Littérature enfantine*. Paris: Association Française pour la lecture, 1988.

Montgomery, Lucy Maud. *Emilie de la Nouvelle Lune*. Montreal: Pierre Tisseyre, 1983.

————. *Emilie de la Nouvelle Lune 2*. Montreal: Pierre Tisseyre, 1988.

————. *Emily's Quest*. Toronto: New Canadian Library, 1989.

Morgenstern, Susie. "400 milliards de Holden Caulfields." *Littérature pour la jeunesse—le roman, L'École des lettres* 1, no. 11 (May 1989): 79–84.

Soriano, Marc. *Guide de littérature pour la jeunesse*. Paris: Flammarion, 1975.

Tansky, Thomas E. "L. M. Montgomery and 'The Alpine Path, So Hard, So Steep.'" *Canadian Children's Literature* 30 (1983): 5–20.

Vérot, Marguerite. "Le Roman psychologique." In *Tendances actuelles de la littérature pour la jeunesse, 1960-1975*. Ed. Raoul Dubois. Paris: Éditions Magnard and Éditions de l'École, 1975.

17

Realistic Stories for Children in the Federal Republic of Germany, 1970–1994: Features and Tendencies

Dagmar Grenz

T he end of the 1960s and the beginning of the 1970s brought with it a decisive change in the children's literature published in the Federal Republic of Germany.[1] A wealth of new themes and motifs, together with a completely new form of writing, developed as a result of the influence of the student movement and its demands for socialistic or antiauthoritarian education. Childlike reality no longer appears as a social period of grace, that is free of social conflicts or in which, if conflicts do occur, they are solved by the children's morality.[2] Children's reality seems to be included far more in social reality and its contrasts. Peter Härtling, for example, in *Das war der Hirbel* (1973) demands of child readers that they deal with the problem of the fate of a mentally handicapped boy whose longing for security and a home is not fulfilled and who, against his will, is finally put in a closed institution. In *Wir pfeifen auf den Gurkenkönig* (1972), Christine Nöstlinger portrays the revolt of a middle-class family against the authoritarian father who is the only one blind enough to believe the lies and flattery of the Kumi-Ori king, who has been pursued by his discontented subjects.

Finally, the book by Ursula Wölfel, *Die grauen und die grünen Felder* (1970), relates the story of lower-class children, children of foreign workers, children in the Third World, and a handicapped boy. Here the children are the victims of poverty, repression, war, dictatorship, prejudices; they are the culprits in that when they stand on the side of the privileged, they take on the prejudices of the adults or they are learning them. It is also expected of the child readers that they recognize the social relationships they are shown in the short stories and that they be willing to help change the situation. Ursula Wölfel clearly expresses the social optimism of the time, which also places great hope in the children, in her foreword: "These stories are true . . . [they] show a world that is not always good, but that can be changed."[3]

The aim of children's literature of the early 1970s is for adolescents "to dismantle questionable authoritarian fixation and social prejudices, to develop their critical faculty . . . [and] to show the need to change social conditions . . . in the sense of humanization."[4] This only applies, however, to the "reforming" trend. The second direction, the socialist one, stems from the theory that the freeing of both adults and children can be achieved only in a socialist society; it wants to lead children to a class struggle. I do not wish to go into these books in detail, but only to say that they are of historical value. The above-mentioned titles from the early 1970s are still highly regarded by critics and are, moreover, read by children; one could almost say that they have become modern classics.

Even so, there is a certain historical distance to them. As students' reactions have shown, some young adults of today consider these books to be old-fashioned, less realistic, because they are too didactic—compared to books of the 1980s and 1990s, which obviously correspond more to the young adults' own concept of childhood and the world of children. This reception clearly shows the aging of even these texts and their historical dimension (despite their topical meaning for children today).

At the end of the 1970s and the beginning of the 1980s new changes were already taking place in German children's literature—even though these changes were less far-reaching than those of 1968–70. These changes have been described and evaluated differently.[5] With Maria Lypp, I would say that after the 1970s had balanced out the deficit of the outward depiction of the world, it is now the aim of children's books to discover the reality of the human inner self, and this, together with the use of new narrative techniques, makes the depiction of childlike subjectivity possible.[6] Social aspects have not necessarily vanished as a result of this; they have remained in the demands of the social environment on children.[7]

It is my intention, by means of the comparative analysis and interpretation of two realistic children's books, chosen exemplarily, to demonstrate the features and tendencies that are characteristic of children's literature of the 1970s and 1980s. The books chosen are of great importance in a receptive-historical context (in view of their resonance among critics, pedagogical agents, and children). For the 1970s I have chosen a children's book that shows individual transitional tendencies. I then analyze a children's book from the 1990s, asking whether new tendencies can be singled out in present-day children's literature. Since historical distance to the present time is missing, there can in no way be the claim of exemplary choice; the title chosen shows only *one* tendency, compared with, to some extent, contradictory tendencies in other children's books.

Peter Härtling's *Oma* (1975), awarded the German Prize for Youth Literature in 1976, and in its thirteenth edition in 1992, relates, as the subtitle says, "the story of Kalle, who loses his parents [in a car accident] and is taken in by his grandmother." The theme is not—as several students in my seminar, considering it from today's expectations, negatively remarked—Kalle's subjectivity, that is the way he gets over his parents' death. It is more about two different generations, grandson and grandmother, living together; the overcoming of the resulting conflicts; the growth of understanding between them; and their dealing with the reality in which they live.

The significance of the outward reality of the story is shown in the structure of the narrative. The narrated time is relatively long; it covers a period of five years from which individual episodes are taken. Besides the grandmother, Kalle, and their flat, there are numerous other figures and scenes; both main figures are portrayed in their social context. The narrative point of view makes possible not only the rendering of thoughts and feelings but also the portrayal of the world. At first the story is told by a mainly self-effacing omniscient narrator who often speaks from Kalle's point of view; at the end of these chapters there is an interior monologue in which the events are seen from the grandmother's point of view in a first-person narrative.

The boy is a self-confident figure: having no problems with reality, able to assert himself, critical, able to deal with conflict, popular with his peers. He overcomes the difficulties with which he is confronted; that he sometimes cries is presented as being quite natural, and is not gone into deeply.

As the boy's new person of reference, the grandmother takes responsibility for her grandson as a matter of course. She gives him a stable emotional relationship in which he finds security, clear orientation, and the possibility of dealing with conflicts. The grandmother is conceived as a mixed character. In spite of being an ingenious woman, she has fears, weaknesses, and failings that the reader is shown through the action and, above all, through the interior monologues. The child reader is given an insight into the inner thoughts of an adult, her insecurities and imperfections, and into the difference between her inner conversations and her outward speech and attitude. This lessens the hierarchy between adult and child, and a more symmetrical relationship is achieved between them.

The grandmother has a further important function within the story. Through her—a woman with her heart in the right place, who has never belonged to the socially privileged and, against social conventions, openly expresses her opinions—the world is explained to Kalle and also to the child readers. Determined by the sociocritical perspectives of the early 1970s, which were aimed at change, the grandmother stands up for tolerance and peace, she defends herself against bureaucracy and interference by the state, and sides with the socially deprived. This occurs in situations or through situation-related comments that are full of humor and that combine recognition with laughter in the reader. The reality is recognizable; despite all difficulties, it can be overcome and, according to sociocritical perspectives, changed. Here realism joins with a final optimistic social perspective.

Although it is a characteristic children's book of the early 1970s, *Oma* also contains tendencies of later children's literature or indicates them:

1. The portrayal of a two-person family, which foreshadows the increasing disintegration of the middle-class nuclear family seen in subsequent children's books
2. The theme of dying and death, which later, against social progressive optimism, places the limitations of people as natural beings in the limelight[8]
3. The insight into the hitherto inaccessible inner life of the adult person of reference and his/her imperfections;[9]
4. The multilayered effect of the narrative perspective, which replaces the traditional omniscient narration or a narrative in the first person, in which the narrating "I" looks back at the experiencing self from a safe distance.[10]

Sonntagskind, by Gudrun Mebs (1983), awarded the German Prize for Youth Literature in 1984 and in its eleventh edition in 1994,[11] portrays an orphan who wishes for "Sunday parents" who will take her to their home. She gets a Sunday mother, and an emotional relationship develops between the two of them within a few weeks. Finally the Sunday mother takes the child on a trial adoption.

The theme of *Sonntagskind* is the child's yearning for love and the fulfillment of this longing through a feeling, loving adult. To be loved for her own sake appears ato be the central necessity of the child, something on which she is existentially dependent. Whereas in *Oma* the relationship between grandmother and grandson is given without question, *Sonntagskind* goes back to the early childhood process of developing the ability to relate or makes up for it in retrospect. Thus the narrative penetrates to deeper psychological levels than *Oma*.

The central point of the book is the child's subjectivity. The world is reduced to only a few scenes and a few exemplary constellations of figures that represent the child's old and new areas of reference. The social context has almost completely been left out. The narrated time covers only five weeks, and of this period, the six Sundays are depicted above all else. The narrative perspective breaks new ground in children's literature.[12] The story is told in the first person, which is a mixture of interior monologue and the portrayal of external elements of action that are embedded in the interior monologue. The innermost thoughts have precedence over what happens outwardly, and the distance between the experiencing and the narrating "I" or the reflecting "I" is very small. There is no concurrence between thoughts and feelings and what appears in the child's utterances in the outside world; the manifold inner speech often confronts the outer speechlessness. Even children, as this book shows, have innermost thoughts that they do not reveal.

The strongly emotional effect of the book lies in the fact that it is directed at empathy and emotion via identification with the child. It addresses in every reader—child as well as adult—the vulnerable, hurt, helpless child who wishes to be loved for his or her own sake. In my opinion, the narrative is indebted to the works of Alice Miller, who influenced educational thought in Germany at the beginning of the 1980s.[13] In place of the desired changes in the social structure came the demand for a loving, empathic relationship between the adult and the child. Only when "adults are aware of their power and 'support' (DeMause) the children, the weak, dependents, and sympathetically help them,"[14] instead of using them for their narcissistic requirements, can the children develop their "real selves"[15] and not need, as adults, to misuse other people. This, in its turn, affects the social level. When children are loved for their own sake, they no longer need to be "reared"; they develop on their own into independent, loving, social beings—as the development of Sunday's Child shows.[16]

The concept of realism in storytelling combines here with the portrayal of a model therapeutic process of emotional growth; from this process, some steps are named, and others are faded out (resistance and transference, which interrupt the growth process—especially with an eight-year-old girl who has always lived in an institution and has never known her parents). The happy ending, however, which is almost like a fairy tale,[17] certainly belongs to the therapeutic model as an optimistic view. The story really touches on the fairy tale: seen from a deeper psychological stand-point, the fairy tale is the symbolic depiction of what is happening in the inner soul; it deals with the maturing process of the child or adult at the end of which, after a phase of suffering or overcoming danger, comes attainment of a new phase of development. As in the fairy tale, which reduces figures and the portrayal of the world to a few elements, so there is in *Sonntagskind*—within the generic requirements of realistic storytelling—a reduction of the world to the elementary theme of yearning for love and the fulfillment of love. In this connection it is significant that the child remains nameless to the end, given the name Sunday's Child (comparable with Lucky Hans or Tom Thumb), and its origin remains uncertain. Like the derided Cinderella or the youngest and most stupid of three brothers, the child is finally raised above her institution brothers and sisters: she not only has a Sunday mother but also is adopted—by a woman who (as in a fairy tale) chose the child without having seen her.

Pischmarie, by Dagmar Chidolue (hardback, 1990; paperback, 1994), has until now been far less successful than *Oma* and *Sonntagskind*. In my opinion, it represents a further development of the tendencies of children's literature, and at the same time it is a reflection of the child's reality today.

Pischmarie is the story of a child who has become conspicuous through her behavior. The story tells of Marie, who, although she is ten years old, still wets her bed and her underpants. Later there is even excrement in her underpants. Even so, it is not Marie who is referred to as being difficult but the environment, to whose lovelessness and lack of understanding she is reacting. Neither her father nor her grandfather has come to terms with the death of her mother, who was killed in a car accident, even though years have gone by; they try to overlook Marie, who reminds them of her mother, as if they could extinguish the past. For her father, Marie exists only when she is a problem, that is when she wets her underpants.

The theme is partly—as with *Sonntagskind*—the child's dependence on love and her helplessness, loneliness, and mutism when she does not get this love. Whereas Sunday's Child has the power to yearn, Marie—due to the stiffness and hardening of her environment—has herself grown stiff. The object of her yearning love is her father with whom she lives; because he ignores her or sees her only as a foe, her wishes lose direction. All that remains for Marie are compensatory dreams and fantasies, which take her even further from reality and more into her problem, wetting herself.

The theme of *Pischmarie* is not only the child but also the adults. The adults are, it seems, very disturbed, and have problems even when they hide their helplessness—as the grandfather and, above all, the father do—behind an authoritarian claim to power. And the loving, understanding grandmother, "the only intact thing in Marie's surroundings,"[18] can, with respect to the situation, only soothe and console; she cannot change Marie's life. The book goes one step further than *Sonntagskind* in that *Pischmarie* sees the child only as a link (the weakest) within the family system; it takes as its central theme—obviously influenced by the increasing importance of systemic forms of therapy—the way the child is at the mercy of adults who cannot adequately deal with themselves or with reality, and are, therefore, not able to treat the child with empathy.

Unlike *Sonntagskind*, there is no fairy-tale solution to the conflict. A change for the better occurs only slowly and laboriously for Marie. That one day she will no longer wet herself appears to be more a possibility than a reality on the level of the narrated present, and only in that the people around her change a little and that she herself receives help from outside. The reason for the beginning of the change is the psychological and physical breakdown of Clara, the father's new wife, through whom movement comes into the stiffened family. After Marie, she is the second weakest link in the family: an adult who impresses Marie as being helpless and afraid, like a child. Marie, who up to this point has pulled away from her stepmother's display of love, realizes that she likes Clara and slowly begins to build a relationship with her; she perceives that her father is anxious about Clara, who is seriously ill, and feels affection for him as a result; and she accepts Clara's offer to seek psychotherapeutic help from a doctor. The father, obviously influenced by Clara, no longer reacts so hysterically when Marie wets herself; Marie, on the other hand, learns to be less afraid of him.[19]

Corresponding to the subject matter, the portrayed extract from reality is greater in *Pischmarie* than in *Sonntagskind* and—relative to the constellation of figures, scenes, and conflicts—more varied. The central scene and core of the conflict, however, remains the family. The story is told in the third person from a self-effacing point of view focusing on the child. It combines elements of external action, dialogues, substitutionary narration, and accounts of Marie's thoughts. Marie's speechlessness is greater than that of Sunday's Child. It is often said that words fail her when she needs to think further. She has not been able to build up a differentiated inner world or differentiated inner speech.

It is important that there are no narrator's commentaries that would make the adults' disturbed behavior visible. Besides the view of Marie, who is not able to appraise but reacts with feelings, perceptions, pictures, or muteness, there is, however, that of the loving, ingenious grandmother, through whose comments or actions the behavior of the figures is either directly or indirectly judged, and thus put into its true light. Even so, the relations here are more difficult for the child reader to understand than in *Sonntagskind*, where the narrative mode is aimed at identification from the child's point of view, or in Härtling's *Oma*, where the grandmother, as one of the two main figures, is present in every scene and where, therefore, everything that happens can be interpreted through her reactions; the grandmother in *Pischmarie* does not have such an important function. Added to this is the fact that Marie, from whose point of view the story is told, is uncertain in her perception of reality; when she feels threatened by her grandparents' constant quarrels, the child readers must irritatedly ask themselves to what extent the grandmother can be regarded as a reliable judgemental authority. Only on a parallel with Marie can the child readers recognize that the grandparents' quarrels are more a ritual, something completely different from the father's outbursts of rage against Marie.

The child readers are burdened with many uncertainties in *Pischmarie*. A complex reality is presented to them in which the child protagonist suffers and in which, to some extent, the adults have neither a guiding function nor emotional reliability; they are massively entangled in their own problems. Or there are (female) adults who are caring and loving, but who as individuals cannot effectively help because the relationships are too complicated or because they are too weak or are also disturbed. Finally, active participation is demanded of the child readers in the interpretation of the portrayed reality, especially the mode of behavior of the adult figures. To a certain extent, the child readers have to find significance on their own.

The interpretation of reality that the book supplies—changes occur only when each individual within the system changes—seems to me to be more pluralistic and less of an ideal than the sociocritical perspective in *Oma* or the empathic sympathy perspective in *Sonntagskind*. *Pischmarie* sides with no one and nothing, and it does not ask anyone to take sides. Nor does it employ interpretive patterns, such as strategies aimed at evoking laughter or emotion. On the whole, the stance adopted is rather skeptical.

Pischmarie is, in my opinion, a radical expression of the advanced social processes of individualization and pluralization that have taken hold of children's lives and are more and more embedded in children's books—this has long been the case in adolescent novels that have as their central theme the adolescent as a problematic individual. The adults in *Pischmarie* and other children's books appear helpless and powerless.[20] They are burdened with their own problems and are no longer able to listen enough to their children. At certain points, help or a partial solution is found by the children, often independent of the parents, through the support of other figures. The children themselves do not live either socially or mentally in a different space than the adults. They are no longer naive and uncomplicated; they are problematic individuals: they suffer, they are lonely, and they are often alone. The depiction of their inner selves occupies a broader space.

These children are no longer written of in simple stories. The narrating techniques have become more complex; literary forms of the psychological novels from the end of the nineteenth century and the beginning of the twentieth century have been taken on (experienced speech, interior monologues, a shifting from external action in favor of inner action, the questioning of whether reality can be explained and controlled). This literature is not as easy to read; it is now presumed that young readers are interested in literature. In addition, these children's books have only a low evasive character; it is no longer a matter of compensatory playful escape from childlike reality, but of dealing with the everyday world.[21]

The process of individualization in children's books began with the differentiation of the childlike inner views and the loneliness of the child in *Sonntagskind*. One can, however, go one step further back. If one follows Hans-Heino Ewers—who, using a modernization theoretical approach, deals with children's literature from the eighteenth century to the present day—it would seem that not only children's literature of the 1980s, but also literature of the 1970s, is part of a modernization push that covers childhood and children's literature from the end of the 1960s.[22] The child is now placed principally on the same level as the adult. Whereby literature of the early 1970s emphasized the clarification of social connections and suppressive mechanisms, children's literature has, since the 1980s, shown the appearance of the "modern subjectivity problematic"[23]; now childlike subjectivity is no longer fundamentally different from that of the adult.

What a further development of the tendency to advanced individualization can look like is shown in the children's book *Wehr dich Mathilda* by Annika Holm (Swedish 1993; German 1994). The child's loneliness appears here in a different form: the child withdraws from her *loving* parents even though she suffers. This book, however, also shows the positive side of individualization, the early independence and new self-confidence of the child.

There is, however, a children's literary anti-tendency toward this progressive individualization. The child is portrayed in a loving, intact family with traditional family roles, with close connections to her mother, living in a world that is reduced to a few figures and a single conflict, and, supported by her parents, she carries out an important, painful step in the development of her personality.[24] The end of *Sonntagskind*—the feeling of being loved—is the start situation of the story, and thus the potential for conflict is eased from the outset. Here, the environment of today's children seems to be an idyll.

Other children's books have modern family relationships as their main topic, for example, a child and her single mother who is a student.[25] The inconsistencies of the everyday world are treated in a playful, comical way, and serious conflicts always resolve themselves. Individualization is portrayed as something that, for the child herself, is not problematic. The humor results partly from the inconsistencies between a childlike lack of prejudice and the traditional adult view; it contains the functions to legitimize and also to partly gloss over the results of modernization.

Are, therefore, humor and idealization the anti-tendencies to the advanced individualization in contemporary children's books? I believe that by 2005, we will be able to see more clearly, and thus better classify the tendencies of children's literature of today.

NOTES

1. I will deal with realistic stories for children (not for young people) that were published in the Federal Republic of Germany (translations included).

2. See. Peter Scheiner, "Realistische Kinder- und Jugendliteratur," in *Kinder- und Jugendliteratur: Ein Handbuch*, ed. Gerhard Haas, 3rd, rev. ed. (Stuttgart: Reclam, 1984), p. 40.

3. Ursula Wölfel, foreword to *Die grauen und die grünen Felder* (Mülheim/Ruhr: Anrich, 1970).

4. Detlev Ram, "Antiautoritäre Kinder- und Jugendliteratur," In *Lexikon der Kinder- und Jugendliteratur*, ed. Klaus Doderer, vol. 1 (Weinheim and Basel: Beltz, 1975), p. 47.

5. See, for example, Winfried Kaminski, "Vom realistischen zum phantastischen Helden. Aspekte des Wandels in der Kinder- und Jugendliteratur seit 1968," in *Neue Helden in der Kinder- und Jugendliteratur*, ed. Klaus Doderer (Weinheim and Munich: Juventa, 1986), pp. 29–30; and Hans-Heino Ewers, "Themen-, Formen- und Funktionswandel der westdeutschen Kinderliteratur seit Ende der 60er, Anfang der 70er Jahre," in *Germanistik* n.s. 2 (1995): 257–278.

6. Maria Lypp, "Der Blick ins Innere. Menschendarstellung im Kinderbuch," *Grundschule* 1 (1989): 24. See also Wilhelm Steffens, "Literarische und didaktische Aspekte des modernen Kinderbuchs," *Die Grundschulzeitschrift* 39 (1990): 30–34, and 40 (1990): 28–35.

7. Bettina Hurrelmann, "Aktuelle Kinder- und Jugendliteratur," *Praxis Deutsch: Aktuelle Kinder- und Jugendliteratur* 111 (1992): 1.

8. See. Kaminski, "Vom realistischen zum phantastischen Helden," pp. 29–30.

9. See Lypp, "Der Blick," p. 26.

10. See Steffens, "Literarische und didaktische Aspekte."

11. It was a radio play in 1986 (see Steffens, "Literarische und didaktische Aspekte," pt. 2, pp. 29, 31).

12. See Steffens, "Literarische und didaktische Aspekte," pt. 2.

13. For example, Alice Miller, *Das Drama des begabten Kindes und die Suche Sach dem wahren Selbst* [The Drama of the Gifted Child and the Search for the Real Self] (Frankfurt: Suhrkamp, 1979); and *Am Anfang war Erziehung* [In the Beginning was Education] (Frankfurt: Suhrkamp, 1980).

14. Quoted in Heidi Gidion, "Gelobt sei, was mitfühlend macht. Über Alice Miller: Am Anfang war Erziehung," *Neue Sammlung* 21 (1981): 164.

15. See Steffens, "Literarische und didaktische Aspekte," pt. 2.

16. In this way Sunday's Child trusts herself to emerge from her withdrawnness and to speak about herself; she trusts herself to show negative feelings such as jealousy, and claims of ownership; and finally, as the child feels secure in the love of the new mother, she gains the ability to share this love with Karli, whom the child previously despised because of his weakness.

17. Here I differ with Reinbert Tabbert, "Ein 'Sonntagskind' als Alltagsheldin? Anmerkungen zu deutschen Kinderbüchern des Jahrgangs 1983," in *Neue Helden*, ed. Klaus Doderer (Weinheim and Munich: Juventa, 1986), especially p. 71. Tabbert was the first to recognize the significance of *Sonntagskind*.

18. Dagmar Chidolue, *Pischmarie* (Hamburg: Dressler, 1990), p. 20.

19. Nor is Marie as helpless as she was in conflicts between the adults. The adults show their helplessness more openly, and Marie can recognize it instead of feeling a victim of them (see Chidolue, *Pischmarie*, p. 107; cf. pp. 22 and 81).

20. See, for example, Mirjam Pressler, *Nickel Vogelpfeifer* (Weinheim and Basel: Beltz & Gelberg, 1986); Dagmar Chidolue, *Ponzl guckt schon wieder* (Weinheim and Basel: Beltz & Gelberg, 1988); Kirsten Boie, *Mit Kindern redet ja keiner* (Hamburg: Oetinger, 1990); Peter Härtling: *Lena auf dem Dach* (Weinheim/Basel: Beltz & Gelberg, 1993); Tormod Haugen's *Die Nachtvögel* (Zurich and Cologne: Benziger, 1978) and *Nattfuglene* (Oslo: Gyldendal Norsk Forlag, 1973) portrayed the child's involvment in his parents' problems, his loneliness, and his inner views very early.

21. See Ewers, "Themenwandel," p. 268.

22. See Ewers, "Themenwandel."

23. Ibid., p. 263.

24. For example, love for an animal and insight into the necessity of separation in Benno Pludra's *Siebenstorch* (Berlin: Der Kinderbuchverlag, 1991) or love for a classmate and the overcoming of the pain of separation in Gudrun Mebs's *Der Mond wird dick und wieder dünn* (Aarau: Sauerländer, 1991).

25. See, for example, Kirsten Boie, *Nella-Propella* (Hamburg: Oetinger, 1994).

REFERENCES

Boie, Kirsten. *Mit Kindern redet ja keiner* [No One Speaks to Children]. Hamburg: Oetinger, 1990.

———. *Ich ganz cool* [Me, Really Cool]. Hamburg: Oetinger, 1992.

———. *Nella-Propella*. Hamburg: Oetinger, 1994.

Chidolue, Dagmar. *Ponzl guckt schon wieder* [Ponzl Is Looking Again]. Weinheim and Basel: Beltz & Gelberg, 1988.

———. *Pischmarie* (Marie the Girl Who Wets Herself). Hamburg: Dressler, 1990.

Ewers, Hans-Heino. "Themen-, Formen- und Funktionswandel der westdeutschen Kinderliteratur seit Ende der 60er, Anfang der 70er Jahre." *Germanistik* n.s. 2 (1995): 257–278.

Gidion, Heidi. "Gelobt sei, was mitfühlend macht. Über Alice Miller: Am Anfang war Erziehung." *Neue Sammlung* 21 (1981): 158–165.

Härtling, Peter. *Das war der Hirbel* [That Was Hirbel]. *Wie Hirbel ins Heim kam, warum er anders ist als andere und ob ihm zu helfen ist.* Weinheim and Basel: Beltz & Gelberg 1973.

———. *Oma* [Grandmother]. *Die Geschichte von Kalle, der seine Eltern verliert und von seiner Großmutter aufgenommen wird.* Weinheim and Basel: Beltz & Gelberg, 1975.

———. *Oma*. HarperCollins, 1977.

———. *Lena auf dem Dach* [Lena on the Roof]. *Die Geschichte von Lena und Lars, die ihren Eltern helfen wollten, Eltern zu sein und dabei entdecken, daß Eltern auch nur Menschen sind.* Weinheim and Basel: Beltz & Gelberg, 1993.

Haugen, Tormod. *Nattfuglene*. Oslo: Gyldendal Norsk Forlag, 1975.

———. *Die Nachtvögel* [The Nightbirds]. Zurich and Cologne: Benziger, 1978.

———. *Nightbirds*. HarperCollins 1985.

Holm, Annika. *Mod, Matilda Markström!* Stockholm: Rabén & Sjögren, 1993.

———. *Wehr dich, Mathilda!* [Defend Yourself, Mathilda!]. *Eine Geschichte aus der Schule.* Munich and Vienna: Hanser, 1994.

Hurrelmann, Bettina. "Aktuelle Kinder- und Jugendliteratur." *Praxis Deutsch: Aktuelle Kinder- und Jugendliteratur* 111 (1992): 9–18.

Kaminski, Winfred. "Vom realistischen zum phantastischen Helden. Aspekte des Wandels in der Kinder- und Jugendliteratur seit 1968." In *Neue Helden in der Kinder- und Jugendliteratur.* Ed. Klaus Doderer. Weinheim and Munich: Juventa, 1986.

Lypp, Maria. "Der Blick ins Innere. Menschendarstellung im Kinderbuch." *Grundschule* 1 (1989): 24–27.

Mebs, Gudrun. *Sonntagskind* [Sunday's Child]. Aarau: Sauerländer, 1983.

———. *Sunday's Child*. New York: Dutton 1986.

———. *Der Mond wird dick und wieder dünn* [The Moon Will Be Full and Then Thin Again]. Aarau: Sauerländer, 1991.

Miller, Alice. *Das Drama des begabten Kindes und die Suche nach dem wahren Selbst.* Frankfurt: Suhrkamp, 1979.

———. *Am Anfang war Erziehung*. Frankfurt: Suhrkamp, 1980.

Nöstlinger, Christine. *Wir pfeifen auf den Gurkenkönig* [We Don't Care a Rap for the Cucumber King]. *Wolfgang Hogelmann erzählt die Wahrheit, ohne auf die Deutschlehrergliederung zu verzichten.* Weinheim and Basel: Beltz & Gelberg, 1972.

———. *Cucumber King*. New York: Dutton, 1985.

Pludra, Benno. *Siebenstorch* [Seven Storks]. Berlin: Der Kinderbuchverlag, 1991.

Pressler, Mirjam. *Nickel Vogelpfeifer* [Nickel Bird Whistler]. Weinheim and Basel: Beltz & Gelberg, 1986.

Scheiner, Peter. "Realistische Kinder- und Jugendliteratur." In *Kinder- und Jugendliteratur. Ein Handbuch*. Ed. Gerhard Haas. 3rd, rev. ed. Stuttgart: Reclam, 1984.

Steffens, Wilhelm. "Literarische und didaktische Aspekte des modernen Kinderbuchs." *Die Grundschulzeitschrift* 39 (1990): 30–34, and 40 (1990): 28–35.

Tabbert, Reinbert: "Ein 'Sonntagskind' als Alltagsheldin? Anmerkungen zu deutschen Kinderbüchern des Jahrgangs 1983." In *Neue Helden in der Kinder- und Jugendliteratur*. Ed. Klaus Doderer. Weinheim and Munich: Juventa, 1986.

Timm, Uwe. *Rennschwein Rudi Rüssel* [Racing Pig Rudi Rüssel]. Zurich: Nagel & Kimche, 1989.

Wölfel, Ursula. *Die grauen und die grünen Felder* [The Gray Fields and the Green Ones]. Mühlheim/Ruhr: Anrich, 1970.

18

Text and Context: Factors in the Development of Children's Literature in Taiwan, 1945–1995, and the Emergence of Young Adult Literature

Shu-Jy Duan

C hildren's literature reflects or transcribes the social life and cultural values in a given society, especially its prevailing notions about childhood and the changing sociocultural conditions of children's lives. As might be expected, the development of children's literature in Taiwan since 1945 has been profoundly affected by the country's complex social, political, and economical history. I will examine the factors that have shaped the evolution of children's literature in Taiwan during this period, and will end with an account of how the emergence of young adult literature has been both impeded and encouraged. My primary concern is how children's literature, especially young adult fiction, has reflected changes in social ideology and, ultimately, has fulfilled its social functions in Taiwan.

HISTORICAL DEVELOPMENT OF CHILDREN'S LITERATURE IN TAIWAN

The development of children's literature is generally an index of economic activities, and children's literature usually develops only with economic prosperity. This is only partly the case with Taiwan, however. The children's book industry began to flourish with the economic prosperity of the 1960s but did not keep abreast of the economic progress of the 1970s and 1980s; in fact, it remained in an almost static state during those two decades.[1]

Due to historical and geographical causes, the development of children's literature in Taiwan since 1945 has been an interaction among three forces: the Chinese mainland culture (brought by the Central Government to Taiwan in 1949), the indigenous culture in Taiwan (Taiwanese, aboriginal, and Hakka), and foreign powers (especially the United States and Japan). The fifty years (1945–1995) of evolution of children's literature in Taiwan can be divided into five phases, corresponding to economic, political, and social developments.[2] The first four stages were defined by Wen-chiung Hong; a fifth stage can now be identified.

Stage I (1945–1963): Stagnation

In 1945, Taiwan was returned to China after fifty years as a Japanese colony. In 1949, the Central Government moved to Taiwan after losing the mainland to the Communists. The government, the new ruling class in Taiwan, sought to establish its social/political/cultural hegemony by suppressing Japanese culture and advocating the Chinese mainland culture. To entrench its ruling status, the government adopted Mandarin Chinese as the official language, wiping out Japanese, Taiwanese, and other local dialects. The promotion of children's literature was viewed as a convenient tool for inculcating Mandarin Chinese.

Children's literature in Taiwan began when the Eastern Publishing Company was established in Taipei in 1945, to publish books for children. In 1948, under the auspices of the Committee for Promoting Mandarin Chinese, *The Mandarin Daily Newspaper* was founded to produce easy readers in large print and with Chinese phonetics. In 1949, a weekly column for children was begun in the government-funded *The Central Daily Newspaper*. In 1951, the Bureau of Education sponsored *The Primary School Student Semimonthly* (for grades 3–6), and in 1953 *The Primary School Student Pictorial Semimonthly* (for K–2), to promote Mandarin Chinese and literacy simultaneously.[3] Thus the government intervened strongly in the development of children's literature in its initial stage. The genres represented in these books were poetry, nursery rhymes, folktales, myths, and didactic narratives, mostly taken from Chinese classics and folklore.

Stage II (1964–1970): Sprouting

After the initial promotion of children's literature by the government, foreign powers began to exercise their influence in Taiwan. The United States and Japan are the two major foreign powers to shape the history of Taiwan since the 1950s. Western culture, represented by the United States, appeared when the Editorial Task Force for Children's Books was set up in 1964 by the Bureau of Education with funding from UNESCO.[4] Experts from the United States improved techniques in the typesetting, formatting, printing, illustration, and writing of children's books. The impact of Japan was to come later.

In 1968, nine-year compulsory education was mandated: six years of primary school and three years of junior high school. Children's literature was incorporated into textbooks to upgrade literacy. In 1965, *The Mandarin Daily Newspaper* published translations of world masterpieces, introducing foreign (mainly American) children's literature. The staple works of children's literature in this stage were folktales, usually retellings from Chinese folklore, or translations from foreign sources. There were also realistic stories dealing with everyday situations, laden with heavy doses of moral didacticism.

Stage III (1971–1979): Growth

Although in this period Taiwan became increasingly isolated diplomatically, the economy boomed and there was a strong demand for children's literature. In 1971, the Primary School Teachers Training Center instituted a children's literature workshop for primary school teachers. This governmental linking of children's literature with primary education accounts for early writers of children's literature in Taiwan being mainly primary school teachers.[5] The official forces that had shaped children's literature were now gradually superseded by large private enterprises. The Hong Chia Chon Group not only began publishing children's books and funded (from 1974) prizes for children's literature. This stimulated a torrent of children's books.

In isolation from the international community, indigenous cultures began to have their voices heard. The call for local color gathered force. Children's literature began to cultivate the native soil instead of transplanting foreign materials or Chinese traditional literature. This self-conscious provincialism was the foundation of realism. The mainstream in this stage was poetry, pioneered by Chi-po Huang, who directed his class of primary school students to write poetry dealing with their daily lives.

Stage IV (1980–1990): Blooming

Generally speaking, the volume of children's books published reflects demand in a society. Given that, it is no wonder that children's literature in Taiwan did not bloom until the 1980s. Around 1980, the GNP in Taiwan exceeded U.S.$2,000. Due to a high percentage of working mothers, day-care centers and kindergartens increased rapidly. In the double-income family, cultural spending became a stable expenditure. Children's welfare was a high priority, and affluent parents spent money on their children: everything relevant to children, including publishing, was lucrative.

Trends in children's literature in this decade were influenced by three elements in the sociopolitical context. First, the readership of children's literature was enlarged and differentiated. Historically, children's literature before the 1980s had aimed at readers in middle childhood (primary school students). In the late 1980s, different readerships began to be identified within the broadly conceived body of children's literature: middle childhood became the pivot between early childhood readers (preschoolers) and the late childhood audience (young adults). Preschoolers became the main consumers of children's literature in the late 1980s. This can be accounted for by the educational system in Taiwan. After the nine years of compulsory education, junior high school graduates take tests for entry to the senior high schools. Three years later, the senior high school graduates take tests for entry to college. Only the preschoolers are exempt from the pressure of examinations. It is no wonder that there was a prevalence of books and magazines for young children, designed to construct intelligence and mold personality. This lucrative market attracted both major publishers and important writers and illustrators of children's books. Literature for preschoolers became *the* representative of children's literature in Taiwan.

Second, the children's literature publishing industry became a battlefield for large private enterprises. The government virtually withdrew, and offered the field to private publishing companies, such as the Eastern Publishing Company, the Hong Chia Chon Cultural Foundation, and the Hsin I Preschool Education Foundation. The common practice was to set up literary prizes for children's literature to attract writers and illustrators, and publish the winners and runners-up. There was also an active market in monthly and weekly magazines for children, and a torrent of children's newspapers, beginning with the release of *The Children's Daily Newspaper* by the Kwang Fu Book Company in 1988. Even foreign powers such as Japan wished to have, and successfully had, a share of the market for children's magazines in Taiwan. The impact of Japan was first visible in 1954, when Shiue-Iou magazine included comic strips. In 1989 *The Little Friend Monthly*, for preschoolers, was released jointly with the Fukutake Bookstore in Japan. Its editing formats and marketing strategies had a lot to teach its counterparts in Taiwan.

Third, there appeared a deluge of Chinese translations of foreign children's books, as local publishers purchased copyrights from well-known foreign publishers, mainly in the United States and Japan. This practice flows from the size of the market for children's books: the major consumers are preschoolers and primary school students, who number only about 2.2 million.[6] The small market and modest prices for children's books compelled publishers to limit their costs. To ensure profits, local publishers sought to translate or adapt foreign children's books, or to retell traditional literature. Translations, adaptations, and retellings constituted about 70 percent of the annual output. The remaining 30 percent was produced by local writers.[7] The practice of more re-creation (translation, adaptation, or retelling) than creation was normal and seemed inevitable for a developing children's literature.

Stage V (since 1990): Intertwining

The development of children's literature in Taiwan since 1945 has been an interaction among Chinese mainland culture, the indigenous cultures in Taiwan, and foreign influences. As a result of political, social, and economic developments in Taiwan and around the world in the early 1990s, these three forces are now intertwining.

With the lifting of martial law in Taiwan in 1987, communication with mainland China was resumed, and writers and illustrators in China became the rising stars of the publishing industry in Taiwan. *The Comicbook Chinese History*, published in Taiwan in 1989 by the Kwang Fu Book Company, was wholly created by writers and illustrators in China. It is common to find a children's book written by a Taiwanese writer and illustrated by an artist from China, or vice versa. For instance, *Reminiscences of Beijing* (1994) was a joint venture of Hai-yin Lin, a respected writer in Taiwan, and Weixing Guan, a celebrated artist in China. Several authors from China have become best-selling writers in Taiwan. Shih-shi Shen's animal fiction, Wen-shiuan Tsau's realistic fiction, and Chih-lu Chang's fantasy are popular with young readers in Taiwan. Writers from Taiwan have won prizes for children's literature in China. The Research Society of Children's Literature for the Two Sides of the Taiwan Strait was set up in 1992 as a result of increasingly intimate dialogue.

Recent years have witnessed a trend towards internationalization of children's books in Taiwan. The Frankfurt Book Fair, the Bologna Book Fair, and the Biennale of Illustrations Bratislava (BIB) have become the major sources of foreign copyrights for local publishers. Japan and the United States are no longer dominant; Europe is the favorite. The introduction of foreign masterpieces for children widens our worldview and stimulates the creativity of local writers and illustrators.

In addition to importing foreign children's books into Taiwan, several publishers export books produced in Taiwan. Yuan Liou Publishing Company released *The Seven Brothers*, *The Chinese Zodiac*, and *The Mouse Bride* in Chinese–English bilingual versions. These beautifully illustrated picture books of Chinese folktales have found an international audience. The Grimm Press is another adventurous publisher, leading the way in internationalizing picture books in Taiwan with works that are collaborations between writers and artists from all over the world. *Modern Fairy Tales* (1994), *Illustrated Short Story Masterpieces* (1995), and *The Illustrated Shakespeare* (1996) are written in Chinese (either as original creations or as adaptations from foreign sources) and illustrated by artists from around the world. These books are internationally well received, and their copyrights have been sold in Germany, France, and Korea. There seems to be a trend to intertwine local and international talents in children's literature; children's books become joint ventures in which the boundaries separating nations disappear, and various cultures cross-fertilize each other.

YOUNG ADULT LITERATURE IN TAIWAN: A BRIEF HISTORY

As the evolution of the notion of adolescence has coincided with the development of literature for young adults in the Western world,[8] so changes in the notions of childhood and adolescence in Taiwan have been relevant to the development of children's literature, specifically young adult literature. Since the 1980s, childhood and young adulthood have to be recognized as two specific stages of life, rather than as rehearsals for the subsequent stages. Also, the educational system in Taiwan has been reformed to allow more choices. As a result, in the late 1980s, young adult literature gradually emerged as a distinct area of book publishing and sales promotion.

Since young adult fiction is fairly recent, there is no long-standing tradition. Until 1964, when Chung-lung Lin wrote *The Heart of A-hei*, there was almost nothing specifically intended as young adult fiction. This story of a lad from a small village in southern Taiwan, who works hard to win trust and respect from his uncle and aunt at home, and from his teachers and classmates at school, reflects the social hardships of the 1960s, and serves as the pioneering landmark of young adult fiction in Taiwan.[9]

Since 1971, the Primary School Teacher Training Center has helped to promote young adult literature through its workshops. As a result, a group of primary school teachers has produced realistic stories depicting poverty in society before the economic takeoff. The 1980s witnessed a watershed in the development of young adult fiction, with the emergence of a second generation of young professional writers.

While literature for preschoolers has flourished in Taiwan since the 1980s, young adult literature has not fared so well. Young adult literature seems to be marginalized by the educational system in Taiwan. The standard textbooks for reading are replete with excerpts from Chinese classics and from modern prose and adult novels, but young adult literature is rarely prescribed reading. Academic pressure makes anything other than textbooks merely leisure reading, irrelevant to the curriculum.

YOUNG ADULT FICTION IN TAIWAN: TUNG LI AND HAI HUANG

Young adult literature in Taiwan still consists mainly translations or adaptations. Since the 1970s, *The Mandarin Chinese Daily Newspaper* has published translations of British and Japanese young adult fiction. Han Shen Publishing Company issued sets of translations in the series World Growth Literature. Translations of Newbery winners and runner-ups are the mainstay of Chih Mau Publishing Company Chung Tong Publishing Company provides excellent adaptations of young adult fiction from around the world.

The main currents of young adult fiction by local writers are realistic stories and historical fiction, with only a handful of writers working with science fiction/fantasy. The most frequent theme for realistic stories is the adjustment of young adults to the physical, emotional, or intellectual changes they experience—the passage from childhood to adulthood. Normally, there is an overt moral message, in which good triumphs over evil and everything turns out fine. Thus the social function of young adult fiction is fulfilled: to help young adults through the process of maturing and make them well-balanced and well-functioning future citizens. Whereas realistic fiction in the United States is painfully honest about cold, harsh reality, realistic young adult fiction in Taiwan is not "realistic." Although teenage pregnancy, abortion, divorce, sexuality, and drug abuse have become hard facts and hot issues in the media in Taiwan, "realistic" young adult fiction generally portrays a naive, cozy world, untouched by harsh reality.

Historical fiction for young adults is part of the cultural/social movement that responds to the calls to "Find Our Roots" and "Meet Our Country." To name just a few, *The Heart of Shiau-uan* (1992), by Jia-chi Guan, centers on the growth of a teenage girl in China during the Sino-Japanese War (1937–1945); *Sunset in Taipei City* (1984), by Iau-ping Jou, narrates different responses of Taiwanese to the Japanese occupation; and *Good-bye, Kinmen* (1984) recounts wars on Kinmen (an island between mainland China and Taiwan) during the 1940s and 1950s.

There are two outstanding contemporary authors of teenage fiction. Si-an Lai (under the pen name Tung Li) and Pi-huang Huang (under the pen name Hai Huang) are productive and well received, and have won almost every prize for children's literature in Taiwan. Tung Li's oeuvre spans the range of young adult fiction in Taiwan. *The New Urn of the Long-Eared God* (1985) is a modern retelling of a traditional folktale. *Stranger in the Green Coat* (1992) narrates a dialogue between a young adult and an imaginary character, his other self. However, Tung Li's strength lies in realistic stories and historical fiction. His realistic stories shimmer with local details, and their colloquial language draws readers into the stories. *The Soaring Sky Hawk* (1985) deals with a group of young adults in a contest involving model airplanes; this contest is a sort of initiation ritual that teaches them to value their friendship. *Good-bye, Tian Ren Jiu* (1985) is about the reunion of seven primary school classmates in Po Hu (an isle between China and Taiwan). The persistence of the splendid tian ren jiu (a native daisy in Po Hu) on the barren soil signifies an unbending life force. Eventually the characters begin to respect the culture and history of this isle. *Doctor, Bu Du and I* (1989) discusses racial prejudice among the three communities in Hwa Lian (a city in eastern Taiwan): the immigrants from China, the Taiwanese, and the aboriginal inhabitants. The story is topical and full of twists and turns, though the ending is somewhat melodramatic and sentimental. *Ke Ma Lan the Youth* (1992), generally recognized as Tung Li's best, is a nostalgic treatment of a tribal tradition of the indigenous people in I Lan (in northeastern Taiwan).

Although realistic stories and historical novels are the dominant genres in young adult fiction in Taiwan, Hai Huang takes the relatively untrodden path of science fiction. His stories are usually mild attacks on aspects of human civilization and technology. *The Bizarre Flight* (1984), vaguely reminiscent of Russell Hoban's *The Mouse and His Child* (1969) and Robert C. O'Brien's *Mrs. Frisby and the Rats of NIMH* (1971), satirizes mankind's scientific achievements and depicts a new race of rats superior to mankind. *Something About the Robots* (1987) probes the master–servant relationships between humans and robots, with robots as the masters and humans as the servants. *Adventures in the Big-Nose Country* (1988) deals with problems of environmental pollution and garbage disposal. The pitiful residents of the Big-Nose Country are burdened with gigantic noses in order to inhale enough fresh air. *Flight to the Future* (1989) narrates the odyssey of a spaceship traveling faster than the speed of light through outer space. Encounters with extraterrestrial beings bring humans to look into the essence of their nature. Overall, however, Hai Huang's science fiction is not as complex in structure or as profound in significance as that by American and European writers.

CONCLUSION

The development of children's literature in Taiwan has been closely intertwined with the social-political-economic evolution. Initially, it served the immediate needs of political/social control and the advocacy of Mandarin Chinese. In the 1960s and 1970s, it was co-opted as an instrument of compulsory education to enhance reading skills for children. In recent years, it has taken on the social missions of cognitive development and personality formation.

Young adult literature is a late bloomer in Taiwan, a small area until the 1980s, when it gradually increased its share of publication as a result of social changes and educational reforms. Yet it has not been well celebrated. There are no such organizations as the National Council of Teachers of English's Assembly on Literature for Adolescents and the American Library Association's Young Adult Library Services Association. The roots of young adult fiction in Taiwan are shallow because of a lack of support from school and public libraries. In Taiwan's youth-oriented society, where every aspect of the young adult market remains relatively strong, young adult fiction still has a long way to go.

NOTES

1. Wen-chiung Hong, *A History of Children's Literature in Taiwan* (Taipei: Chuan Wen, 1994) and *Reflections on Children's Literature* (Taipei: Chuan Wen, 1994) (both in Chinese).

2. Wen-chiung Hong, "Observations on the Development of Children's Literature in Taiwan from 1945 to 1990" and "The Developmental Trends of Young Adult Fiction in Taiwan from 1945 to 1990," both in *Chronicle for Children's Literature: 1945–1990*, ed. Wen-chiung Hong et al. (Taipei: Society of Children's Literature, the ROC, 1991) (both in Chinese).

3. Ge-rung Chiou, *Historical Materials for Children's Literature: 1945–1989* (Taipei: Fu Tsen, 1990) (in Chinese).

4. Wen-chiung Hong et al., eds., *Chronicle for Children's Literature: 1945–1990* (in Chinese) (Taipei: Society of Children's Literature, the ROC, 1991) (in Chinese); and Wen-chiung Hong et al., eds., *A History of Chinese Children's Literature: 1945–1990* (Taipei: Society of Children's Literature, the ROC, 1991) (in Chinese).

5. Chiou, *Historical Materials*.

6. Hong, *History of Children's Literature* and *Reflections on Children's Literature*.

7. Ibid.

8. Alleen Nilson and Kenneth Donelson, eds. *Literature for Today's Young Adults*, 2nd ed. (Glenview, Ill.: Scott, Foresman, 1993).

9. Lin Tong Fu, *Introduction to Young Adult Fiction* (Taipei: Fu Tsen, 1994) (in Chinese).

REFERENCES

Chiou, Ge-rung. *Historical Materials for Children's Literature: 1945–1989* Taipei: Fu Tsen, 1990. (In Chinese).
Fu, Lin Tong. *Introduction to Young Adult Fiction*. Taipei: Fu Tsen, 1994. (In Chinese).
Hong, Wen-chiung. "The Developmental Trends of Young Adult Fiction in Taiwan from 1945 to 1990." In *Chronicle for Children's Literature: 1945–1990*. Ed. Wen-chiung Hong et al. Taipei: Society of Children's Literature, the ROC, 1991. (In Chinese).
———. "Observations on the Development of Children's Literature in Taiwan from 1945 to 1990." In *Chronicle for Children's Literature: 1945–1990*. Ed. Wen-chiung Hong et al. Taipei: Society of Children's Literature, the ROC, 1991. (In Chinese).
———. *A History of Children's Literature in Taiwan*. Taipei: Chuan Wen, 1994.
———. *Reflections on Children's Literature*. Taipei: Chuan Wen, 1994.
Hong, Wen-chiung et al., eds. *Chronicle for Children's Literature: 1945–1990*. Taipei: Society of Children's Literature, the ROC, 1991. (In Chinese).
Hong, Wen-chiung et al., eds. *A History of Chinese Children's Literature: 1945–1990*. Taipei: Society of Children's Literature, the ROC, 1991. (In Chinese).
Nilson, Alleen, and Kenneth Donelson, eds. *Literature for Today's Young Adults*. 2nd ed. Glenview, Ill.: Scott, Foresman, 1993.

Part VI

Reconceptualizing the Past

An Awfully Big Adventure? Representations of the Second World War in British Children's Books of the 1960s and 1970s

Dieter Petzold

THE SECOND WORLD WAR AND CHILDREN'S FICTION

Although it seems that stories about war have interested children ever since historical fiction became available to them, there are relatively few children's books on the Second World War on record. Whereas an essay on adult novels about the Second World War metaphorically speaks of "a floodlike river" of books,[1] the corresponding phrase in a survey of children's books is "a spate of novels."[2] In that survey, eleven titles of books by British authors are mentioned; in another, probably the most thorough to date, the number is twenty-five.[3] Of course, in the decades following the war, adults had a most vital interest in coming to terms with an experience that for many must have been the most shattering of their lives; it may not be equally obvious why children should be told about an event that is, after all, history to them. However, the urge of the older generation to explain itself to the younger is natural, I suppose; and the books we are dealing with were written, in David James's words, "by those whose formative years were spent scattered over sundry pastoral retreats of the British isles, awaiting news from home, or cramped into shelters hoping only for survival."[4]

Considering this autobiographical impetus, the same critic's verdict seems equally plausible: "For the most part the novels . . . are either over-elaborate attempts to document the war or self-indulgent exercises in nostalgia; sometimes they are both."[5] It seems to me, though, that there are more reasons than just the autobiographical one to account for "the reluctance of so many of our writers to probe the troublesome psychological and spiritual questions that war should provoke."[6] After all, writers of fiction have to deal not only with their own experiences, and their own ways of interpreting the past, but also with generic conventions that—possibly quite unconsciously—shape the literary expressions of these experiences, if not the experiences themselves. In addition, authors of children's books often feel restricted by what they, and the general public, assume to be the limited understanding of their audience.

In spite of our sentimental reluctance to admit tales of war into the nursery, there is a long-standing tradition of war stories read by children. It is not at all unlikely that children were among Homer's first audience; in any case, his story of the fall of Troy has been retold for children countless times. Just as history books are full of wars, so are historical novels, which were soon adopted (for that very reason, I suspect) by children. The line of historical novels describing warfare in great detail stretches from Sir Walter Scott's *Ivanhoe* and James Fenimore Cooper's *Last of the Mohicans* through Frederick Marryat's *Children of the New Forest* and Robert Louis Stevenson's *Black Arrow* to the yarns spun by G. A. Henty, Captain W. E. Johns, Rosemary Sutcliff and countless contemporary writers.[7] In most of these novels, adventure and war are so densely interwoven that they amount to much the same thing. Along with this go certain sets of attitudes, values, and ideas—in short, ideologies—that certainly differ according to the times of composition and the personalities of the authors, yet tend to have certain things in common. Books like these tend to extol, for instance, personal courage, energy, resourcefulness, and, of course, loyalty and patriotism. Needless to say, these are also considered "manly" virtues that were highly valued, particularly in the nineteenth and early twentieth century.

The experiences of the two world wars and subsequent instances of organized mass murder in various places (and a number of other factors) have made us rather suspicious of such sets of values. According to David Craig and Michael Egan, "in the First World War, 5 percent of the fatal casualties were civilian; in the second, 44 percent; in the Korean War, 88 percent; and in the war in Vietnam, 91 percent."[8] How can an awareness of the brutality of modern total wars create anything but despair? The problem, as I see it, is not just political and moral but also aesthetic; it has to do with form as well as with content: What can be an adequate artistic response to this despair?

For an expression of this modern sensibility, the conventional telling of war stories hardly seems adequate. Since it is fettered to the patterns of adventure fiction, it is in constant danger of inadvertently glorifying, if not war itself, then at least the individual war effort. Serious adult war fiction has responded to this dilemma either by reverting to pure documentation or by "turn[ing] war experience into comedy, fantasy, science-fiction, satire, and other modes which so rearrange and 'exaggerate' that we are no longer on the plane of what could literally happen."[9]

None of these alternatives, it seems, are open to children's books about the Second World War. As is so often the case, children's literature lags behind the development of adult fiction. In addition, the special British perspective on the war was apt to further a more conservative approach. British chroniclers of the Second World War faced none of the excruciating moral predicaments their German colleagues, for instance, had to deal with. From the British point of view, the rights and wrongs of this war were clear: this was an obvious case of self-defense. Heroism and patriotism, only recently cut down to size by the poets of the First World War, could be reinstalled as noble virtues. Praising heroic deeds was not necessarily tantamount to glorifying war as such; unlike the First World War, this war was regarded not as a noble mission but rather as a "bloody nuisance" that had to be seen through.

PASTORAL RETREATS

War stories for children are inevitably stories about how war affects children. Surprisingly, in quite a number of the books under scrutiny, the answer to the question of how war affects children seems to be: Not very much, really. To twelve-year-old Carrie and her younger brother Nick, in Nina Bawden's famous book *Carrie's War* (1973), the war means evacuation to a remote village in Wales, and little else; it is, as Mary Cadogan and Patricia Craig put it a little ungraciously, "used . . . simply as a device to get the parents out of the way."[10] War has little to do with the story that unfolds, which is about the protagonist's vain attempt to come to terms with the complexities of adult relationships. What Carrie experiences is a war only in a very loosely metaphorical, ironic sense: hers is a struggle for emotional survival in what she perceives as a hostile environment—a struggle that escalates into a short outburst of destructiveness that, because it is based on a superstition, is quite ineffective but burdens her with feelings of guilt for years to come.

War is equally remote, and definitely part of the world of adults, not of children, in Penelope Lively's *Going Back* (1975). Again, and even more persistently, the war is presented as part of an adult's childhood memories. These memories create a pastoral world in which the most important effects of the war are the father's absence (bringing relief rather than regret) and the presence of a young man, a conscientious objector working on a nearby farm. The nostalgic view of childhood is made more poignant by being set against the background of a distant war whose horrors are hardly mentioned but are present in the adult narrator's consciousness. In the last resort, though, the pastoral mode reasserts itself against the demands of the subject of war.[11]

HEROIC DEEDS

The proper mode of war fiction, however, is of course the heroic. It is inevitably present in all those stories in which children do not escape into the (however ambiguously presented) pastoral world of evacuation but stay at home to live through the horrible reality of air raids and the no less real fear of invasion. Authors of such stories must face the dilemma that the tellers of pastoral fiction avoid: How can you describe the horrors of war without glamorizing them by presenting them within the context of a "gripping yarn"? How can you tell stories of endurance and heroism without making war seem like "an awfully big adventure"?[12]

For a large part of the book, it seems as if Jill Paton Walsh is trying to do precisely this in her first war story, *The Dolphin Crossing* (1967). Set in an unnamed place on the coast of Kent, the first half of the story describes the growth of friendship between two adolescent boys, upper-middle-class John, whose father is a captain in the merchant marine, and working-class Pat, an evacuee from London, whose father is in the army. The exceptional situation of the war helps to overcome class prejudice; with

Pat's help, John and his mother are "doing their bit" by converting an old stable into living quarters for the evacuees.

At first sight, it seems that an innate sense of responsibility and fair play is all it takes to make the two boys natural patriots; but in fact Walsh is careful to show how public life is steeped in patriotism: posters and newsreels, the classmates' contempt for conscientious objectors, a teacher reading *Mein Kampf* to John and making him translate Herodotus' account of the battle of Marathon, and Churchill's famous "blood, toil, tears, and sweat" speech (which is quoted at length) all combine to instill a sense of patriotic obligation in the boys.

Thus prepared, the boys' secret decision to take part in the famous rescue of the British army trapped at Dunkirk in June 1940 seems almost unavoidable—and it is by no means condemned. The subsequent description of the rescue action certainly does not spare the reader the horrors of war; but its main purpose is to show the toughness, courage, determination, and moral commitment of the boys—in short, their heroism.

At one point, Walsh shows an awareness not only of the physical but also of the moral cost of heroism. When John discovers that the ship meant to carry the rescued troops to England has been sunk at night by a German U-boat, he gives way to unbridled hatred: "He hated [the men in the U-boat]. He imagined being able to revenge himself, and with savage pleasure he thought of kicking them in the face, breaking arms, letting rip with a machine gun, watching pain and blood."[13] This gut feeling is presented as being stronger than John's brother's warning that hatred is always evil. It is implicitly justified by the narrator, just as John's actions as a whole are justified and applauded by his parents and acknowledged even by his brother, who revokes his status as a conscientious objector. Even though the happy ending is subdued by a coda that involves the death of John's friend Pat, the plot as a whole conforms to the basic pattern of the adventure story. In the last resort, the gravitational pull of the adventure pattern is stronger than the author's unflinching realism in the description of the horrors of war. The result is, indeed, a kind of glorification: if not of war as such, then certainly of the selfless, individual heroic deed.[14]

THE AMBIGUITIES OF ADVENTURE

Like all adventure stories, *The Dolphin Crossing* can be read as a parable of maturation, although John and Pat show few traces of childishness to begin with. In Robert Westall's *The Machine-Gunners* (1975), the protagonists are only slightly younger, but they are definitely children. They are just as resourceful as John and Pat, but much more confused about what is going on and what they are doing. But then, so are most adults in the book, apart from the main character's father.

Westall shows how ordinary children adapt to war: in general, they manage to integrate the extraordinary into their daily routine. They collect war souvenirs as they would collect stamps or cigarette pictures during peacetime. A sense of grotesque unrealness seems to envelop the horrors of war like a protective cover, although the bombs falling on homes, and the death and destruction they cause, are real enough. The book is brimming with grotesque characters and situations: Chas's grandmother, who regards Hitler as her personal enemy, and Mrs. Spalding, who is caught in an awkward position "on the outside lav" when the air raid begins,[15] and whose sentimental rhetoric triggers some ludicrously inappropriate imagery in Chas's mind: "The bomb fell right on his little room where he was lying innocent asleep. They found not one little piece of him. He's with the angels now. Chas had an absurd picture of angels piecing together some unknown innocent's arms and legs, as if he was a jigsaw puzzle."[16]

Adults rarely have time for their children, who mostly live in their own world of school life, games, rivalries, and bullying. However, the borders between the adults' world, where the war is a grim reality, and the children's world, where war intrudes occasionally but is kept at bay by the children's limited sense of reality, are blurred in several ways. On the one hand, the two worlds converge insofar as some adults' institutions, in particular the police, the Home Guard, and the Polish Free Army, are shown to be quite as incompetent and given to playing absurd war games as the children are. They meet more seriously when Chas and his friends steal a machine gun in perfect working condition from a downed German airplane and manage to set it up in a reinforced air raid shelter on the grounds of a bombed-out mansion.

The children have created their "Fortress Caparetto" as a base from which to fight German airplanes, but it comes to mean much more to them. Although built around a deadly weapon, the fortress is a kind of home to them (quite literally, to some), a place where they can retreat into a world of make-believe. As the children swear to look after Nicky, the orphan boy believed dead by the authorities, "Fortress Caparetto became more than a game; it became a nation. And the Germans ceased to be the only enemies. All the adults were a kind of enemy now, except John [the half-wit who helped them build the shelter]."[17] What the children are defending is their childhood.

The machine gun, paradoxically, becomes the center of a precarious utopia that is so peaceful that it can even accommodate what should be the Enemy—Rudi, the German airman. Rudi and the children become friends because they are essentially in the same situation of powerlessness.[18] As long as they shy away from using their weapons, they live in a kind of pastoral idyll—an idyll, however, that is even more precarious than idylls normally are. It is destroyed in the end, paradoxically, by the impulse that created it in the first place: the children's dream of heroic adventure. As the adults close in on the children to prevent their war game from turning deadly , the children find themselves caught between two realities, the one heroic, the other prosaic, but both equally nightmarish: "The world had two faces. Which was the true one? The world of the long night of waiting, of Stukas and Panzers, stormtroopers and death? Or the world of day, of punishments, hidings and magistrate's court?"[19]

Shouting, "Go away! Go away! Sod off, you bastards. Leave us *alone*!,"[20] they shoot and, tragically, wound or perhaps kill Rudi, the only friend they have among the adults. Their adventure is over—and is found to be rather silly and not "awfully big" at all.

Thus, Westall manages to undercut the ideological dynamics of his motif. His wry humor and his use of the grotesque counteract the pathos the story might otherwise demand. To a modern sensibility, the children's senseless act seems an apt emblem of the mad logic, the absurd irrationality, of war in general.

NOTES

1. Holger Klein et al., eds., *The Second World War in Fiction* (London: Macmillan, 1984), p. 3.

2. David L. James, "Recent World-War-II Fiction: A Survey," *Children's Literature in Education* 8, no. 2 (1977): 71.

3. Mary Cadogan and Patricia Craig, *Women and Children First: The Fiction of Two World Wars* (London: Gollancz, 1978), chap. 11. In an earlier chapter, Cadogan and Craig also deal with books written during or immediately after the war. For reasons of space and compactness, I will confine myself here to a discussion of books that may be regarded as part of the "New Realism" in children's literature. Rather than attempt another survey, I shall conduct only a few case studies of some outstanding specimens of the genre.

4. James, "Recent World-War-II Fiction," p. 71. The authors discussed here were born between 1925 (Bawden) and 1937 (Walsh). Peter Hollindale quotes Robert Westall as having written *The Machine-Gunners* "for his son Christopher, then age twelve, 'to show him how life had been for me at twelve. I wanted to invite him back into my world and let the two generations, just for a moment, stand side by side in time'" ("Westall's Kingdom," *Children's Literature in Education* 25, no. 3 [1994]: 148. One story that is clearly autobiographical is Judith Kerr's *The Other Way Round* (London: Collins, 1975).

5. James, "Recent World-War-II Fiction," p. 71.

6. Ibid.

7. For an assessment of the last three writers' contribution to the history of children's war fiction, see Margery Fisher, *The Bright Face of Danger* (Boston: The Horn Book, 1986), pp. 349–663, 372–77.

8. David Craig and Michael Egan, *Extreme Situations: Literature and Crisis from the Great War to the Atom Bomb* (London: Macmillan, 1979), p. 1.

9. Ibid., p. 37. Conspicuous examples are Joseph Heller's *Catch 22* and Kurt Vonnegut, Jr.'s *Slaughterhouse-Five*.

10. Cadogan and Craig, *Women and Children First*, p. 266.

11. The persistent pastoralism and the insistence on the autonomy of childhood place Lively's book in the tradition of late-nineteenth-century fiction. Like Kenneth Grahame's *The Golden Age* (1895) and *Dream Days* (1898), *Going Back* is not really a children's book, as the author herself acknowledges in her preface to the 1991 edition.

12. The quotation is from *Peter Pan*. What interests me in this context is not whether "to die" or "to live" is "an awfully big adventure," but the fact that to Barrie's archetypal boy, "an awfully big adventure" seems to be the highest term of praise.

13. Jill Paton Walsh, *The Dolphin Crossing* (Harmondsworth: Penguin, 1970), p. 116.

14. In contrast, Walsh's second war story, *Fireweed* (1969), avoids patriotic messages. In this respect, Rees is hardly justified in lumping the two books together (see David Rees, *The Marble in the Water* [Boston: The Horn Book, 1980], pp. 142–143). Though advertised as "a gripping war-time adventure" (cover of the Puffin edition), this is essentially a love story of a boy and a girl trying to create some private space for themselves in the chaos of London during the blitz.

15. Robert Westall, *The Machine-Gunners* (Harmondsworth: Penguin, 1977), p. 53.

16. Ibid., p. 90.

17. Ibid., p. 94.

18. For Westall's use of an individual German to counterpoise the stereotyped image of the Nazi Germans, see Emer O'Sullivan, *Friend or Foe: The Image of Germany and the Germans in British Children's Fiction from 1870 to the Present* (Tübingen: Narr, 1990), pp. 279–290.

19. Ibid., pp. 181–182.

20. Ibid., p. 182.

REFERENCES

Bawden, Nina. *Carrie's War*. 1973. Harmondsworth: Penguin, 1974.

Cadogan, Mary, and Patricia Craig. *Women and Children First: The Fiction of Two World Wars*. London: Gollancz, 1978.

Craig, David, and Michael Egan. *Extreme Situations: Literature and Crisis from the Great War to the Atom Bomb*. London: Macmillan, 1979.

Fisher, Margery. *The Bright Face of Danger*. Boston: The Horn Book, 1986.

Hollindale, Peter. "Westall's Kingdom." *Children's Literature in Education* 25, no. 3 (1994): 147–154.

James, David L. "Recent World-War-II Fiction: A Survey." *Children's Literature in Education* 8, no. 2 (1977): 71–79.

Kerr, Judith. *The Other Way Round*. London: Collins, 1975.

Klein, Holger, et al., eds. *The Second World War in Fiction*. London: Macmillan, 1984.

Lively, Penelope. *Going Back*. 1975. Harmondsworth: Penguin, 1991.

O'Sullivan, Emer. *Friend and Foe: The Image of Germany and the Germans in British Children's Fiction from 1870 to the Present*. Tübingen: Narr, 1990.

Rees, David. *The Marble in the Water: Essays on Contemporary Writers of Fiction for Children and Young Adults*. Boston: Horn Book, 1980.

Walsh, Jill Paton. *The Dolphin Crossing*. 1967. Harmondsworth: Penguin, 1970.

———. *Fireweed*. 1969. Harmondsworth: Penguin, 1971.

Westall, Robert. *The Machine-Gunners*. Harmondsworth: Penguin, 1975.

20

Topsy-Turvy World: New Trends In Modern Russian Children's Literature

Olga Mäeots

Political changes that have taken place in Russia since 1985 have considerably influenced children's literature. New names have appeared, new literary associations have come into being, new children's periodicals have been published.

Some historical facts: in 1989, young authors and illustrators established a literary association of their own, The Black Hen. They placed themselves in opposition to the official literature of the past that was based on the ideological dogmas of the Communist regime. At the same time, they proclaimed their desire to revive the best traditions of classical Russian children's literature, to create books full of humor and lyrical optimism in which an author acts not as a teacher but as a friend who wants to help rather than to supervise.

Their first collective publication, which appeared in *Pioneer*, the periodical for teenagers, in 1990, was met with suspicion by critics and with approval by readers. The same year, they published a book, *Ku-ka-re-ku* (Cock-a-doodle-doo). The thick volume contained poems and novels by young authors and their elder colleagues, as well as articles about contemporary artists and interviews. The book was illustrated by young artists. The authors were united by the desire to create a book full of fantasy and humor. The Black Hen made its first appearance as a brightly colored rooster.

Ku-ka-re-ku appeared almost simultaneously with the first issue of a new children's periodical, *Tramvaj* (The Tram). This vehicle was driven by the same company, under the leadership of two poets, Andrei Usachev and Tim Sobakin. *Tramvaj* differed considerably from earlier children's periodicals. It was both funny and cognitive, and had an attractive appearance.

It should be stressed that these bright and cheerful works appeared in Russia during the gloomy period of the deepest economic crisis, which, for children, meant no food, no Christmas presents, the troubled expressions of the grown-ups.

The birth of this new children's literature took place at a time when adult literature was in crisis. For the lengthy period known as Perestroika, adult fiction was suppressed by publicistic writings. Thus, children's literature took the lead. To explain this situation, one should remember that under the Communist regime, children's literature gave many talented writers the opportunity to escape from ideological supervision through the world of fantasy. That was how we got our best children's poets and writers: Daniil Kharms, Yuri Olesha, Genrikh Sapgir, and others. The young generation of children's writers inherited their traditions and were better prepared to overcome various disasters—and, what is more, they felt a responsibility toward children and could not allow themselves to waste time.

One of the main tasks of children's literature is to educate children and to prepare them for the adult world. What do we Russians know about our society? Our past was full of lies and absurdities, our present seems to have no sense, our future is rather vague and disquieting. Thus literature attempts to help children to escape the horrifying influence of the totalitarian past, to find their way through the mist of modern life, and to provide a remedy against future disasters. The best remedy is laughter. It encourages people to oppose ideological dogmas, helps them to become individuals.

The ideological pressure deformed children's literature. Many so-called masterpieces appeared; their main value was their ideological purity. Most of them hadn't the slightest trace of literary talent. The following example of poetry for young children was a popular song:

> I look with admiration at my little red flag,
> On great holidays I take it with me
> When we march along the streets.
> I walk with my little flag,
> I hold my little flag in my hand.[1]

And now try to imagine what parents and children felt when they read this: "A local committee of the Communist Party made 1,756 slogans for the celebration of the next anniversary of the Great October Revolution. It is known that 37 people took part in the demonstration. How many slogans did each participant have to carry so that not a single slogan was wasted?"[2]

The author of this mathematical problem is a famous Russian writer, Grigori Oster. He can be classified neither as new nor as young, for he started his literary career more than twenty years ago. Oster attempted to parody out-of-date school textbooks that did not reflect political changes in the country. In the early 1990s, he wrote *The Nonsense Book of Problems*. Parody is often considered to be beyond a child's apprehension, but I believe that any child can feel the absurdity of the situation described in the problem, or at least can calculate the answer.

New children's writers not only try to destroy the lies of the past; they are eager to present a truthful picture of the modern world. But this "real world" often turns into a topsy-turvy world full of absurdity and nonsense. The spirit of nonsense, being an echo of real life, penetrates various genres of children's literature. This phenomenon is easy to explain: our modern life, as well as our past, is full of the absurd. We live in it and we write about it.

Modern nonsense literature, which seems so strikingly new and exotic, is nevertheless deeply rooted in Russian culture. One of its main sources is Russian folklore: nursery rhymes and numerous topsy-turvies. Among the predecessors of modern nonsense literature are famous representatives of nineteenth-century Russian classical literature: Nikolai Gogol and Mikhail Saltykov. Another important source of inspiration is the European nonsense tradition, primarily English literature of the nineteenth century. (Modern nonsense and absurd literature was, until quite recently, practically unknown in Russia.) There are more than a dozen translations of Lewis Carroll's books by well-known Russian writers and poets, such as Vladimir Nabokov, Boris Zakhoder, and Nina Demurova. Poems by Edward Lear also are very popular and have inspired numerous imitations. Brilliant new translations of nonsense classics have been published recently. They were done by distinguished Russian poets who also write nonsense poetry of their own: Grigory Kruzkov, Marina Boroditskaya, Evgenii Kluev. Russian poets admit the influence of the European tradition on their work.

Born in folklore, the nonsense tradition quickly found its way into children's literature. There is a long tradition of nonsense poetry in Russian children's literature: Sasha Chernii, Kornej Chukovsky, Daniil Kharms, Oleg Grigorjev. They used nonsense against the common sense of the society, to break the official doctrine that suppressed individuality and to let in the fresh air of fantasy. The nonsense tradition existed in Soviet literature, but it never received official approval. Furthermore, the works of Daniil Kharms were considered by critics to be "a protest against the dictatorship of the proletariat."[3]

The creation of a parallel topsy-turvy world is not a form of escapism (the fantasy world is better suited for this purpose) but, rather, an attempt to protect one's individuality: "There are two ways of escaping the house of Common-sense—by breaking the windows or by upsetting the furniture, by the magic Fairyland or by the topsy-turvydom of Nonsense."[4] Individuals locked in a totalitarian society are unable to "break the window"; however, they can demonstrate their protest by "upsetting the furniture," by deliberately breaking laws and conventions.

That is the main difference between Russian and European nonsense traditions: nonsense literature in the West creates a "completely different world, rather than merely distort or invent the familiar world"[5]; nonsense is considered mostly a linguistic or philosophical game. All these features belong to Russian literature as well, "but in addition to their timeless, universal relevance, the writings make specific comments on the concrete social and political . . . conditions prevalent in Soviet Russia at a particular historical moment."[6] Russian writers are more politically active than their Western colleagues.

Most of the new authors started their careers when revolutionary enthusiasm was degenerating into hypocrisy and fear. Independent thinking was considered a dreadful crime. The only way to protect one's individuality was to laugh. A new genre of folklore appeared in the 1970s as a reaction to offical hypocrisy and absurdity—nonsense anecdotes. Here is an example:

Two hippos are sitting in their nest, knitting. They notice two elephants flying above in the sky.
—Look, elephants!

—Never mind! They might have a nest nearby.

Such anecdotes are still very popular, especially with children. They can be considered as the direct predecessors of modern nonsense literature. Let's compare. Here is a poem by Vladimir Druk:

> A Tale
> A broom was flying.
> —Mother, asked Kolja,
> Do brooms really fly?
> —Certainly not, answered mother.
> And the broom fell.[7]

It was the fall of the totalitarian regime and the abolition of censorship that made it possible for the Russian nonsense tradition to appear in printed form. This story appeared in *Tramvaj* in December 1990:

> A Herring Is Released
> —Let's eat some herring! suggested my father.
> I stuck a can-opener into a can. The can exploded with
> a bang and a herring flew out.
> It started flying under the ceiling, crying:
> —Freedom! Freedom![8]

This story, by Tim Sobakin, could be at first considered a mere joke; but if one takes into account the date of its publication, one finds traces of the economic crisis (when a can of herring was a real treat) and signs of the political struggles between democrats and Communists, the echoes of numerous demonstrations. So this strange story, in its peculiar way, reflects the contemporary situation in the country.

"You may call it 'nonsense' if you like, but I've heard nonsense, compared with which that would be a sensible dictionary,"[9] said by the Red Queen in *Alice in Wonderland*, seems to reflect modern writers' desire to outdo their colleagues. The topsy-turvy world in modern Russian literature has nothing in common with a fantasy Wonderland; it is an ordinary world, the world children live in, where an ordinary balcony can be turned into an ordinary military base (Yurij Viira) and where a diver can suddenly emerge in the ordinary bath-tub (Igor Shevchuk).

Children also contribute to this competition; their nonsense poems and short stories are often published in *Tramvaj*. The success of topsy-turvies with children can be explained by children's passion for the incongruous, for the absurd, which we can trace in their apprehension of nursery rhymes where, for example, "the village rode past the peasant." And what is more, a child enjoys nonsense as a mental play that helps him "to master his concept of the world around him."[10]

Grigori Oster wrote a burlesque book of good manners that became the children's top best-seller, *The Textbook of Bad Advice*. The moral values in the book are deliberately turned upside down. The author adresses himself to naughty children who don't want to obey adults. Here are some examples:

1. Matches are the best toys for a bored child.
2. If you get lost
and a policeman asks your address,
don't miss your chance to see the world!
You should answer
that you live under a big palm tree
and are brought up by monkeys.
3. Don't touch anything.
Do not interfere.
Just step quietly aside
And stay in a corner.
Don't move
Until you get old.[11]

If the first two examples can be considered to be a mere joke, the last one presents a motto of life.

Kornei Chukovsky, in his essay "The Sense of Nonsense Verse," wrote about the educational value of topsy-turvies: "The function of similar rhymes and stories is obvious, for every 'wrong' the child realizes what is 'right' and every departure from the normal strengthens his conception of the normal. Thus he values even more highly his firm, realistic orientation."[12] Grigori Oster uses this quality of nonsense as an educational device, but his aim is not just to bring up a polite child; his goal is a thinking individual who won't be deceived by ideological and political tricks.

Nonsense seldom appears in a pure form as "nonsense for nonsense's sake." It is usually mixed with more distinguishable genres, such as parody. Tim Sobakin, one of the leading figures of the "new wave," published a book of poems, *Letters to the Cow*. The poet meets a cow and helps her to button her coat. They become friends. The cow appears to be an advanced worker, her main desire being "to give more milk to the beloved motherland." Their correspondence, presented in funny verse, can be considered a parody of the popular genre of the past. It is a combination of humor, pure nonsense, word games, parody, and skillful stylization. Though the goal of the parody can be clear only to adults, children consider these poems to be just funny. But they also have a very important result, for if later a child meets a similar "piece of poetry," he or she won't be deceived by its pretentiousness, and will consider it to be a well-known joke, or even a parody of real life. One of the main aims of parody is to root out obsolete literary genres and devices, and to make way for the fresh and new. Thus the inclusion of parody in the world of children's literature pursues both ideological and literary aims contributing to the revival of children's literature. And nonsense can be very useful in this regard.

Nonsense literature is known for the boldness of its language, for its experiments with words, for numerous elaborate word games and puns. This capacity of nonsense to brighten up literary production is widely used by modern Russian writers and poets. It helps them to enliven their children's books, to do away with the old, faded clichés and the triviality of official children's literature of the past.

Among the merits of nonsense literature are its optimism, tolerance, and sympathy. Nonsense literature teaches children not only to despise evil and hypocrisy but also to cherish variety and appreciate the company of curious people.

As mentioned above, Russian writers admit their relationship to classical English nonsense literature, first to the work of Lewis Carroll. But a comparison of the two traditions helps to reveal the differences. G. K. Chesterton considered the books of Lewis Carroll to be a sort of "intellectual holiday"; Wonderland appears to be a place where respectable Victorians escaped from a "very comfortable and secure England."[13] And they were sure to find themselves among the same "Victorian furniture" at the end of the adventure. That is how it was in England in Carroll's time. But a century later in Russia, we have a different situation. Contemporary Russian society can be called neither secure nor comfortable. It is a changing world. And when they go on an "intellectual holiday," writers and readers plan never to return; they look for a better fortune, they really try to jump out of the house they are locked in.

The ability of nonsense to reconstruct the normal world is used by children's writers as a remedy against all kinds of ideological oppression. The topsy-turvy world created by Russian authors resembles the absurdity of the real world more than that of realistic literature. It presents the grotesque image of real life, so children's aspiration for "right" and "normal" makes them create a new reality—an ideal to strive for—that differs from the one they live in now and the one they find in nonsense books. Thus nonsense is used not only to destroy but also to create.

NOTES

1. Anonymous. All translations are mine.

2. Grigori Oster, *Protivnye zadachi* (Moscow: Nezavisimaia Gazeta, 1992), p. 11.

3. L. Nilvich, "Reaktsionnoje zonglerstvo," *Smena*, April 9, 1930.

4. Emile Cammaerts, *The Poetry of Nonsense* (London: George Routledge & Sons, 1925), p. 28.

5. Thomas Joyce, "'There Was an Old Man . . .': The Sense of Nonsense Verse," *Children's Literature Association Quarterly* 10, no. 3 (1985): 119.

6. George Gibian, "Introduction: Daniil Kharms and Alexander Vvedensky," in *Russia's Lost Literature of the Absurd* (Ithaca, N. Y.: Cornell University Press, 1971), p. 29.

7. *Ku-ka-re-ku* (Moscow: Slovo, 1990), p. 12.

8. *Tramvaj*, December 1990, p. 18.

9. Lewis Carroll, *The Complete Illustrated Works* (London: Chancellor Press, 1987), p. 142.

10. Kornei Chukovsky, *From Two to Five* (Berkely: University of California Press, 1968), p. 101.

11. Grigori Oster, *Vrednye sovety* (Moscow: Posman, 1994), pp. 6, 7, 57.

12. Chukovsky, *From Two to Five*, p. 102.

13. G. K. Chesterton, *The Spice of Life and Other Essays* (Beaconsfield, U.K.: Darwen Finlayson, 1964), p. 68.

21

Children's Literature in Totalitarian and Post-totalitarian Society

Vincas Auryla

The view of world children's literature since 1945 would not be complete if we neglected one anomaly—children's literature produced by totalitarian regimes. I will touch upon one of the most bizarre cultural phenomena: Soviet children's literature written after the Second World War. Its genesis, evolution, and transformations will be illustrated by examples from children's literature of the Baltic nations, especially Lithuania, which is typical of literatures in the regions under Soviet influence.

At the end of the Second World War, many nations gained independence, and their cultural renaissance began. However, the nations of Eastern Europe, after becoming free from the fascist plague, fell into the clutches of the Communist regime. Three Baltic republics—Estonia, Latvia and Lithuania—were bound to the Soviet slave ship with strong and heavy chains. For fifty years, they existed under a dictatorship that aimed to create the utopian Homo Sovieticus. For the Baltic states, the Second World War didn't end until 1993, when the last soldiers of the occupation army left their territories.

The ideology of the so-called Soviet society, maintained by force, burst like a soap bubble. Today, we are trying to liberate ourselves from the class, atheistic, and bureaucratic ideology based on hatred, turning instead toward democracy and Christian Western European culture. Millions of copies of Soviet books for children will, from now on, be left to rot in the libraries. As researchers of children's literature, we are faced with the task of examining honestly and objectively the development of Soviet children's literature since 1945. Without a scholarly investigation of the origin, evolution, and transformation of Soviet children's literature, it will not be possible to write a comprehensive history of children's literature in the whole world, in specific regions, or in the nations that once belonged to the Soviet system. The questions we keep asking today are: Why did talented writers cooperate with the regime, falsifying their books for young readers? How was the "newspeak" of Soviet children's literature created, with words lacking meaning and social realism lacking realism? How did such concepts as humanism, patriotism, and internationalism mutate in children's literature?

Why did certain literary devices invade children's literature: euphemisms, paralipsis, hidden meaning, and so on? Furthermore, every historical period—Stalin's, Khrushchev's, Brezhnev's, and Gorbachev's—had its own specific traits.

The most dramatic period was the years of Stalin's terror. That was the era of censorial realism in children's literature, based on the concept of two economic (capitalism and socialism) and two ethical (Soviet and bourgeois) systems in the world. Of course, the genuine struggle during these years was not between socialism and capitalism, but between democracy and dictatorship.

Children's literature in the West is based on an ethical system oriented toward love for humankind with all its positive and negative qualities. Soviet children's literature was based on a system of ethical values where the notions of good and evil were inseparable. "Bad" qualities were considered to be the consequences of private property and the selfish instincts caused by it, not inherent parts of a human being.

Thus the depiction of the Soviet people and their way of life during the Stalin period was a direct result of the often-repeated statement, "The socialist system is superior to the capitalist." All the troubles and misfortunes of the Soviet people, even noxious insects in the collective farms' fields, were ascribed to saboteurs, secret agents, unvanquished class enemies, and other anti-Soviet elements. Essential traditions of national education were rejected, treated as remnants of nationalism. Internationalism was depicted superficially, as a mob of people driven together, without any mutual interest or sympathy.

Among the approved masterpieces of Soviet children's literature were a documentary story written by Vitaly Gubarev and a poem by Stepan Shchipachov, both portraying the teenager Pavlik Morozov, who denounced his father to the secret police as an enemy of the Soviet regime. The books appeared in Lithuanian translations in 1948 and 1952, respectively.

By the end of the war, many talented writers from the Baltic states had emigrated to the West. Those remaining faced a dilemma: to surrender to Communist Party pressure and adapt their books to the primitive ideology of class struggle, or to be honest and choose the traditional, eternal themes of children's literature. The brutal regime left no choice. In the late 1940s, repressions against writers increased. Many were frightened, and tried to squeeze their works into prescribed formulas. Two Lithuanian writers who challenged the dictatorship were murdered without trial: Kazys Bajerčius in 1946 and Kazys Jakubėnas in 1950. Intimidated writers either abandoned children's literature or found themselves caught by the policy of stick and carrot.

During the first ten years in postwar Lithuania, as in other Baltic states, several stereotypes emerged in children's literature:

1. A radical child, imbued with the new ideology, neglects his or her own childhood, and is involved with adult affairs: creating collective farms, inviting people to meetings to fight for peace or protest against the Vietnam war.

2. Adventures can be depicted only if children take part in the struggle against resistance, the so-called "bandits" (national armed resistance against Soviet occupation lasted until 1952 in Lithuania).

3. Religious children are bored on Sundays because they have to go to church, while young Communists are hiking and playing. Clergy are reactionary, instigating children's opposition to the Soviet regime.
4. Parents and older people are outdated in their worldview because they have lived under capitalism. Children attend Soviet schools, and are members of the Young Communist League; therefore they have more progressive views. In a short story, a little girl sits down to write an application to join a collective farm on behalf of her doubting father.
5. Two childhoods are contrasted. In the capitalist world, a black boy suffers discrimination; in the socialist country, he feels like a respectable person. In other countries, children are either spoiled bourgeois no-goods or poor, suffering, working-class kids; in the Soviet Union, children of all social classes and races are equals and friends. They go to summer camps by the Black Sea, and the Great Leader and the Party take care of them. Judge by the book titles: *Two Childhoods*, *Negro Johnny*, *A Vietnam Soldier*, among many others.

Until the denouncement of Stalin's personality cults, children's literature in the Baltic states was normative, false, and uniform, involving narrow themes and problems. We call it the literature of censorial realism because it was written according to strict rules prescribed by Party censors. Fairy tales, allegories, adventures, detective stories, and other genres that did not fit the frame of censorial realism were banned. The short poem "Oželis Kvaišelis," (A Silly Little Goat, 1951), by Kostas Kubilinskas, using fairy-tale motifs, was severely criticized with absurd argumentation, for instance, that the fairy-tale form could take the readers' imagination to a transcendental world (!). No volume of poetry or prose could appear without obligatory ideological themes: Soviet festivals, military patriotic events, the great builders of communism, young Communists, Party members, collective farms, and friendship among Soviet nations. Militarist propaganda gained a foothold. From infancy, children were exposed through books to aggressiveness and cruel fanaticism masked as hatred of the class enemy. Children's literature was framed by the Cold War. Children were deprived of reading for pleasure, and their imaginations were restricted.

After Stalin's death, an ideological thaw began. Children's writers were allowed to adjust to child psychology. The fairy tale was fully exonerated. Imagery was once again tolerated in children's books. This new form of children's literature, which can tentatively be called metaphorical realism, influenced the child's aesthetic perception of the world and at the same time stimulated a longing for a just life.

During this period, several types of artistic portrayal of the world emerged. Some writers turned back to national culture, depicting lifestyles, customs, and other ethnical values settled over the course of centuries, thus restoring an old system of rural culture. *Jurgio Paketurio klajonės* (The Wanderings of Jurgis Paketuris, 1963), by Kazys Boruta, reminds us of Baron von Munchausen or Till Elenspiegel.

Another strategy was to portray an allegoric world of despotic rulers and oppressed masses, as in *Už nevarstomų durų* (Behind the Closed Door, 1978), by Kazys Saja, and *Gilės nuotykiai Ydų šalyje* (The Adventures of Acorn in the Land of Vices, 1964), by Vytautas Petkevičius. Fairy tales and fantasy touched upon many burning moral, social, and national problems of that time. The legend-inspired novel by Vytautas Petkevičius, *Molio Motiejus žmonių karalius* (Clay Matthew the King of People,

1978), covers several centuries of a nation's existence and its struggle against enemies. The diligent people of Duonuva (Bread Land) are suffering from the rule of the bloodsucker Birbyzas. A clay statue begins to speak and live, seeing the damage caused by the oppressors. Thus a proud and freedom-loving human being is born from clay—an insensitive and unconscious matter; however, he will turn back into clay if he ever apologizes to a scoundrel. The allegoric clay Matthew gives freedom to the land of Duonuva, defeats the oppressors, and becomes a ruler who seeks freedom amd justice. But, paradoxically, free people start grumbling. Little by little fear disappears because there is no more suffering anxiety gives way to satiety; love disappears because there is no hatred. Only boredom remains, and people become mummies, encased in settled rules. Clay Matthew does not find any universal truths. Every man and every nation has its own truth.

During the so-called years of stagnation, U.S. President Ronald Reagan called the Soviet Union "the empire of evil." In Kaunas, in Lithuania, a young man burned himself to protest against evil. The instability of families, increasing alcoholism, low prestige of education, double standards, the rise of the Soviet mafia and gangs of frustrated, violent teenagers affected the nature of the "hard realism." Vytautas Račickas depicted a teenage suicide in his first book, *Zuika Padūkėlis* (Zuika, the Imp, 1985), which became a best-seller. Many famous mainstream writers, such as Vytautas Bubnys, Kazys Saja, and Algimantas Zurba, also wrote for children. In his poems addressed to teenagers, Juozas Erlickas defied the Soviet line and parodied the official poetry glorifying happy socialist childhood.

Mikhail Gorbachev's reform ideas stimulated a critical attitude on the part of writers. Upon the collapse of the totalitarian system, writers turned back to the portrayal of eternal values, such as the unity of man and nature, history and eternity. World harmony in the poetry of Antanas Vaičiulaitis, Vytautas Tamulaitis, and Bernardas Brazdžionis is opposed to distorted humanism, vulgar materialism, the pragmatism of technical civilization, and vain Soviet ambitions and illusions. These writers depart from traditional values, such as beauty and love. Poetry based on mythological sources reaches high artistic levels, at the same time reflecting subtle psychological experiences of the child—for instance, in the poems of Martynas Vainilaitis, Janina Degutytė, and Leonardas Gutauskas. Fantasy is turning away from social themes and grotesque allegories, toward universal philosophical issues. Mythical plots are interwoven with questions about the meaning of life, the damaging influence of civilization, and human behavior in different situations. In her book *Robotas ir Peteliškė* (The Robot and the Butterfly, 1978), Vytaute Žilinskaitė opposes a rational and narrow-minded robot and a kindhearted, beautiful, and emotional butterfly. Her fantastic book *Kelionė į Tandadriką* (A Journey to Tandadrika, 1984), depicts some toys that, on New Year's Eve, fly away from a dump to a dreamland called Tandadrika, where they find an infinite world facing ecological and moral problems. The purpose of the journey is to find the human essence. The animals in the story—a grasshopper missing a leg and an earthworm hanging on a hook in a lake—symbolize a saint who has given his wealth to the poor, yet is still able to share moments of happiness with other people.

When the nation risked losing its identity in the Communist society, many famous Lithuanian poets, even the official and established Lenin Prize laureates, such as Eduardas Mieželaitis and Jonas Avyžius, wrote for children, sometimes balancing on the edge of the permissible and using their authority to maintain the prestige of children's literature. Five children's writers signed the Declaration of Independence of Lithuania and became members of Parliament.

What, then, is the situation of children's literature after the fall of the totalitarian regime? Totalitarianism was in tragic conflict with human integrity. It was not able to destroy it, but it still deformed it. During the transitional period toward democratic ideals, low and brutal human instincts surfaced, which society was supposed to overcome not by repressive means but by education. Since 1990, juvenile delinquency in Lithuania has increased fourfold. Many children are dropping out of school. Libraries are closing because of insufficient state funding. Manuscripts for children's books wait forever at the publishers because book printing is no longer subsidized. Children's writers are experiencing a crisis. The market is filled with commercial books, written by scribblers, that undermine the image of children's literature. It seems to have completely lost its previous prestige.

During the period of national revival, Lithianians in exile warned against the danger of an invasion of mass culture from the West. Today, Western popular culture is flooding Lithuania. Some forecasts state that in the next ten years, up to 20 percent of young Lithuanians will lose all ties with national culture.

Is there a way to preserve national identity? One possibility, being implemented in Lithuania today, is to establish new publishing houses that will consistently bring out national children's literature and engage authors to write for children. Among such endeavors, novels based on national history have started to appear. Other means are extensive book promotion and children's literature research. The international context is especially important, since children's literature around the world is similar because it has its source in myth. Only by supporting children's literature of good quality can we withstand the aggressive invasion of mass culture.

REFERENCES

Boruta, Kazys. *Jurgio Paketurio klajonės*. Vilnius, 1963.
Kubilinskas, Kostas. "Oželis Kvaišelis." Vilnius, 1951.
Petkevičius, Vytautas. *Gilės nuotykiai Ydų šalyje*. Vilnius, 1964.
———*Molio Motiejus žmonių karalius*). Vilnius, 1978.
Račickas, Vytautas. *Zuika Padūkėlis*. Vilnius, 1985.
Saja, Kazys. *Už nevarstomų durų*. Vilnius, 1978.
Žilinskaitė, Vytaute. *Robotas ir Peteliškė*. Vilnius, 1978.
———. *Kelionė į Tandadriką*. Vilnius, 1984.

Selected Bibliography

Ariès, Philippe. *Centuries of Childhood: A Social History of Family Life*. Trans. Robert Baldick. New York: Random House, 1962.

Attebury, Brian. *The Fantasy Tradition in American Literature: From Irving to Le Guin*. Bloomington: Indiana University Press, 1980.

Avery, Gillian, and Julia Briggs, eds. *Children and Their Books: A Collection of Essays to Celebrate the Work of Iona and Peter Opie*. Oxford: Clarendon Press, 1989.

Beckett, Sandra. "La Littérature de jeunesse au Canada francophone: De la Colonisation à la conquête du monde." In *La Littérature de jeunesse au croisement des cultures*. Ed. Jean Perrot and Pierre Bruno. Le Perreux: CRDP d'Ile-de-France, Académie de Créteil, 1993.

———. "From the Art of Rewriting for Children to the Art of Crosswriting Child and Adult: the Secret of Michel Tournier's Dual Readership." In *Voices from Far Away. Current Trends in International Children's Literature Research* 24. Ed. Maria Nikolajeva. Stockholm: Centrum för Barnkulturforskning vid Stockholms Universitet, 1995.

———. *Les Grands Romanciers écrivent pour les enfants 1945–1995*. Geneva and Paris: La Nacelle, forthcoming.

Bravo-Villasante, Carmen. *Historia de la literatura infantil española*. Madrid: Escuela Española, 1986.

Brooks, Peter. *Reading for the Plot: Design and Intention in Narrative*. New York: Knopf, 1984.

Bunbury, Rhonda, ed. *A Decade of Research in Children's Literature*. Geelong, Australia: International Research Society for Children's Literature, 1995.

Butts, Dennis, ed. *Stories and Society: Children's Literature in Its Social Context*. Basingstoke and London: Macmillan, 1992.

Caradec, François. *Histoire de la littérature enfantine en France*. Paris: Albin Michel, 1977.

Carpenter, Humfrey, and Mari Prichard. *The Oxford Companion to Children's Literature*. London: Oxford University Press, 1984.

Cawelti, John G. *Adventure, Mystery, and Romance: Formula Stories as Art and Popular Culture*. Chicago: University of Chicago Press, 1976.

Chambers, Aidan. "The Reader in the Book." *Signal* 23 (1977). Reprinted in *Booktalk: Occasional Writings on Literature and Children*. London: Bodley Head, 1985.

Chernyavskaya, Irina, ed. *Zarubezhnaya detskaya literatura*. 2nd ed. Moscow: Prosveshcheniye, 1982.

Chiou, Ge-rung. *Historical Materials for Children's Literature: 1945–1989*. Taipei: Fu Tsen, 1990. (In Chinese).

Chukovsky, Kornei. *From Two to Five*. Berkeley: University of California Press, 1963.

Cott, Jonathan. *Pipers at the Gates of Dawn: The Wisdom of Children's Literature*. New York: Random House, 1983.

Coveney, Peter. *The Image of Childhood, the Individual and Society*. Harmondsworth: Penguin, 1967.

Crago, Hugh. "Cultural Categories and the Criticism of Children's Literature." *Signal* 30 (1979): 140–150.

Craig, David, and Michael Egan. *Extreme Situations: Literature and Crisis from the Great War to the Atom Bomb*. London: Macmillan, 1979.

Crouch, Marcus. *The Nesbit Tradition: The Children's Novel in England 1945–1970*. London: Ernest Benn, 1972.

Cullinan, Bernice E. *Literature and the Child*. 2nd ed. San Diego: Harcourt Brace Jovanovich, 1989.

Deane, Paul. *Mirrors of American Culture: Children's Fiction Series in the Twentieth Century*. Metuchen, N.J., and London: Scarecrow Press, 1991.

Doderer, Klaus, ed. *Neue Helden in der Kinder- und Jugendliteratur*. Weinheim and Munich: Juventa, 1986.

Egoff, Sheila A. *Thursday's Child: Trends and Patterns in Contemporary Children's Literature*. Chicago: American Library Association, 1981.

———. *Worlds Within: Children's Fantasy from the Middle Ages to Today*. Chicago: American Library Association, 1988.

Egoff, Sheila, G. T. Stubbs, and L. F. Ashley, eds. *Only Connect: Readings on Children's Literature*. 2nd ed. Toronto: Oxford University Press, 1980.

Escarpit, Denise. *La Littérature d'enfance et de jeunesse en Europe: Panorama historique*. Paris: Presses Universitaires de France, 1981.

Ewers, Hans-Heino. "Themen-, Formen- und Funktionswandel der westdeutschen Kinderliteratur seit Ende der 60er, Anfang der 70er Jahre." *Germanistik* n.s. 2 (1995): 257–278.

——— ed. *Komik im Kinderbuch: Erscheinungsformen des Komischen in der Kinder- und Jugendliteratur*. Weinheim and Munich: Juventa, 1992.

Ewers, Hans-Heino, Maria Lypp, and Ulrich Nassen, eds. *Kinderliteratur und Moderne: Ästhetische Herausforderungen der Kinderliteratur im 20 Jahrhundert*. Weinheim and Munich: Juventa, 1990.

Eyre, Frank. *British Children's Books in the Twentieth Century*. London: Longman, 1971.

Featherstone, Mike, ed. *Cultural Theory and Cultural Change*. London: Sage, 1992.

Fisher, Margery. *The Bright Face of Danger*. London: Hodder and Stoughton, 1986.

Fraser, James H., ed. *Society and Children's Literature*. Boston: Godine, 1978.

Fu, Lin Tong. *Introduction to Young Adult Fiction*. Taipei: Fu Tsen, 1994. (In Chinese).

Gilead, Sarah. "Magic Abjured: Closure in Children's Fantasy Fiction." *PMLA* 106 (1991): 277–293.

Goldberg, David Theo, ed. *Multiculturalism: A Critical Reader*. Cambridge, Mass.: Blackwell, 1994.

Griswold, Jerry. *Audacious Kids: Coming of Age in America's Classic Children's Books*. New York and Oxford: Oxford University Press, 1992.

Haas, Gerhard, ed. *Kinder- und Jugendliteratur: Zur Typologie und Funktion einer literarischen Gattung*. Stuttgart: Reclam, 1974.

————. *Kinder- und Jugendliteratur. Ein Handbuch.* 3rd, rev. ed. Stuttgart: Reclam, 1984.

Hagemann, Sonja. *Barnelitteratur i Norge 1914–1970.* Oslo: Aschehoug, 1974.

Hazard, Paul. *Books, Children, and Men.* Trans. Marguerite Mitchell. Boston: Horn Book, 1944.

Hellman, Ben. *Barn- och ungdomsboken i Sovjetryssland. Från oktoberrevolutionen 1917 till perestrojkan 1986.* Stockholm: Rabén and Sjögren, 1991.

Hendrickson, Linnea. *Children's Literature: A Guide to the Criticism.* Boston: G. K. Hall, 1987.

Higonnet, Margaret R. "Narrative Fractures and Fragments." *Children's Literature* 15 (1987): 37–54.

Hollindale, Peter. "Ideology and the Children's Book." *Signal* 55 (1988): 3–22.

Hollins, Robert A., and Howard D. Pearce, eds. *The Scope of the Fantastic—Culture, Biography, Themes, Children's Literature.* Westport, Conn.: Greenwood Press, 1985.

Hong, Wen-chiung. "The Developmental Trends of Young Adult Fiction in Taiwan from 1945 to 1990." In *Chronicle for Children's Literature: 1945–1990.* Ed. Wen-chiung Hong et al. Taipei: Society of Children's Literature, the ROC, 1991. (In Chinese).

————. "Observations on the Development of Children's Literature in Taiwan from 1945 to 1990." In *Chronicle for Children's Literature: 1945–1990.* Ed. Wen-chiung Hong et al. Taipei: Society of Children's Literature, the ROC, 1991. (In Chinese).

————. *A History of Chinese Children's Literature: 1945–1990.* Taipei: Society of Children's Literature, the ROC, 1991. (In Chinese).

Hong, Wen-chiung. *A History of Children's Literature in Taiwan.* Taipei: Chuan Wen, 1994.

————. *Reflections on Children's Literature.* Taipei: Chuan Wen, 1994. (In Chinese).

Hong, Wen-chiung, et al., eds. *Chronicle for Children's Literature: 1945–1990.* Taipei: Society of Children's Literature, the ROC, 1991. (In Chinese).

Hunt, Peter. "Necessary Misreadings: Directions in Narrative Theory for Children's Literature." *Studies in the Literary Imagination* 18 (1985): 107–121.

————. *Criticism, Theory, and Children's Literature.* Cambridge, Mass.: Blackwell, 1991.

————. *An Introduction to Children's Literature.* Oxford: Oxford University Press, 1994.

————, ed. *Literature for Children: Contemporary Criticism.* London: Routledge, 1993.

Inglis, Fred. *The Promise of Happiness: Value and Meaning in Children's Literature.* Cambridge: Cambridge University Press, 1981.

Jackson, Rosemary. *Fantasy: The Literature of Subversion.* London: Methuen, 1981.

Kaminski, Winfred. *Jugendliteratur und Revolte: Jugendprotest und seine Spiegelung in der Literatur für junge Leser.* Frankfurt, dipa, 1982.

————. "Vom realistischen zum phantastischen Helden. Aspekte des Wandels in der Kinder- und Jugendliteratur seit 1968." In *Neue Helden in der Kinder- und Jugendliteratur.* Ed. Klaus Doderer. Weinheim and Munich: Juventa, 1986.

Kensinger, Faye Riter. *Children of the Series and How They Grew; Or, A Century of Heroines and Heroes, Romantic, Comic, Moral.* Bowling Green, Ohio: Bowling Green State University Popular Press, 1987.

Kermode, Frank. *The Sense of an Ending: Studies in the Theory of Fiction.* New York: Oxford University Press, 1967.

Kies, Cosette. *Young Adult Horror Fiction.* New York: Twayne, 1992.

Kirkpatrick, D. L., ed. *Twentieth-Century Children's Writers.* 3rd ed. Chicago: St. James, 1989.

Krüger, Anna. *Die erzählende Kinder- und Jugendliteratur im Wandel: Neue Inhalte und Formen im Kommunikations- und Sozialisationsmittel Jugendliteratur.* Frankfurt: Diesterweg, 1980.

Kuznets, Lois. *When Toys Come Alive: Narratives of Animation, Metamorphosis, and Development*. New Haven and London: Yale University Press, 1994.

Landsberg, Michele. *The World of Children's Books*. London: Simon & Schuster, 1988.

Larrick, Nancy. "The All-White World of Children's Books." *Saturday Review*, September 11, 1965, pp. 63–85.

Leeson, Robert. *Children's Books and Class Society: Past and Present*. London: Writers and Readers Publishing Cooperative, 1977.

Lesnik-Oberstein, Karín. *Children's Literature: Criticism and the Fictional Child*. Oxford: Clarendon Press, 1994.

Lochhead, Marion. *The Renaissance of Wonder in Children's Literature*. Edinburgh: Canongate, 1977.

MacLeod, Anne Scott. *A Moral Tale*. Hamden, Conn.: Archon Books, 1975.

Madore, Edith. *La Littérature pour la jeunesse au Québec*. Montreal: Éditions Boréal, 1994.

Malarte, Claire-Lise. "The French Fairy-Tale Conspiracy." *The Lion and the Unicorn* 12, no. 2 (1988): 112–120.

Martin, Wallace. *Recent Theories of Narrative*. Ithaca, N.Y.: Cornell University Press, 1986.

Mattenklott, Gundel. *Zauberkreide: Kinderliteratur seit 1945*. Stuttgart: J. B. Metzler, 1989.

McGillis, Rod. *The Nimble Reader: Literary Theory and Children's Literature*. New York: Twayne, 1996.

Morrison, Toni. *Playing in the Dark: Whiteness and the Literary Imagination*. New York: Vintage, 1992.

Niall, Brenda. *Australia Through the Looking Glass: Children's Fiction 1830–1980*. Brunswick: Melbourne University Press, 1984.

Nikolajeva, Maria. *The Magic Code*. Goteborg: Almqvist & Wiksell International, 1988.

———. *Children's Literature Comes of Age: Toward a New Aesthetics*. New York and London: Garland, 1995.

———. "Russian Children's Literature Before and After Perestroika." *Children's Literature Association Quarterly* 20, no. 3 (Fall 1995): 105–111.

———, ed. *Aspects and Issues in the History of Children's Literature*. Westport, Conn.: and London: Greenwood Press, 1995.

———. *Voices from Far Away. Current Trends in International Children's Literature Research* 24. Stockholm: Centrum för Barnkulturforskning vid Stockholms Universitet, 1995.

Nilson, Alleen, and Kenneth Donelson, eds. *Literature for Today's Young Adults*. 2nd ed. Glenview, Ill.: Scott, Foresman, 1993.

Nodelman, Perry. *Words About Pictures: The Narrative Art of Children's Books*. Athens and London: University of Georgia Press, 1988.

———. "The Other: Orientalism, Colonialism, and Children's Literature." *Children's Literature Association Quarterly* 17, no. 1 (Spring 1992): 29–35.

———. *The Pleasures of Children's Literature*. White Plains, N.Y.: Longman, 1992.

O'Dell, Felicity Ann. *Socialization Through Literature: The Soviet Example*. Cambridge: Cambridge University Press, 1978.

O'Sullivan, Emer. *Friend and Foe: The Image of Germany and the Germans in British Children's Fiction from 1870 to the Present*. Tübingen: Narr, 1990.

Otten, Charlotte F., and Gary D. Schmidt, eds. *The Voice of the Narrator in Children's Literature: Insights from Writers and Critics*. Westport, Conn.: Greenwood Press, 1989.

Perrot, Jean. *Art baroque, art d'enfance*. Nancy: Presses Universitaires de Nancy, 1991.

———, ed. *Culture, texte et jeune lecteur*. Actes du Xe Congrès de l'IRSCL, Paris, September 1991. Nancy: Presses Universitaires de Nancy, 1993.

Rees, David. *The Marble in the Water: Essays on Contemporary Writers of Fiction for Children and Young Adults.* Boston: Horn Book, 1980.

―――. *Painted Desert, Green Shade: Essays on Contemporary Writers for Children and Young Adults.* Boston: Horn Book, 1984.

Rose, Jacqueline. *The Case of Peter Pan; or, The Impossibility of Children's Fiction.* London: Macmillan, 1984.

Rustin, Margaret, and Michael Rustin. *Narratives of Love and Loss: Studies in Modern Children's Fiction.* London and New York: Verso, 1987.

Sadker, Myra Pollack, and David Miller Sadker. *Now upon a Time: A Contemporary View of Children's Literature.* New York: Harper & Row, 1977.

Saxby, Maurice. *A History of Australian Children's Literature 1941–1970.* Sydney: Wentworth, 1971.

―――. *The Proof of the Puddin': Australian Children's Literature 1970–1990.* Sydney: Ashton Scholastic, 1993.

Shavit, Zohar. *Poetics of Children's Literature.* Athens and London: University of Georgia Press, 1986.

Sims, Rudine. *Shadow and Substance: Afro-American Experience in Contemporary Children's Fiction.* Urbana, Ill.: National Council of Teachers of English, 1982.

Soriano, Marc. *Guide de la littérature pour la jeunesse.* Paris: Flammarion, 1975.

Spacks, Patricia Meyer. *The Adolescent Idea: Myths of Youth and the Adult Imagination.* New York: Basic Books, 1981.

Steffens, Wilhelm. "Literarische und didaktische Aspekte des modernen Kinderbuchs." *Die Grundschulzeitschrift* 39 (1990): 30–34; 40 (1990): 28–35.

Stephens, John. "Advocating Multiculturalism: Migrants in Australian Children's Literature After 1972." *Children's Literature Association Quarterly* 15, no. 4 (1990): 180–185.

―――. *Language and Ideology in Children's Fiction.* London and New York: Longman, 1992.

―――. "Post-Disaster Fiction: The Problematics of a Genre," *Papers: Explorations into Children's Literature* 3, no. 3 (1992): 126–130.

Tabbert, Reinbert. "The Impact of Children's Books: Cases and Concepts." *Children's Literature in Education* 10 (1979): 92–102, 144–150.

Townsend, John Rowe. *A Sounding of Storytellers: New and Revised Essays on Contemporary Writers for Children.* New York: Lippincott, 1979.

Vérot, Marguerite. "Le Roman psychologique." In *Tendances actuelles de la littérature pour la jeunesse.* Paris: Éditions Magnard and Éditions de l'École, 1975.

Walsh, Jill Paton. "Realism, Fantasy and History: Facts in Fiction." *Canadian Children's Literature* 48 (1987): 7–14.

Watkins, Tony. "Cultural Studies, New Historicism and Children's Literature." In *Literature for Children: Contemporary Criticism.* Ed. Peter Hunt. London: Routledge, 1993.

Zipes, Jack. *Fairy Tales and the Art of Subversion: The Classical Genre for Children and the Process of Civilization.* London: Heinemann, 1983.

―――. *The Brothers Grimm: From Enchanted Forests to the Modern World:* New York: Routledge, 1988.

―――, ed. *Don't Bet on the Prince: Contemporary Feminist Fairy Tales in North America and England.* Aldershot, U.K.: Gower; New York: Methuen, 1986.

―――. *The Trials and Tribulations of Little Red Riding Hood: Versions of the Tale in Sociocultural Context.* New York: Routledge, 1993.

Index

The Abduction (Newth), 60
Admission to the Feast (Beckman), 88
Adventures in the Big-Nose Country (Huang), 159
The Adventures of Pinocchio (Collodi), 86
The Adventures of Tom Sawyer (Twain), 86
Aesop, 36, 39
Alain-Fournier. *See* Fournier, Henri Alban
Alcott, Louisa May, 29 n.9, 36
Alice, 55
Alice in Wonderland (Carroll), 51, 54, 55, 85
Alles Rainer Zufall (Dirx), 54–55
All We Know (French), 107–13
Althusser, Louis, 9, 12
American Werewolf in London (Landis), 103
Andrews, V. C., 101
Anna Keeps Her Promise (Bergström), 86
Anne of Green Gables (Montgomery), 85
Annelie in the Depths of the Night (Dros), 45–46
Annetje Lie in het holst van de nacht (Dros), 45–46
Arbeitsgruppen, 51
Ariès, Philippe, 35, 37, 51

Arthur, King, 36, 39, 92
Ash Road (Southall), 107
Austen, Jane, 37
The Australian Ugliness (Boyd), 109
Australia Through the Looking Glass (Niall), 113 n.9
Avyžius, Jonas, 181

Babar, 55
Babar the Little Elephant (Brunhoff), 85
Babysitter (Stine), 104
Babysitter II (Stine), 104
Babysitter books (Stine), 100, 103
Babysitter's Club, 4
Bajerčius, Kazys, 178
Bakhtin, Mikhail, 85
Barrie, James, 40
Barth, John, 95
Barthes, Roland, 54
Basis Verlag, 51
Bates, A., 101, 102
Bawden, Nina, 165
Beach Party (Stine), 103
Beasts of Suburbia (Ferber), 110
Beauty and the Beast (Disney film), 39
Beavis and Butthead, 40
Becker, Jörg, 51
Beezus and Ramona (Cleary), 25
Belsvik, Rune, 60, 62
Berquin, Arnaud, 138 n.1

Betsy's First Day at the Day-care Center (Wolde), 88
Bettelheim, Bruno, 39, 76–77
Beyond the Chocolate War (Cormier), 66–70
Big, 41 n.12
The Bizarre Flight (Huang), 159
Black Arrow (Stevenson), 164
The Black Hen, 171
Blade Runner, 18
Block, Francesca Lia, 17, 20–21
Blood and Lace series, 101, 102
Blume, Judy, 39, 133, 136, 139 n.7
The Boggart (Cooper), 91–96
Bonaparte, Napoleon, 61
Books, Children, and Men (Hazard), 3, 5–9
Booth, Wayne, 26
Boréal Inter, 138 n.2
Boroditskaya, Marina, 173
Borrobil (Dickinson), 87
The Borrowers (Norton), 85, 86
The Borrowers Afloat (Norton), 86
The Borrowers Aloft (Norton), 86
Bortførelsen (Newth), 60
Boruta, Kazys, 179
Boyd, Robin, 109
The Boyfriend (Stine), 103
Brazdžionis, Bernardas, 180
Breaktime (Chambers), 88
Brezhnev, Leonid, 178
Broken Date (Stine), 102
The Brontë, 37
Brooks, Bruce, 118
Brooks, Peter, 71 n.16
Brother Eagle, Sister Sky (Jeffers), 117
The Brothers Lionheart (Lindgren), 86
Brueghel, Pieter, 35
Bubnys, Vytautas, 180
The Bulletin (Australia), 109
Burns, George, 41 n.12
"The Bush Undertaker" (Lawson), 109
Butler, Francelia, 24
Butler, Judith, 12
The Butter Battle Book (Seuss), 40

Cadogan, Mary, 165, 168 n.3
Camp Fear (Ellis), 103, 104

The Canon and the Common Reader (Kaplan and Rose), 29 n.9
Capone, Al, 37
Carby, Hazel, 116
Carpenter, John, 103
Carrie's War (Bawden), 165
Carroll, Lewis, 36, 55, 94
The Catcher in the Rye (Salinger), 126
Catching Salamanders (Kusters), 44
The Centerberg Tales (McCloskey), 88
The Central Daily Newspaper (Taiwan), 154
Certeau, Michel de, 23
Chambers, Aidan, 27–28
Chang, Chih-lu, 156
Charlie and the Chocolate Factory (Dahl), 87
Charlotte's Web (White), 51, 89
Chernii, Sasha, 173
Chidolue, Dagmar, 145–47
Child Loving: The Erotic Child and Victorian Culture (Kincaid), 7
The Children of Green Knowe (Boston), 86, 87
Children of the New Forest (Marryat), 164
The Children of the Noisy Village, 86
The Children's Daily Newspaper (Taiwan), 156
Children Without Childhood (Winn), 37
The Chimneys of Green Knowe (Boston), 87
The Chinese Zodiac, 157
The Chocolate War (Cormier), 29, 66–70
Chukovsky, Kornej, 173, 175
Cinderella, 62, 145
Cinderella (Disney film), 40
Cleary, Beverly, 23–29, 126
Climb a Lonely Hill (Norman), 107
Coïncidence Jeunesse, 138 n.2
Coleman, Gary, 37
College Weekend (Stine), 102
Comet in Moominland (Jansson), 89
The Comicbook Chinese History, 156
Coming Down to Earth (Price), 18, 19, 21 n.4
Commager, Henry Steele, 36–37, 39
Coogan, Jackie, 37

Cooper, James Fenimore, 37, 60, 164
Cooper, Susan, 91–96
The Coral Island (Ballantyne), 87
Cormier, Robert, 66–70, 72, n.20, 139
   n.7
La Courte Échelle, 132, 138 n.2
Craig, David, 164
Craig, Patricia, 165, 168 n.3
Critical Essays on American
   Postmodernism (Trachtenberg), 95
"Criticism and Children's Literature"
   (Hunt), 46
*Criticism, Theory, and Children's
   Literature* (Hunt), 50
Cross, Gillian, 75–80
Crutcher, Chris, 127–28, 129
The Cuckoo Clock (Molesworth), 87
The Cucumber King (Nöstlinger), 52
Cunningham, Sean S., 103
Curious George (Rey), 85, 87
Cusick, Richie Tankersley, 99, 101, 102

Dagens Nyheter, 50
Dahrendorf, Malte, 51
The Dark Is Rising (Cooper), 88, 93
The Dark Is Rising series (Cooper),
   91, 92, 95
Das war der Hirbel (Härtling), 141
David Copperfield (Dickens), 85
Dawn of Fear (Cooper), 92
Deadly Relations (Locke), 102
Deane, Paul, 70 n.4
Dear Mili (Sendak), 39
Dear Mr. Henshaw (Cleary), 24
Deesje (van Leeuwen), 45
Degutytė, Janina, 180
DeLuca, Geraldine, 24
DeMause, Lloyd, 144
Demers, Dominique, 132–38
*Den som kysser i vinden blæs ikkje bort
   aleine* (Belsvik), 60, 62
Le Dernier des raisins (Plante), 138 n.3
Dick, Philip, 18
Dickens, Charles, 36, 37
Die Softly (Pike), 102
Dirx, Jörn Peter, 54–55
Disney, Walt, 11, 39, 40
Do Androids Dream of Electric Sheep
   (Dick), 18
Doctor, Bu Du and I (Lai), 159

Doctor Who "Robots of Death," 18
Doderer, Klaus, 51
The Dolphin Crossing (Walsh), 165–66
Donovan, John, 126
Dracula (Stoker), 100, 103
Dream Days (Grahame), 168 n.11
Dros, Imme, 45
Dynasty, 60

Échos, 138, n.2
Ecstasia (Block), 19, 20–21 n.4
Egan, Michael, 164
Egoff, Sheila, 91
Eight Children and a Truck (Vastly), 86
Eighteen Again, 41 n.12
Einstein, Albert, 95
Eliade, Mircea, 135
Elkind, David, 37
Ellis, Carol, 101, 102, 103
Ellis, Edward Sylvester, 60
Elidor (Garner), 87, 89
Emil and the Detectives (Kästner), 86
Emil's Pranks (Lindgren), 86
Emily Climbs (Montgomery), 86
Emily of New Moon (Montgomery), 85
Emily of New Moon series
   (Montgomery), 132–38
An Enemy at Green Knowe (Boston), 87
Ericsson, Stig, 60
Erisman, Fred, 71 n.6
Eurydice, 20
Ewers, Hans Heino, 147

The Facts and Fictions of Minna Pratt
   (MacLachlan), 88
The Famous Five (Blyton), 86
Fatal Attraction (Lyne), 103
Fear Street series, 101
Featherstone, Mike, 23–24
Felsen, Henry, 126
Final Exam (Bates), 102
Fireweed (Walsh), 168 n.14
The First Two Lives of Lukas-Kasha
   (Alexander), 89
Fitzhugh, Louise, 66–70, 71 n.11
Five on a Treasure Island (Blyton), 85
Flight to the Future (Huang), 159
Flossie and the Fox (McKissack),
   120–21

Flowers in the Attic (Andrews), 101
Forever (Blume), 39
Fournier, Henri Alban (pseud. Alain-
    Fournier), 133
French, Simon, 107–13
Freud, Sigmund, 71 n.16, 76–77, 95
Frey, Charles, 27
Friday and Robinson (Tournier), 88
Friday the 13th (Cunningham), 103
Frommlet, Wolfgang, 51
*From the Mixed-up Files of Mrs. Basil
    E. Frankweiler* (Konisburg), 88
The Future Trap (Jinks), 17–18, 21 n.4

Gaarder, Jostein, 61–62
Galax-Arena (Rubenstein), 19–20
Gavroche, 133
Geisel, Theodor Seuss (pseud. Dr.
    Seuss), 39–40
*Die Geschichte von der Verjagung und
    Ausstopfung des Königs* (Röhrbein),
    51
Ghost (Zucker), 103
Ghostbusters, 103
Gilés nuotykiai Ydų šalyje
    (Petkevičius), 179
The Girlfriend (Stine), 103
The Giver (Lowry), 24–25, 29 n.4
Gleeson, Libby, 75
Gogol, Nikolai, 173
Going Back (Lively), 165, 168 n.11
Goldberg, David Theo, 115
The Golden Age (Grahame), 168 n.11
Good-bye, Kinmen, 158
Good-bye, Tian Ren Jiu (Lai), 158
Goosebumps series, 4, 101
Gorbachev, Mikhail, 178
Grahame, Kenneth, 168 n.11
Gramsci, Antonio, 9
Le Grand Meaulnes (Alain-Fournier),
    133
Les Grands Sapins ne meurent pas
    (Demers), 132
Die grauen und die grünen Felder
    (Wölfel), 141
Great Expectations (Dickens), 29
The Great Gilly Hopkins (Paterson), 87
The Grey King (Cooper), 93
Griffith, John, 27

Grigorjev, Oleg, 173
Gripe, Maria, 59–60, 62–63
Guan, Jia-chi, 158
Guan, Weixing, 156
Gubarev, Vitaly, 178
Gulliver's Travels (Swift), 37
Gutauskas, Leonardas, 180

Hai Huang. *See* Huang, Pi-huang
Halloween (Carpenter), 103
Hanks, Tom, 41 n.12
The Happy Lion (Duvoisin), 85
Hardison, O. B., Jr., 18
Harell, Janice, 104
Harper & Row, 39
Harriet the Spy (Fitzhugh), 66–70, 85
Harris, Jesse, 101, 102
Härtling, Peter, 141, 142
Hartnett, Sonja, 16–17, 21 n.4
Haugen, Tormod, 55, 58, 62, 149 n.20
Haunted (Stine), 102, 103
Hazard, Paul, 3–4, 5–10
The Heart of A-hei (Lin), 157
The Heart of Shiau-uan (Guan), 158
Heather Has Two Mommies (Newman),
    88
Heidi, 85
Heidi (Spyri), 86
Heller, Agnes, 23
Henty, George Albert, 164
Héritage, 138 n.2
Herrnstein-Smith, Barbara, 68, 72 n.25
Hitler, Adolf, 95, 166
Un Hiver de tourmente (Demers), 132,
    139 nn.5, 9
Hoban, Russell, 39, 159
Hoh, Diane, 101
Hollindale, Peter, 121, 168 n. 4
Holm, Annika, 148
Holmås, Stig, 60
Homecoming (Voigt), 88
The Hong Chia Chon Group, 155
Hook (Spielberg), 40
House of Horrors series, 101
Huang, Pi-huang (pseud. Hai Huang),
    158, 159
Huckleberry Finn, 133
Hugo, Victor, 133
Hugo and Josephine (Gripe), 86
Hunt, Peter, 27, 46, 50, 72 n.22, 76

The Hurried Child (Elkind), 37

I Am the Cheese (Cormier), 88
The Ice Is Coming (Wrightson), 88
Ideas for Australian Cities (Stretton),
    110
I'll Get There. It Better Be Worth the
    Trip (Donovan), 126
The Illustrated Shakespeare, 157
Illustrated Short Story Masterpieces,
    157
Ils dansent dans la tempête (Demers),
    132, 136
The Immortal (Pike), 104
In Search of Nancy Drew (Haugen), 88
Instead of a Dad (Thorvall), 88
Into the Woods (Sondheim), 39
Iphigenia in Tauris (Euripides), 85
The Island (Paulsen), 87
Island of the Blue Dolphins (O'Dell), 87
Ivanhoe (Scott), 164

Jacob Have I Loved (Paterson), 86, 88
Jacob Two-two Meets the Hooded Fang
    (Richler), 87–88
Jakubėnas, Kazys, 178
James, David, 163
James and the Giant Peach (Dahl), 86
Jane Eyre (Brontë), 85
Janne, min vän (Pohl), 60
Jarrell, Randall, 39
Jeffers, Susan, 117
Jinks, Catherine, 17–18, 21 n.4
Johnny, My Friend (Pohl), 60, 87
Johns, Captain W. E., 164
Josephine (Gripe), 86
Jou, Iau-ping, 158
Journey (MacLachlan), 87
Joyce, William, 119–20, 121
Jung, Carl Gustav, 77
Jurgio Paketurio klajonės (Boruta), 179
Just William (Crompton), 86

Kabalmysteriet (Gaarder), 61–62
Kafka, Franz, 55
Kaplan, Carey, 29 n.9
Karlson on the Roof (Lindgren), 85
Kästner, Erich, 50
Keeping Secrets (Haugen), 89

Kelionė į Tandadriką (Žilinskaitė), 180
Ke Ma Lan the Youth (Lai), 159
Kermode, Frank, 68
Khrushchev, Nikita,178
Kies, Cosette, 101
Kincaid, James, 7, 8
King, Stephen, 101, 103
The Kingdom by the Sea (Westall), 89
Kipling, Rudyard, 78
Kissing in the Wind (Belsvik), 60
Kluev, Evgenii, 173
Krüss, James, 50
Kruzkov, Grigory, 173
Kubilinskas, Kostas, 179
Ku-ka-re-ku, 171
Kusters, Wiel, 44
Kuznets, Lois, 4–5
The Kwang Fu Book Company, 156

Lacan, Jacques, 10–11
Lai, Si-an (pseud. Tung Li), 158–59
La Mancha, Don Quixote de, 55
The Land Beyond (Gripe), 87
Landis, John, 103
The Land of Green Ginger (Langley),
    87
Language and Ideology in Children's
    Fiction (Stephens), 9
Larrick, Nancy, 115
Lasse's Grandfather Is Dead (Eurelius),
    88
The Last Battle (Lewis), 88
Last of the Mohicans (Cooper), 164
Lauren, Ralph, 102
Lawson, Henry, 109
Lear, Edward, 54
Lefebvre, Henri, 23
Le Guin, Ursula, 96
L'Engle, Madeleine, 126
Leprince de Beaumont, Mme., 138 n.1
Lesnik-Oberstein, Karín, 27
Letters to the Cow (Sobakin), 175
Lewis, C. S., 94
Like Father, like Son, 41 n.12
Lin, Chung-lung, 157
Lin, Hai-yin, 156
Lindgren, Astrid, 49, 59
The Lion, the Witch and the Wardrobe
    (Lewis), 87

The Literary Heritage of Childhood: An Appraisal of Children's Classics in the Western Tradition (Frey and Griffith), 27

Little Black Sambo (Bannerman), 85

The Little Friend Monthly (Taiwan), 156

Little Lord Fauntleroy (Burnett), 85

Little Men (Alcott), 65

The Little Prince (Saint-Exupéry), 85

The Little Princess (Burnett), 85

Little Red Riding Hood, 76, 77

Little Red Riding Hood (Perrault), 77

The Little Witch (Preussler), 85

Little Women (Alcott), 29 n.9, 65

Lively, Penelope, 165

Les livres, les enfants, et les hommes (Hazard), 3, 5–9

Locke, John, 36

Locke, Joseph, 101, 102

The Locker (Cusick), 102

Longfellow, Henry Wadsworth, 37

The Long Secret (Fitzhugh), 66–70, 71 n.12

Looking for Alibrandi (Marchetta), 88

Lowry, Lois, 24–25, 28

Lucky Hans, 145

Lurie, Alison, 51, 54

Lyne, Adrian, 103

Lypp, Maria, 54, 142

The Machine-Gunners (Westall), 166–67, 168 n.4

Mack, Louise, 65

MacLeod, Anne Scott, 138

Maffesoli, Michel, 23

Le Magasin des adolescents (Leprince de Beaumont), 138

The Magic Bed-knob (Norton), 87

Magic by the Lake (Eager), 88

The Magic City (Nesbit), 87

The Magic Code (Nikolajeva), 91

The Magic Finger (Dahl), 87

The Magic Tunnel (Emerson), 87

The Magic Walking-stick (Buchan), 87

Malena Starts School (Lindqvist), 88

Malot, Hector, 70 n.3

The Mandarin Chinese Daily Newspaper (Taiwan), 158

The Mandarin Daily Newspaper (Taiwan), 154, 156

Marie-Lune series (Demers), 133

Marryat, Frederick, 164

Marshall, James, 38–39

Marvin Redpost: Why Pick on Me? (Sachar), 24

Mary Poppins (Travers), 55, 85

Mary Poppins Comes Back (Travers), 86

Mattenklott, Gundel, 49

McAuliffe, Chris, 110, 113

McGillis, Roderick, 70, n.5

McKissack, Patricia, 120–21

Mebs, Gudrun, 144–48, 149 n.24

Mein Kampf (Hitler), 166

Meštrović, Stjepan, 15, 16, 19–20

Mickey Mouse, 55

Midnight Is a Place (Aiken), 88

Mieželaitis, Eduardas, 181

Miller, Alice, 144

Miller, J. Hillis, 68, 71 n.18

Milton, John, 92

Mio, My Son (Lindgren), 87

Miroirs of American Culture (Deane), 70 n.4

Modern Fairy Tales, 157

Molio Motiejus žmonių karalius (Petkevičius), 179–80

Moll Flanders (Defoe), 85

Momo (Ende), 87

Der Mond wird dick und wieder dünn (Mebs), 149 n.24

Montgomery, Lucy Maud, 132–38

Moominland in November (Jansson), 89

Moore, Dudley, 41 n.12

More, Hannah, 36

Morgenstern, Susie, 136

Morozov, Pavlik, 178

Morrison, Toni, 116

Mouse and His Child (Hoban), 39, 159

The Mouse Bride, 157

The Moves Make the Man (Brooks), 118

Mowgli, 78

Mrs. Frisby and the Rats of NIMH (O'Brien), 159

My Daddy Says Your Daddy Is in Prison (Thorvall), 88

My Secret Admirer (Ellis), 102

Nabokov, Vladimir, 173
Die Nachtvögel (Haugen), 149 n.20
Napoli, Donna Jo, 18–19, 21 n.4
Nattfuglene (Haugen), 149 n.20
Naylor, Phyllis Reynolds, 28
Neverland (Forward), 88
Newbery, John, 36
Newman, Charles, 54
Newth, Mette, 60, 63
The New Urn of the Long-Eared God (Lai), 158
New York Times, 117
Niall, Brenda, 113 n.9
Nightmare Matinee (Garth), 104
Nightmare on Elm Street, 103
Night of the Living Dead, 103
Nikolajeva, Maria, 91, 95
Nodelman, Perry, 25
The Nonsense Book of Problems (Oster), 172
Norman, Lilith, 107
Nöstlinger, Christine, 52, 141

O'Brien, Robert C., 159
Oedipus Rex (Sophocles), 85
Old Yeller, 40
Olesha, Yuri, 172
Oma (Härtling), 142–43, 144, 146, 147
Ong, Walter, 54
Orality and Literacy (Ong), 54
Orfe (Voigt), 19, 20, 21 n.4
Orientalism (Said), 4
Orpheus, 20
O'Sullivan, Emer, 169 n.18
Oster, Grigori, 172, 174–75
Outside Over There (Sendak), 39
"Oželis Kvaišelis" (Kubilinskas), 179

A Pack of Lies (MacCaughrean), 88
"Paradigm Shift in Plot Models: An Outline of the History of Narratology" (Ronen), 71 n.16
Paradise Lost (Milton), 92
Park's Quest (Paterson), 88
Parley, Peter, 36
Peirce, C.S., 116
Perrault, Charles, 5, 36, 77
Peter Pan (Barrie), 40, 88, 168 n.12
Peter Rabbit (Potter), 85
Petkevičius, Vytautas, 179

Petronius, 77
Pflieger, Pat, 24
The Phantom Tollbooth (Juster), 87
Pike, Christopher, 101, 102
Pilgrim's Progress (Bunyan), 36
Pioneer (Russia), 171
Pippi Longstocking (Lindgren), 49, 86
The Pirates of the Deep Green Sea (Linklater), 85
Pischmarie (Chidolue), 145–47
Plante, Raymond, 138 n.3, 139, n.9
Playing in the Dark: Whiteness and the Literary Imagination (Morrison), 116
Pludra, Benno, 149 n.24
Plumb, J. H., 35
Plutarch, 36
Pocahontas, 40
Poe, Edgar Allan, 37
Poetic Closure: A Study of How Poems End (Herrnstein-Smith), 72 n.25
Pohl, Peter, 55, 60
Pollyanna (Porter), 40
The Possession (Harris), 102
Postman, Neil, 36, 37, 39
The Power series, 101
Price, Susan, 17, 18, 19, 21 n.4
The Primary School Student Pictorial Semimonthly (Taiwan), 154
The Primary School Student Semimonthly (Taiwan), 154
The Prince of the Pond (Napoli), 18
Psycho, 103

Québec/Amérique, 132, 138 n.3

Rabén, Hans, 49
Račickas, Vytautas, 180
Ramona books, 23–29
Ramona and Her Father (Cleary), 25
Ramona and Her Mother (Cleary), 25
Ramona Forever (Cleary), 25
Ramona Quimby Age 8 (Cleary), 25, 28
Ramona the Brave (Cleary), 25
Ramona the Pest (Cleary), 25, 29, 85
Random House, 28
Reading for the Plot (Brooks), 71, n.16
Reagan, Ronald, 180
The Real Elvis (Gripe), 88

Recent Theories of Narrative (Martin),
  71 n.7
Red Shift (Garner), 88
Rees, David, 168 n.14
Reimer, Mavis, 102
Reminiscences of Beijing (Guan and
  Lin), 156
René, 136
"Representations of Place in Australian
  Children's Picture Books" (Stephens),
  114 n.9
Rice, Anne, 101
The River at Green Knowe (Boston), 87
Robin Hood, 36
Robinson Crusoe (Defoe), 5, 37
Robotas ir Peteliškė (Žilinskaitė), 180
Roman Plus, 138 n.2
Romulus and Remus, 78
Ronen, Ruth, 71 n.16
Ronia, the Robber's Daughter
  (Lindgren), 59
Ronja rövardotter (Lindgren), 59
A Room of Her Own (Gripe), 88
The Root Cellar (Lunn), 87
Rose, Ellen Cronan, 29 n.9
Rose, Jacqueline, 8
Roter Elefant, 51
Rousseau, Jean-Jacques, 36
Rubenstein, Gillian, 17, 19–20, 21 n.4

Sachar, Louis, 24
Said, Edward, 4
Saja, Kazys, 179, 180
Salinger, J. D., 126
Sally Sjørøverdatter (Tenfjord), 61
Saltykov, Mikhail, 173
Sans famille (Malot), 70 n.3, 88
Santa Calls (Joyce), 119–20
Sapgir, Genrikh, 172
Sarah, Plain and Tall (MacLachlan), 86
Sartre, Jean–Paul, 39
Scieszka, John, 52
Scott, Walter, 37, 164
Seaward (Cooper), 93–94
Sebestyen, Ouida, 118–19
The Secret Island (Verne), 87
The Secret Seven (Blyton), 86
Sendak, Maurice, 39, 46
"The Sense of Nonsense Verse"
  (Chukovsky), 175

Serraillier, Ian, 70 n.3
Seuss, Dr. *See* Geisel, Theodor Seuss
Seven Blind Mice (Young), 80
The Seven Brothers, 157
Sexton, Anne, 39
Shadow (Gripe), 59–60
Shadow and Substance (Sims), 115
Shadow Zone series, 101
Shavit, Zohar, 27
Shchipachov, Stepan, 178
Shen, Shih–shi, 156
Shevchuk, Igor, 175
Shields, Brooke, 37
Showalter, Elaine, 29 n.9
Siebenstorch (Pludra), 149 n.24
Silent Stalker (Cusick), 99–101, 102,
  104
Silver, Long John, 61
Silver on the Tree (Cooper), 93
The Silver Sword (Serraillier), 70 n.3
Simpson, Bart, 40, 102
Sims, Rudine, 115
Singer, Isaac Bashevis, 27, 39
Sklovsky, Victor, 68, 72 n.24
Skriket fra jungelen (Haugen), 60
The Soaring Sky Hawk (Lai), 158
Socrates, 61
The Solitaire Mystery (Gaarder), 61–62
Something About the Robots (Huang),
  159
Sondheim, Stephen, 39
Sonntagskind (Mebs), 144–48, 149 n.17
Southhall, Ivan, 104
Spack, Patricia, 126
Spielberg, Stephen, 40
The Spring When Everything Happened
  (Beckman), 88
Stalin, Joseph, 178, 179
"The Stepchild in the Basement: Trends
  in Series Book Research" (Erisman),
  71 n.6
Stephens, John, 9, 21 n.2, 114 n.9
Stepping Stone Books, 28
Stevenson, Robert Louis, 36, 61, 164
Stine, R. L., 100, 101, 102, 103
*The Stinky Cheese Man and Other
  Fairly Stupid Tales* (Scieszka), 52
Stoker, Bram, 100
Storm Boy (Thiele), 107
Strange Objects (Crew), 89

Stranger in the Green Coat (Lai), 158
Straub, Peter, 101
Stretton, Hugh, 110
Struwwelpeter, 55
Sunset in Taipei City (Jou), 158
Superman, 55
Sutcliff, Rosemary, 164

Tabbert, Reinbert, 149 n.17
Tarka the Otter (Williamson), 85
Tarzan, 55
Teens (Mack), 65
Temple, Shirley, 37
Tenfjord, Jo, 61
The Textbook of Bad Advice (Oster),
    174–75
Théorie de la littérature (Sklovsky), 72
    n.24
Thiele, Colin, 107
"Three Fallacies About Children's
    Books" (Chambers), 27–28
The Three Little Pigs, 78
Tiffin, Helen, 108
The Time Garden (Eager), 88
Tistou of the Green Thumbs (Druon), 85
Todorov, Tzvetan, 85
The Toll Bridge (Chambers), 89
Tompkins, Jane, 26, 29
Tom Thumb, 145
Torgovnick, Marianna, 68
Touchstones series, 27
Townsend, John Row, 139 n.6
Trachtenberg, Stanley, 95
Tramvaj (Russia), 171, 175
Transformations (Sexton), 39
A Traveller in Time (Uttley), 85
Treasure Island (Stevenson), 61, 87
The Treasure Seekers (Nesbit), 85
Tsau, Wen-shiuan, 156
Tucker, Nicholas, 27
Tuck Everlasting (Babbitt), 87
Tung Li. *See* Lai, Si-an
Turner, Graeme, 108
Twain, Mark, 36, 133

Unclaimed Treasures (MacLachlan), 88,
    89
Usachev, Andrei, 171
Uses of Enchantment (Bettelheim), 39
Už nevarstom ų durų (Saja), 179

Vaičiulaitis, Antanas, 180
Vainilaitis, Martynas, 180
Vampire Twins: A Trilogy (Harell), 104
van Leeuwen, Joke, 45
van Lieshout, Ted, 44, 45
Verne, Jules, 36
A Vietnam Soldier, 179
Viira, Yurij, 175
Voigt, Cynthia, 17, 21 n.4

Wallace, Martin, 71 n.7
Walsh, Jill Paton, 165–66, 168 n.14
Watkins, Tony, 116, 120
We Are All in the Dumps with Jack &
    Guy (Sendak), 39
Weber, Lenore, 126
Wehr dich Mathilda (Holm), 148
The Well-Wishers (Eager), 88
Werther, 136
Westall, Robert, 166–67, 168 n.4, 169
    n.18
Westmark (Alexander), 87
When Hitler Stole Pink Rabbit (Kerr),
    87
Where the Wild Things Are (Sendak),
    46, 87
White, Patrick, 109
The Wierdstone of Brisingamen
    (Garner), 87
Wiesner, David, 4
Wilful Blue (Hartnett), 16–17, 21 n.4
Williams, Raymond, 9
Williams, Robin, 40
Winn, Marie, 35, 37
Winnie-the-Pooh (Milne), 85, 86
Wir pfeifen auf den Gurkenkönig
    (Nöstlinger), 52, 141
The Wizard of Earthsea (Le Guin), 85
The Wizard of Oz (Baum), 85
Wolf (Cross), 75–80, 88
Wölfel, Ursula, 141
The Wolfman, 103
Wolgast, Heinrich, 50
Women and Children First: The Fiction
    of Two World Wars (Cadogan and
    Craig), 168 n.3
The Wonderful Adventures
    (Wernström), 88
The Wonderful Adventures of Nils
    (Lagerlöf), 88

Wordsworth, William, 36
Words by Heart (Sebestyen), 118–19
Worlds Within (Egoff), 91

Young, Ed, 80
You Only Grow Old Once! (Seuss), 40
Yuan Liou Publishing Company, 157

Zakhoder, Boris, 173
Zauberkreide (Mattenklott), 50
Zeppelin (Haugen), 89
Žilinskaitė, Vytaute, 180
Zipes, Jack, 77
Zucker, Jerry, 103
Zuika Padūkėlis (Račickas), 180
Zurba, Algimantas, 180

About the Editor and Contributors

SANDRA L. BECKETT is professor of French at Brock University in St. Catharines, Ontario, Canada, where she teaches French literature and Francophone children's literature. Her research focuses on contemporary French fiction for adults and children. She is the author of three books on the novelist Henri Bosco. She has recently completed a book titled *Les Grands Romanciers écrivent pour les enfants, 1945–1995*, devoted to important twentieth-century French novelists who have written for both children and adults, and is currently researching a book on intertextuality in children's literature. She also has published numerous articles on the contemporary French novel, as well as on French and French-Canadian children's literature.

VINCAS AURYLA is a professor at Vilnius Pedagogical University, head librarian at the Children's Literature Center of the Lithuanian National Library, member of the Lithuanian Writers' Union, and literary critic. He has published a history of Lithuanian children's literature in two volumes; an anthology of Lithuanian children's prose, poetry, and drama in three volumes; and books, articles, and essays on Lithuanian children's literature in Russian, Polish, and other languages. His current interest is the theory and history of children's literature.

SUSAN CLANCY has spent many years teaching in primary and secondary schools. On receiving a master's degree in children's literature, she became a literacy education lecturer at Charles Sturt University, Wagga Wagga, Australia, where she now develops and teaches children's literature courses for both students and practicing teachers. Her particular interests are folk tales and fairy tales, picture books, and reader response.

SHU-JY DUAN holds a Ph.D. (1994) from the Program of Language, Literature, and Reading, Department of Educational Theory and Practice, The Ohio State University. She is an associate professor in the Department of Foreign Languages and International Communications, Shih Chien College, Taipei, Taiwan. The subjects she teaches include an introduction to Western literature, as well as English and American literature. Her areas of interest include children's literature, folklore, and literacy. She is currently involved in two projects: "Young Adult Fiction in Taiwan" and "A Comparative Study of Heroes in Mythology."

DAGMAR GRENZ is professor at Hamburg University, and formerly at the University of Cologne. She was a board member of the IRSCL from 1985 to 1989, and organized the 8th International Congress of the IRSCL at Cologne in 1987. Her publications include *Mädchenliteratur* (1981), an investigation of girls' fiction in the eighteenth and nineteenth centuries, and a number of articles and essays on German-language children's and youth literature from the eighteenth century to the present.

JERRY GRISWOLD teaches literature at San Diego State University and has been a visiting professor at UCLA, the University of Connecticut, and the University of California, San Diego. He is the author of *The Children's Books of Randall Jarrell* (University of Georgia Press) and *Audacious Kids: Coming of Age in America's Classic Children's Books* (Oxford University Press). He has published some 100 essays in *Paris Review, The Nation, New Republic,* the *New York Times Book Review,* and elsewhere. He writes regularly for the *Los Angeles Times.*

DANIEL D. HADE is associate professor at the Pennsylvania State University. His work focuses on the study of children's literature, particularly the nature and quality of the experiences readers have with children's literature. He is interested in the social contexts (especially classrooms) within which readers read and interpret literature, and the interpretive stances that children and teachers assume toward a piece of literature. His recent work has examined ideological differences among advocates of literature-based instruction, and how children's reading is shaped by the ways in which writers produce, scholars critique, and teachers mediate children's literature, as well as the assumptions about children as readers held by these adults.

BETTINA KÜMMERLING-MEIBAUER studied German philology, art history, and philosophy at the universities of Cologne, London, and Lund. Her dissertation deals with the fairy tales of Hofmannstahl, Musil, and Döblin. She teaches children's literature at the University of Tübingen. Her area of research is German and Scandinavian children's literature, picture book theory, and the relationship between children's literature and other media. She is working on an encyclopedia of international children's classics that deals with approximately 350 classic children's books from 50 countries (it will be published by Metzler).

DEBORAH STEVENSON is the assistant editor of the Bulletin of the Center for Children's Books, located at the University of Illinois Graduate School of Library and Information Science. A graduate student in the English Department of the University of Chicago, she is completing her doctoral dissertation on children's literature and contemporary culture.

ÅSFRID SVENSEN received her M.A. from the University of Oslo in 1963. Lecturer in Scandinavian literature at the same university since 1971, she has been a professor from 1993. She has written a textbook on methods of interpreting literature, and books and articles on fantastic literature and on Scandinavian authors of adult literature, as well as articles on children's literature.

DANIELLE THALER, originally from France, has lived in Canada for many years. She teaches at the University of Victoria in British Columbia and is past president of the Canadian Association of College and University Professors of French. Her publications reflect her interest in the nineteenth-century novel—*Peuple, femme, hystérie: La Clinique de l'amour chez les frères Goncourt* (1986)—and in children's literature: *Était-il une fois? Panorama de la critique France–Canada* (1989). She regularly contributes reviews and articles to *Canadian Children's Literature* and is presently writing a book on the subject of youth literature as a genre.

ANNE DE VRIES is head of the Dutch Center for Children's Literature (The Hague) and lecturer at the Free University (Amsterdam) in the Department of Dutch Literature. His research concerns the history of Dutch children's literature and responses to children's literature.

ISBN 0-313-30145-X

EAN

HARDCOVER BAR CODE

ANNE SCOTT MACLEOD is professor of children's literature at the College of Library and Information Services, University of Maryland. She is the author of *A Moral Tale: Children's Literature and American Culture, 1820–1860* (Archon Books, 1975, 1990) and *American Childhood: Essays on Children's Literature in the 19th and 20th Centuries* (University of Georgia Press, 1994), as well as numerous articles on children's literature, with special attention to the connections between children's books and culture. She was president of IRSCL (1985–1989); has been an active member of the Children's Literature Association since 1975; was a member of Executive Board (1985–1988), and has served on various committees.

OLGA MÄEOTS graduated from the Scandinavian Department of St. Petersburg University. While still an undergraduate she took great interest in medieval Swedish literature, and has written several articles based on her medieval studies. At present she works at the Library for Foreign Literature, Moscow, where she is head of the Children's Literature Department. She has published translations and several papers on English and Scandinavian children's literature.

RODERICK MCGILLIS has published over fifty articles and has edited MacDonald's "Princess" books for Oxford (World's Classics), and *For the Childlike: George MacDonald's Fantasy for Children* (a collection of essays; Scarecrow Press). He is also the author of two books for Twayne: *Quick Text, Nimble Reader: Literary Theory and Children's Literature* (1996) and *A Little Princess* (forthcoming in Twayne's Masterworks series).

EVA-MARIA METCALF teaches German and Swedish at the University of Minnesota. She is the author of a book on Astrid Lindgren (Twayne, 1995) and has published articles on German and Scandinavian children's literature in *Children's Literature, ChLA Quarterly, The Lion and the Unicorn*, and German and Swedish journals; she is also a contributor to *Children's Literature Abstracts*. Currently, she is working on a book for Garland Press about the Austrian author Christine Nöstlinger.

MARIA NIKOLAJEVA is an associate professor in the Department of Comparative Literature, University of Stockholm, where she teaches children's literature and literary theory. Her research emphasis is on the theory and poetics of children's literature. She is the author of *The Magic Code: The Use of Magical Patterns in Fantasy for Children* (1988) and *Children's Literature Comes of Age: Toward a New Aesthetics* (1995), and the editor of several volumes on children's literature, and has published a large number of articles and essays. In 1993 she was a Fulbright scholar at the University of Massachusetts, Amherst. She also has published several books for children. She is the current president of the IRSCL.

PERRY NODELMAN is a professor of English at the University of Winnipeg, Manitoba, Canada, where he teaches children's literature, popular literature, and courses in literary conventions and strategies. He has published about ninety articles in academic journals, most of them on various aspects of children's literature. He also has written two books on the subject: *Words About Pictures: The Narrative Art of Children's Picture Books* (University of Georgia Press) and *The Pleasures of Children's Literature* (Longman USA); a second edition of the latter appeared in 1995. He is also the author of two fantasy novels for children—*The Same Place but Different* (Groundwood in Canada, Simon & Schuster in the United States—and, in collaboration with Carol Matas, *Of Two Minds* (Bain and Cox/Blizzard in Canada; Simon & Schuster in the United States). Sequels of both are in progress.

BEVERLEY PENNELL is a postgraduate assistant at the University of Western Sydney (Nepean), where she is working on her doctorate. She is currently on study leave from the New South Wales Department of School Education, having been head teacher (English) for seven years in a coeducational comprehensive high school. Her academic interest in children's literature grew out of her classroom experiences. Her other areas of academic interest are the nature and purpose of student writing in secondary school, and organizational change paradigms in the management of secondary schools and tertiary institutions.

DIETER PETZOLD is associate professor of English literature at the University of Erlangen-Nuremberg. He also has taught at the universities of St. Andrews (Scotland), of North Carolina (United States), and of British Columbia (Canada). In addition to numerous articles on children's literature, he has published books on English nonsense literature, English literary fairy tales, J. R. R. Tolkien, and Robinson Crusoe. He is currently editing a volume on fantasy in film and literature.

CAROLE SCOTT is undergraduate dean, and a member of the English and Comparative Literature Department, at San Diego State University. Her initial studies in children's literature have focused upon late-nineteenth- and early-twentieth-century British works, with a special interest in parallel universes and their special laws. More recently, the rapidly changing demographics of southern California have stimulated her interest in cross-cultural and multicultural themes. She is a founding member of the San Diego Children's Literature Circle and secretary of IRSCL.

JOHN STEPHENS is associate professor of English at Macquarie University, Sydney, where he teaches, among other things, children's literature and medieval literature, and runs a thriving M.A. program in children's literature. His research interests are mainly in children's literature, discourse analysis, and medieval literature. He is the author of *Literature, Language and Change* (1990; with Ruth Waterhouse), *Language and Ideology in Children's Fiction* (1992), and *Reading the Signs: Sense and Significance in Written Texts* (1992).